The Humour of Homer
and Other Essays

Pizzetta, photo Carallo, 1889.   Walker & Cockerell, ph. sc.

S. Butler.

The Humour of Homer and Other Essays

By
Samuel Butler

Edited by
R. A. Streatfeild

With a biographical sketch of the author by Henry
Festing Jones, and a portrait in photogravure from
a photograph taken in 1889

Essay Index Reprint Series

Originally published by: Mitchell Kennerley

BOOKS FOR LIBRARIES PRESS, INC.
FREEPORT, NEW YORK

First Published 1914
Reprinted 1967

LIBRARY OF CONGRESS CATALOG CARD NUMBER:
67-30178

PRINTED IN THE UNITED STATES OF AMERICA

Contents

Introduction

By R. A. Streatfeild

THE nucleus of this book is the collection of essays by Samuel Butler, which was originally published by Mr. Grant Richards in 1904 under the title *Essays on Life, Art and Science,* and reissued by Mr. Fifield in 1908. To these are now added another essay, entitled "The Humour of Homer," a biographical sketch of the author kindly contributed by Mr. Henry Festing Jones, which will add materially to the value of the edition, and a portrait in photogravure from a photograph taken in 1889—the period of the essays.

"The Humour of Homer" was originally delivered as a lecture at the Working Men's College in Great Ormond Street on the 30th January, 1892, the day on which Butler first promulgated his theory of the Trapanese origin of the *Odyssey* in a letter to the *Athenæum.* Later in the same year it was published with some additional matter by Messrs. Metcalfe and Co. of Cambridge. For the next five years Butler was engaged upon researches into the origin and authorship of the *Odyssey,* the results of which are embodied in his book *The Authoress of the "Odyssey,"* originally published by Messrs. Longman in 1897. Butler incorporated a good deal of "The Humour of Homer" into *The Authoress of the "Odyssey,"* but the section relating

to the *Iliad* naturally found no place in the later work.
For the sake of this alone " The Humour of Homer "
deserves to be better known.   Written as it was for
an artisan audience and professing to deal only with
one side of Homer's genius, " The Humour of Homer "
must not, of course, be taken as an exhaustive statement of Butler's views upon Homeric questions.   It
touches but lightly on important points, particularly
regarding the origin and authorship of the *Odyssey*,
which are treated at much greater length in *The
Authoress of the " Odyssey."*

Nevertheless, "The Humour of Homer" appears to me
to have a special value as a kind of general introduction
to Butler's more detailed study of the *Odyssey*.   His
attitude towards the Homeric poems is here expressed
with extraordinary freshness and force.   What that
attitude was is best explained by his own words : " If
a person would understand either the *Odyssey* or any
other ancient work, he must never look at the dead
without seeing the living in them, nor at the living
without thinking of the dead.   We are too fond of
seeing the ancients as one thing and the moderns as
another."   Butler did not undervalue the philological
and archæological importance of the *Iliad* and the
Odyssey, but it was mainly as human documents that
they appealed to him.   This, I am inclined to suspect,
was the root of the objection of academic critics to
him and his theories.   They did not so much resent
the suggestion that the author of the *Odyssey* was a
woman ; they could not endure that he should be
treated as a human being.

Of the remaining essays two were originally delivered
as lectures ; the others appeared first in *The Universal
Review* in 1888. 1889 and 1890.   I should perhaps

Introduction

explain why two other essays which also appeared in
The Universal Review are not included in this collection. The first of these, entitled " L'Affaire Holbein-Rippel," relates to a drawing of Holbein's " Danse des
Paysans " in the Basle Museum, which is usually
described as a copy, but which Butler believed to be
the work of Holbein himself. This essay requires
to be illustrated in so elaborate a manner that it was
impossible to include it in a book of this size. The
second essay, which is a sketch of the career of the
sculptor Tabachetti, was published as the first section
of an article, entitled "A Sculptor and a Shrine," of
which the second part is here given under the title
" The Sanctuary of Montrigone." The section devoted
to the sculptor contains all that Butler then knew
about Tabachetti, but since it was written various
documents have come to light, principally through the
investigations of Cavaliere Francesco Negri, of Casale
Monferrato, which negative some of Butler's conclusions. Had Butler lived, I do not doubt that he
would have revised his essay in the light of Cavaliere
Negri's discoveries, the value of which he fully recognized. As it stands the essay requires so much
revision that I have decided to omit it altogether and
to postpone giving English readers a full account of
Tabachetti's career until a second edition of Butler's
" Ex Voto," in which Tabachetti's work is discussed
in detail, is required. Meanwhile I have given a brief
summary of the main facts of Tabachetti's life in a
note (p. 195) to the essay on " Art in the Valley of
Saas." Anyone who desires further details concerning
the sculptor and his work will find them in Cavaliere
Negri's pamphlet " Il Santuario di Crea " (Alessandria, 1902).

The three essays grouped together under the title *The Deadlock in Darwinism* may be regarded as a postscript to Butler's four books on evolution, viz. *Life and Habit, Evolution Old and New, Unconscious Memory,* and *Luck or Cunning?* When these essays were first published in book form in 1904, I ventured to give a brief summary of Butler's position with regard to the main problem of evolution. I need now only refer readers to Mr. Festing Jones's biographical sketch and, for fuller details, to the masterly introduction contributed by Professor Marcus Hartog to the new edition of *Unconscious Memory* (A. C. Fifield, 1910), and recently reprinted in his *Problems of Life and Reproduction* (John Murray, 1913), in which Butler's work in the field of biology and his share in the various controversies connected with the study of evolution are discussed with the authority of a specialist.

R. A. STREATFEILD.

July, 1913.

Sketch of the Life

of

Samuel Butler

Author of *Erewhon*

(1835–1902)

by
Henry Festing Jones

Note

THIS sketch of Butler's life, together with the portrait which forms the frontispiece to this volume, first appeared in December, 1902, in The Eagle, the magazine of St. John's College, Cambridge. I revised the sketch and read it before the British Homœopathic Association at 43 Russell Square, London, W.C., on the 9th February, 1910 ; some of Butler's music was performed by Miss Grainger Kerr, Mr. R. A. Streatfeild, Mr. J. A. Fuller Maitland, and Mr. H. J. T. Wood, the secretary of the Association. I again revised it and read it before the Historical Society of St. John's College, Cambridge, in the combination room of the college on the 16th November, 1910 ; the Master (Mr. R. F. Scott), who was also Vice-Chancellor of the University, was in the chair, and a vote of thanks was proposed by Professor William Bateson, F.R.S.

As the full Memoir of Butler on which I am engaged is not yet ready for publication, I have again revised the sketch, and it is here published in response to many demands for some account of his life.

H. F. J.

August, 1913.

Sketch of the Life of Samuel Butler

Author of *Erewhon*

(1835–1902)

SAMUEL BUTLER was born on the 4th December, 1835, at the Rectory, Langar, near Bingham, in Nottinghamshire. His father was the Rev. Thomas Butler, then Rector of Langar, afterwards one of the canons of Lincoln Cathedral, and his mother was Fanny Worsley, daughter of John Philip Worsley of Arno's Vale, Bristol, sugar-refiner. His grandfather was Dr. Samuel Butler, the famous headmaster of Shrewsbury School, afterwards Bishop of Lichfield. The Butlers are not related either to the author of *Hudibras*, or to the author of the *Analogy*, or to the present Master of Trinity College, Cambridge.

Butler's father, after being at school at Shrewsbury under Dr. Butler, went up to St. John's College, Cambridge ; he took his degree in 1829, being seventh classic and twentieth senior optime ; he was ordained and returned to Shrewsbury, where he was for some time assistant master at the school under Dr. Butler. He married in 1832 and left Shrewsbury for Langar. He was a learned botanist, and made a collection of dried plants which he gave to the Town Museum of Shrewsbury.

Butler's childhood and early life were spent at Langar among the surroundings of an English country rectory, and his education was begun by his father. In 1843, when he was only eight years old, the first great event in his life occurred ; the family, consisting of his father and mother, his two sisters, his brother and himself, went to Italy. The South-Eastern Railway stopped at Ashford, whence they travelled to Dover in their own carriage ; the carriage was put on board the steamboat, they crossed the Channel, and proceeded to Cologne, up the Rhine to Basle and on through Switzerland into Italy, through Parma, where Napoleon's widow was still reigning, Modena, Bologna, Florence, and so to Rome. They had to drive where there was no railway, and there was then none in all Italy except between Naples and Castellamare. They seemed to pass a fresh custom-house every day, but, by tipping the searchers, generally got through without inconvenience. The bread was sour and the Italian butter rank and cheesy—often uneatable. Beggars ran after the carriage all day long and when they got nothing jeered at the travellers and called them heretics. They spent half the winter in Rome, and the children were taken up to the top of St. Peter's as a treat to celebrate their father's birthday. In the Sistine Chapel they saw the cardinals kiss the toe of Pope Gregory XVI, and in the Corso, in broad daylight, they saw a monk come rolling down a staircase like a sack of potatoes, bundled into the street by a man and his wife. The second half of the winter was spent in Naples. This early introduction to the land which he always thought of and often referred to as his second country made an ineffaceable impression upon him.

In January, 1846, he went to school at Allesley, near Coventry, under the Rev. E. Gibson. He seldom referred to his life there, though sometimes he would say something that showed he had not forgotten all about it. For instance, in 1900 Mr. Sydney C. Cockerell, now the Director of the Fitzwilliam Museum, Cambridge, showed him a medieval missal, laboriously illuminated. He found that it fatigued him to look at it, and said that such books ought never to be made. Cockerell replied that such books relieved the tedium of divine service, on which Butler made a note ending thus :

Give me rather a robin or a peripatetic cat like the one whose loss the parishioners of St. Clement Danes are still deploring. When I was at school at Allesley the boy who knelt opposite me at morning prayers, with his face not more than a yard away from mine, used to blow pretty little bubbles with his saliva which he would send sailing off the tip of his tongue like miniature soap bubbles ; they very soon broke, but they had a career of a foot or two. I never saw anyone else able to get saliva bubbles right away from him and, though I have endeavoured for some fifty years and more to acquire the art, I never yet could start the bubble off my tongue without its bursting. Now things like this really do relieve the tedium of church, but no missal that I have ever seen will do anything except increase it.

In 1848 he left Allesley and went to Shrewsbury under the Rev. B. H. Kennedy. Many of the recollections of his school life at Shrewsbury are reproduced for the school life of Ernest Pontifex at Roughborough in *The Way of All Flesh*, Dr. Skinner being Dr. Kennedy.

During these years he first heard the music of Handel ; it went straight to his heart and satisfied a longing which the music of other composers had only awakened and intensified. He became as one of the listening brethren who stood around " when Jubal struck the chorded shell " in the *Song for Saint Cecilia's Day :*

> Less than a god, they thought, there could not dwell
> Within the hollow of that shell
> That spoke so sweetly and so well.

This was the second great event in his life, and henceforward Italy and Handel were always present at the bottom of his mind as a kind of double pedal to every thought, word, and deed. Almost the last thing he ever asked me to do for him, within a few days of his death, was to bring *Solomon* that he might refresh his memory as to the harmonies of " With thee th' unsheltered moor I'd trace." He often tried to like the music of Bach and Beethoven, but found himself compelled to give them up—they bored him too much. Nor was he more successful with the other great composers ; Haydn, for instance, was a sort of Horace, an agreeable, facile man of the world, while Mozart, who must have loved Handel, for he wrote additional accompaniments to the *Messiah,* failed to move him. It was not that he disputed the greatness of these composers, but he was out of sympathy with them, and never could forgive the last two for having led music astray from the Handel tradition and paved the road from Bach to Beethoven. Everything connected with Handel interested him. He remembered old Mr. Brooke, Rector of Gamston, North Notts, who had been present at the Handel Commemoration in 1784, and his great-aunt, Miss Susannah Apthorp, of Cambridge, had known a lady who had sat upon Handel's knee. He often regretted that these were his only links with " the greatest of all composers."

Besides his love for Handel he had a strong liking for drawing, and, during the winter of 1853–4, his family again took him to Italy, where, being now eighteen, he looked on the works of the old masters with intelligence.

In October, 1854, he went into residence at St. John's College, Cambridge. He showed no aptitude for any particular branch of academic study, nevertheless he impressed his friends as being likely to make his mark. Just as he used reminiscences of his own schooldays at Shrewsbury for Ernest's life at Roughborough, so he used reminiscences of his own Cambridge days for those of Ernest. When the Simeonites, in *The Way of All Flesh*, " distributed tracts, dropping them at night in good men's letter boxes while they slept, their tracts got burnt or met with even worse contumely." Ernest Pontifex went so far as to parody one of these tracts and to get a copy of the parody " dropped into each of the Simeonites' boxes." Ernest did this in the novel because Butler had done it in real life. Mr. A. T. Bartholomew, of the University Library, has found, among the Cambridge papers of the late J. Willis Clark's collection, three printed pieces belonging to the year 1855 bearing on the subject. He speaks of them in an article headed " Samuel Butler and the Simeonites," and signed A. T. B. in the *Cambridge Magazine*, 1st March, 1913 ; the first is " a genuine Simeonite tract ; the other two are parodies. All three are anonymous. At the top of the second parody is written ' By S. Butler, March 31.' " The article gives extracts from the genuine tract and the whole of Butler's parody.

Besides parodying Simeonite tracts, Butler wrote various other papers during his undergraduate days,

B

some of which, preserved by one of his contemporaries, who remained a lifelong friend, the Rev. Canon Joseph M'Cormick, now Rector of St. James's, Piccadilly, are reproduced in *The Note-Books of Samuel Butler* (1912).

He also steered the Lady Margaret first boat, and Canon M'Cormick told me of a mishap that occurred, on the last night of the races in 1857. Lady Margaret had been head of the river since 1854, Canon M'Cormick was rowing 5, Philip Pennant Pearson (afterwards P. Pennant) was 7, Canon Kynaston, of Durham (whose name formerly was Snow), was stroke, and Butler was cox. When the cox let go of the bung at starting, the rope caught in his rudder lines, and Lady Margaret was nearly bumped by Second Trinity. They escaped, however, and their pursuers were so much exhausted by their efforts to catch them that they were themselves bumped by First Trinity at the next corner. Butler wrote home about it :

11 March, 1857. Dear Mamma : My foreboding about steering was on the last day nearly verified by an accident which was more deplorable than culpable the effects of which would have been ruinous had not the presence of mind of No. 7 in the boat rescued us from the very jaws of defeat. The scene is one which never can fade from my remembrance and will be connected always with the gentlemanly conduct of the crew in neither using opprobrious language nor gesture towards your unfortunate son but treating him with the most graceful forbearance ; for in most cases when an accident happens which in itself is but slight, but is visited with serious consequences, most people get carried away with the impression created by the last so as to entirely forget the accidental nature of the cause and if we had been quite bumped I should have been ruined, as it is I get praise for coolness and good steering as much as and more than blame for my accident and the crew are so delighted at having rowed a race such as never was seen

before that they are satisfied completely. All the spectators saw the race and were delighted ; another inch and I should never have held up my head again. One thing is safe, it will never happen again.

The *Eagle*, " a magazine supported by members of St. John's College," issued its first number in the Lent term of 1858 ; it contains an article by Butler " On English Composition and Other Matters," signed " Cellarius " :

Most readers will have anticipated me in admitting that a man should be clear of his meaning before he endeavours to give it any kind of utterance, and that, having made up his mind what to say, the less thought he takes how to say it, more than briefly, pointedly and plainly, the better.

From this it appears that, when only just over twenty-two, Butler had already discovered and adopted those principles of writing from which he never departed.

In the fifth number of the *Eagle* is an article, " Our Tour," also signed " Cellarius " ; it is an account of a tour made in June, 1857, with a friend whose name he Italianized into Giuseppe Verdi, through France into North Italy, and was written, so he says, to show how they got so much into three weeks and spent only £25 ; they did not, however, spend quite so much, for the article goes on, after bringing them back to England, " Next day came safely home to dear old St. John's, cash in hand 7d."[1]

Butler worked hard with Shilleto, an old pupil of

[1] I am indebted to one of Butler's contemporaries at Cambridge, the Rev. Dr. T. G. Bonney, F.R.S., and also to Mr. John F. Harris, both of St. John's College, for help in finding and dating Butler's youthful contributions to the *Eagle*.

his grandfather, and was bracketed 12th in the Classical Tripos of 1858. Canon M'Cormick told me that he would no doubt have been higher but for the fact that he at first intended to go out in mathematics ; it was only during the last year of his time that he returned to the classics, and his being so high as he was spoke well for the classical education of Shrewsbury.

It had always been an understood thing that he was to follow in the footsteps of his father and grandfather and become a clergyman ; accordingly, after taking his degree, he went to London and began to prepare for ordination, living and working among the poor as lay assistant under the Rev. Philip Perring, Curate of St. James's, Piccadilly, an old pupil of Dr. Butler at Shrewsbury.[1] Placed among such surroundings, he felt bound to think out for himself many theological questions which at this time were first presented to him, and, the conclusion being forced upon him that he could not believe in the efficacy of infant baptism, he declined to be ordained.

It was now his desire to become an artist ; this, however, did not meet with the approval of his family, and he returned to Cambridge to try for pupils and, if possible, to get a fellowship. He liked being at Cambridge, but there were few pupils and, as there seemed to be little chance of a fellowship, his father wished him to come down and adopt some profession. A long correspondence took place in the course of which many alternatives were considered. There are letters about his becoming a farmer in England, a tutor, a homœopathic doctor, an artist, or a publisher, and the possibilities of the army, the bar, and dip-

---

[1] This gentleman, on the death of his father in 1866, became the Rev. Sir Philip Perring, Bart.

lomacy. Finally it was decided that he should emigrate to New Zealand. His passage was paid, and he was to sail in the *Burmah*, but a cousin of his received information about this vessel which caused him, much against his will, to get back his passage money and take a berth in the *Roman Emperor*, which sailed from Gravesend on one of the last days of September, 1859. On that night, for the first time in his life, he did not say his prayers. " I suppose the sense of change was so great that it shook them quietly off. I was not then a sceptic ; I had got as far as disbelief in infant baptism, but no further. I felt no compunction of conscience, however, about leaving off my morning and evening prayers—simply I could no longer say them."

The *Roman Emperor*, after a voyage every incident of which interested him deeply, arrived outside Port Lyttelton. The captain shouted to the pilot who came to take them in :

" Has the *Robert Small* arrived ? "

" No," replied the pilot, " nor yet the *Burmah*."

And Butler, writing home to his people, adds the comment : " You may imagine what I felt."

The *Burmah* was never heard of again.

He spent some time looking round, considering what to do and how to employ the money with which his father was ready to supply him, and determined upon sheep-farming. He made several excursions looking for country, and ultimately took up a run which is still called Mesopotamia, the name he gave it because it is situated among the head-waters of the Rangitata.

It was necessary to have a horse, and he bought one for £55, which was not considered dear. He wrote home that the horse's name was " Doctor " : " I hope he is a

Homœopathist." From this, and from the fact that he had already contemplated becoming a homœopathic doctor himself, I conclude that he had made the acquaintance of Dr. Robert Ellis Dudgeon, the eminent homœopathist, while he was doing parish work in London. After his return to England Dr. Dudgeon was his medical adviser, and remained one of his most intimate friends until the end of his life. Doctor, the horse, is introduced into *Erewhon Revisited ;* the shepherd in Chapter XXVI tells John Higgs that Doctor " would pick fords better than that gentleman could, I know, and if the gentleman fell off him he would just stay stock still."

Butler carried on his run for about four and a half years, and the open-air life agreed with him ; he ascribed to this the good health he afterwards enjoyed. The following, taken from a notebook he kept in the colony and destroyed, gives a glimpse of one side of his life there ; he preserved the note because it recalled New Zealand so vividly.

April, 1861. It is Sunday. We rose later than usual. There are five of us sleeping in the hut. I sleep in a bunk on one side of the fire ; Mr. Haast,[1] a German who is making a geological survey of the province, sleeps upon the opposite one ; my bullock-driver and hut-keeper have two bunks at the far end of the hut, along the wall, while my shepherd lies in the loft among the tea and sugar and flour. It was a fine morning, and we turned out about seven o'clock.

The usual mutton and bread for breakfast with a pudding made of flour and water baked in the camp oven after a joint of meat—Yorkshire pudding, but without eggs. While we were at breakfast a robin perched on the table

[1] The late Sir Julius von Haast, K.C.M.G., appointed Provincial Geologist in 1860, was ennobled by the Austrian Government and knighted by the British. He died in 1887.

and sat there a good while pecking at the sugar. We went on breakfasting with little heed to the robin, and the robin went on pecking with little heed to us. After breakfast Pey, my bullock-driver, went to fetch the horses up from a spot about two miles down the river, where they often run ; we wanted to go pig-hunting.

I go into the garden and gather a few peascods for seed till the horses should come up. Then Cook, the shepherd, says that a fire has sprung up on the other side of the river. Who could have lit it ? Probably someone who had intended coming to my place on the preceding evening and has missed his way, for there is no track of any sort between here and Phillips's. In a quarter of an hour he lit another fire lower down, and by that time, the horses having come up, Haast and myself—remembering how Dr. Sinclair had just been drowned so near the same spot—think it safer to ride over to him and put him across the river. The river was very low and so clear that we could see every stone. On getting to the river-bed we lit a fire and did the same on leaving it ; our tracks would guide anyone over the intervening ground.

Besides his occupation with the sheep, he found time to play the piano, to read and to write. In the library of St. John's College, Cambridge, are two copies of the Greek Testament, very fully annotated by him at the University and in the colony. He also read the *Origin of Species*, which, as everyone knows, was published in 1859. He became " one of Mr. Darwin's many enthusiastic admirers, and wrote a philosophic dialogue (the most offensive form, except poetry and books of travel into supposed unknown countries, that even literature can assume) upon the *Origin of Species* " (*Unconscious Memory*, close of Chapter I). This dialogue, unsigned, was printed in the *Press*, Canterbury, New Zealand, on 20th December, 1862. A copy of the paper was sent to Charles Darwin, who forwarded it to a, presumably,

English editor with a letter, now in the Canterbury Museum, New Zealand, speaking of the dialogue as " remarkable from its spirit and from giving so clear and accurate an account of Mr. D's theory." It is possible that Butler himself sent the newspaper containing his dialogue to Mr. Darwin ; if so he did not disclose his name, for Darwin says in his letter that he does not know who the author was. Butler was closely connected with the *Press*, which was founded by James Edward FitzGerald, the first Superintendent of the Province, in May, 1861 ; he frequently contributed to its pages, and once, during FitzGerald's absence, had charge of it for a short time, though he was never its actual editor. The *Press* reprinted the dialogue and the correspondence which followed its original appearance on 8th June, 1912.

On 13th June, 1863, the *Press* printed a letter by Butler signed " Cellarius " and headed " Darwin among the Machines," reprinted in *The Note-Books of Samuel Butler* (1912). The letter begins :

" Sir : There are few things of which the present generation is more justly proud than of the wonderful improvements which are daily taking place in all sorts of mechanical appliances " ; and goes on to say that, as the vegetable kingdom was developed from the mineral, and as the animal kingdom supervened upon the vegetable, " so now, in the last few ages, an entirely new kingdom has sprung up of which we as yet have only seen what will one day be considered the antediluvian types of the race." He then speaks of the minute members which compose the beautiful and intelligent little animal which we call the watch, and of how it has gradually been evolved from the clumsy brass clocks of the thirteenth century. Then comes the question : Who will be man's successor ? To which the answer is : We are ourselves creating our own successors. Man will become to the machine what the horse and the dog are to man ; the conclusion being that machines are, or are becoming, animate.

In 1863 Butler's family published in his name *A First Year in Canterbury Settlement*, which, as the preface states, was compiled from his letters home, his journal and extracts from two papers contributed to the *Eagle*. These two papers had appeared in the *Eagle* as three articles entitled " Our Emigrant " and signed " Cellarius." The proof sheets of the book went out to New Zealand for correction and were sent back in the *Colombo*, which was as unfortunate as the *Burmah*, for she was wrecked. The proofs, however, were fished up, though so nearly washed out as to be almost undecipherable. Butler would have been just as well pleased if they had remained at the bottom of the Indian Ocean, for he never liked the book and always spoke of it as being full of youthful priggishness ; but I think he was a little hard upon it. Years afterwards, in one of his later books, after quoting two passages from Mr. Grant Allen and pointing out why he considered the second to be a recantation of the first, he wrote : " When Mr. Allen does make stepping-stones of his dead selves he jumps upon them to some tune." And he was perhaps a little inclined to treat his own dead self too much in the same spirit.

Butler did very well with the sheep, sold out in 1864 and returned via Callao to England. He travelled with three friends whose acquaintance he had made in the colony ; one was Charles Paine Pauli, to whom he dedicated *Life and Habit*. He arrived in August, 1864, in London, where he took chambers consisting of a sitting-room, a bedroom, a painting-room and a pantry, at 15 Clifford's Inn, second floor (north). The net financial result of the sheep-farming and the selling out was that he practically doubled his capital, that is to say he had about £8000. This he left in New Zealand, invested on mortgage at 10 per cent, the then current rate in the colony ; it produced more than enough for him to live upon in the very simple way that suited him best, and life in the Inns of Court resembles life at Cambridge in that it reduces the cares of housekeeping to a minimum ; it suited him so well that he never changed his rooms, remaining there thirty-eight years till his death.

He was now his own master and able at last to turn to painting. He studied at the art school in Streatham Street, Bloomsbury, which had formerly been managed by Henry Sass, but, in Butler's time, was being carried on by Francis Stephen Cary, son of the Rev. Henry Francis Cary, who had been a school-fellow of Dr. Butler at Rugby and is well known as the translator of Dante and the friend of Charles Lamb. Among his fellow-students was Mr. H. R. Robertson, who told me that the young artists got hold of the legend, which is in some of the books about Lamb, that when Francis Stephen Cary was a boy and there was a talk at his father's house as to what profession he should take up, Lamb, who was present, said :

" I should make him an apo-po-pothe-Cary."

They used to repeat this story freely among themselves, being, no doubt, amused by the Lamb-like pun, but also enjoying the malicious pleasure of hinting that it might have been as well for their art education if the advice of the gentle humorist had been followed. Anyone who wants to know what kind of an artist F. S. Cary was can see his picture of Charles and Mary Lamb in the National Portrait Gallery.

In 1865 Butler sent from London to New Zealand an article entitled " Lucubratio Ebria," which was published in the *Press* of 29th July, 1865. It treated machines from a point of view different from that adopted in " Darwin among the Machines," and was one of the steps that led to *Erewhon* and ultimately to *Life and Habit*. The article is reproduced in *The Note-Books of Samuel Butler* (1912).

Butler also studied art at South Kensington, but by 1867 he had begun to go to Heatherley's School of Art in Newman Street, where he continued going for many years. He made a number of friends at Heatherley's, and among them Miss Eliza Mary Anne Savage. There also he first met Charles Gogin, who, in 1896, painted the portrait of Butler which is now in the National Portrait Gallery. He described himself as an artist in the Post Office Directory, and between 1868 and 1876 exhibited at the Royal Academy about a dozen pictures, of which the most important was " Mr. Heatherley's Holiday," hung on the line in 1874. He left it by his will to his college friend Jason Smith, whose representatives, after his death, in 1910, gave it to the nation and it is now in the National Gallery of British Art. Mr. Heatherley never went away for a holiday ; he once had to go out of town on business and did not return till the next day ; one of the students asked him how he had got on, saying no doubt he had enjoyed the change and that he must have found it refreshing to sleep for once out of London.

" No," said Heatherley, " I did not like it. Country air has no body."

The consequence was that, whenever there was a holiday and the school was shut, Heatherley employed the time in mending the skeleton ; Butler's picture represents him so engaged in a corner of the studio. In this way he got his model for nothing. Sometimes he hung up a looking-glass near one of his windows and painted his own portrait. Many of these he painted out, but after his death we found a little store of them in his rooms, some of the early ones very curious. Of the best of them one is now at Canterbury, New Zealand, one at St. John's College, Cambridge, and one at the Schools, Shrewsbury.

This is Butler's own account of himself, taken from a letter to Sir Julius von Haast ; although written in 1865 it is true of his mode of life for many years :

I have been taking lessons in painting ever since I arrived, I was always very fond of it and mean to stick to it ; it suits me and I am not without hopes that I shall do well at it. I live almost the life of a recluse, seeing very few people and going nowhere that I can help—I mean in the way of parties and so forth ; if my friends had their way they would fritter away my time without any remorse ; but I made a regular stand against it from the beginning and so, having my time pretty much in my own hands, work hard ; I find, as I am sure you must find, that it is next to impossible to combine what is commonly called society and work.

But the time saved from society was not all devoted to painting. He modified his letter to the *Press* about " Darwin among the Machines " and, so modified, it appeared in 1865 as " The Mechanical Creation " in the *Reasoner*, a paper then published in London by Mr. G. J. Holyoake. And his mind returned to the con-

siderations which had determined him to decline to be
ordained. In 1865 he printed anonymously a pamphlet
which he had begun in New Zealand, the result of his
study of the Greek Testament, entitled *The Evidence
for the Resurrection of Jesus Christ as given by the
Four Evangelists critically examined.* After weighing
this evidence and comparing one account with another,
he came to the conclusion that Jesus Christ did not
die upon the cross. It is improbable that a man
officially executed should escape death, but the
alternative, that a man actually dead should return
to life, seemed to Butler more improbable still and
unsupported by such evidence as he found in the
gospels. From this evidence he concluded that Christ
swooned and recovered consciousness after his body
had passed into the keeping of Joseph of Arimathæa.
He did not suppose fraud on the part of the first
preachers of Christianity ; they sincerely believed that
Christ died and rose again. Joseph and Nicodemus
probably knew the truth but kept silence. The idea
of what might follow from belief in one single supposed
miracle was never hereafter absent from Butler's mind.

In 1869, having been working too hard, he went
abroad for a long change. On his way back, at the
Albergo La Luna, in Venice, he met an elderly Russian
lady in whose company he spent most of his time there.
She was no doubt impressed by his versatility and
charmed, as everyone always was, by his conversation
and original views on the many subjects that interested
him. We may be sure he told her all about himself and
what he had done and was intending to do. At the end
of his stay, when he was taking leave of her, she said :

" Et maintenant, Monsieur, vous allez créer,"
meaning, as he understood her, that he had been

looking long enough at the work of others and should now do something of his own.

This sank into him and pained him. He was nearly thirty-five, and hitherto all had been admiration, vague aspiration and despair ; he had produced in painting nothing but a few sketches and studies, and in literature only a few ephemeral articles, a collection of youthful letters and a pamphlet on the Resurrection ; moreover, to none of his work had anyone paid the slightest attention. This was a poor return for all the money which had been spent upon his education, as Theobald would have said in *The Way of All Flesh.* He returned home dejected, but resolved that things should be different in the future. While in this frame of mind he received a visit from one of his New Zealand friends, the late Sir F. Napier Broome, afterwards Governor of Western Australia, who incidentally suggested his rewriting his New Zealand articles. The idea pleased him ; it might not be creating, but at least it would be doing something. So he set to work on Sundays and in the evenings, as relaxation from his profession of painting, and, taking his New Zealand article, "Darwin among the Machines," and another, "The World of the Unborn," as a starting point and helping himself with a few sentences from *A First Year in Canterbury Settlement,* he gradually formed *Erewhon.* He sent the MS. bit by bit, as it was written, to Miss Savage for her criticism and approval. He had the usual difficulty about finding a publisher. Chapman and Hall refused the book on the advice of George Meredith, who was then their reader, and in the end he published it at his own expense through Messrs. Trübner.

Mr. Sydney C. Cockerell told me that in 1912 Mr.

Bertram Dobell, second-hand bookseller of Charing
Cross Road, offered a copy of *Erewhon* for £1 10s. ; it
was thus described in his catalogue : " Unique copy
with the following note in the author's handwriting on
the half-title : ' To Miss E. M. A. Savage this first copy
of *Erewhon* with the author's best thanks for many
invaluable suggestions and corrections.' " When Mr.
Cockerell inquired for the book it was sold. After
Miss Savage's death in 1885 all Butler's letters to her
were returned to him, including the letter he wrote
when he sent her this copy of *Erewhon*. He gave her
the first copy issued of all his books that were published
in her lifetime, and, no doubt, wrote an inscription in
each. If the present possessors of any of them should
happen to read this sketch I hope they will communicate with me, as I should like to see these books.
I should also like to see some numbers of the *Drawing-
Room Gazette*, which about this time belonged to or was
edited by a Mrs. Briggs. Miss Savage wrote a review
of *Erewhon*, which appeared in the number for 8th
June, 1872, and Butler quoted a sentence from her
review among the press notices in the second edition.
She persuaded him to write for Mrs. Briggs notices of
concerts at which Handel's music was performed.
In 1901 he made a note on one of his letters that he
was thankful there were no copies of the *Drawing-Room
Gazette* in the British Museum, meaning that he did
not want people to read his musical criticisms ;
nevertheless, I hope some day to come across back
numbers containing his articles.

The opening of *Erewhon* is based upon Butler's
colonial experiences ; some of the descriptions remind
one of passages in *A First Year in Canterbury Settlement*, where he speaks of the excursions he made with

Doctor when looking for sheep-country. The walk over the range as far as the statues is taken from the Upper Rangitata district, with some alterations ; but the walk down from the statues into Erewhon is reminiscent of the Leventina Valley in the Canton Ticino. The great chords, which are like the music moaned by the statues, are from the prelude to the first of Handel's *Trois Leçons ;* he used to say :

"One feels them in the diaphragm—they are, as it were, the groaning and labouring of all creation travailing together until now."

There is a place in New Zealand named Erewhon, after the book ; it is marked on the large maps, a township about fifty miles west of Napier in the Hawke Bay Province (North Island). I am told that people in New Zealand sometimes call their houses Erewhon and occasionally spell the word Erehwon which Butler did not intend ; he treated wh as a single letter, as one would treat th. Among other traces of Erewhon now existing in real life are Butler's Stones on the Hokitika Pass, so called because of a legend that they were in his mind when he described the statues.

The book was translated into Dutch in 1873 and into German in 1897.

Butler wrote to Charles Darwin to explain what he meant by the " Book of the Machines " : " I am sincerely sorry that some of the critics should have thought I was laughing at your theory, a thing which I never meant to do and should be shocked at having done." Soon after this Butler was invited to Down and paid two visits to Mr. Darwin there ; he thus became acquainted with all the family and for some years was on intimate terms with Mr. (now Sir) Francis Darwin.

It is easy to see by the light of subsequent events

that we should probably have had something not unlike *Erewhon* sooner or later, even without the Russian lady and Sir F. N. Broome, to whose promptings, owing to a certain diffidence which never left him, he was perhaps inclined to attribute too much importance. But he would not have agreed with this view at the time ; he looked upon himself as a painter and upon *Erewhon* as an interruption. It had come, like one of those creatures from the Land of the Unborn, pestering him and refusing to leave him at peace until he consented to give it bodily shape. It was only a little one, and he saw no likelihood of its having any successors. So he satisfied its demands and then, supposing that he had written himself out, looked forward to a future in which nothing should interfere with the painting. Nevertheless, when another of the unborn came teasing him he yielded to its importunities and allowed himself to become the author of *The Fair Haven*, which is his pamphlet on the Resurrection, enlarged and preceded by a realistic memoir of the pseudonymous author, John Pickard Owen. In the library of St. John's College, Cambridge, are two copies of the pamphlet with pages cut out ; he used these pages in forming the MS. of *The Fair Haven*. To have published this book as by the author of *Erewhon* would have been to give away the irony and satire. And he had another reason for not disclosing his name ; he remembered that as soon as curiosity about the authorship of *Erewhon* was satisfied, the weekly sales fell from fifty down to only two or three. But, as he always talked openly of whatever was in his mind, he soon let out the secret of the authorship of *The Fair Haven*, and it became advisable to put his name to a second edition.

c

One result of his submitting the MS. of *Erewhon* to Miss Savage was that she thought he ought to write a novel, and urged him to do so. I have no doubt that he wrote the memoir of John Pickard Owen with the idea of quieting Miss Savage and also as an experiment to ascertain whether he was likely to succeed with a novel. The result seems to have satisfied him, for, not long after *The Fair Haven*, he began *The Way of All Flesh*, sending the MS. to Miss Savage, as he did everything he wrote, for her approval and putting her into the book as Ernest's Aunt Alethea. He continued writing it in the intervals of other work until her death in February, 1885, after which he did not touch it. It was published in 1903 by Mr. R. A. Streatfeild, his literary executor.

Soon after *The Fair Haven* Butler began to be aware that his letter in the *Press*, " Darwin among the Machines," was descending with further modifications and developing in his mind into a theory about evolution which took shape as *Life and Habit;* but the writing of this very remarkable and suggestive book was delayed and the painting interrupted by absence from England on business in Canada. He had been persuaded by a college friend, a member of one of the great banking families, to call in his colonial mortgages and to put the money into several new companies. He was going to make thirty or forty per cent instead of only ten. One of these companies was a Canadian undertaking, of which he became a director ; it was necessary for someone to go to headquarters and investigate its affairs ; he went, and was much occupied by the business for two or three years. By the beginning of 1876 he had returned finally to London, but most of his money was lost and his financial position for the next ten years caused him very serious anxiety. His personal expenditure was already so low that it was hardly possible to reduce it, and he set to work at his profession more industriously than ever, hoping to paint something that he could sell, his spare time being occupied with *Life and Habit*, which was the subject that really interested him more deeply than any other.

Following his letter in the *Press*, wherein he had seen machines as in process of becoming animate, he went on to regard them as living organs and limbs which we had made outside ourselves. What would follow if we reversed this and regarded our limbs and organs as machines which we had manufactured as parts of our bodies ? In the first place, how did we come to make them without knowing anything about it ? But then, how comes anybody to do anything unconsciously ? The answer usually would be : By habit. But can a man be said to do a thing by habit when he has never done it before ? His ancestors have done it, but not he. Can the habit have been acquired by them for his benefit ? Not unless he and his ancestors are the same person. Perhaps, then, they are the same person.

In February, 1876, partly to clear his mind and partly to tell someone, he wrote down his thoughts in a letter to his namesake, Thomas William Gale Butler, a fellow art-student who was then in New Zealand ; so much of the letter as concerns the growth of his theory is given in *The Note-Books of Samuel Butler* (1912) and a résumé of the theory will be found at the end of the last of the essays in this volume, " The Deadlock in Darwinism."

In September, 1877, when *Life and Habit* was on the

eve of publication, Mr. Francis Darwin came to lunch
with him in Clifford's Inn and, in course of conversation, told him that Professor Ray Lankester had
written something in *Nature* about a lecture by Dr.
Ewald Hering of Prague, delivered so long ago as
1870, "On Memory as a Universal Function of Organized Matter." This rather alarmed Butler, but he
deferred looking up the reference until after December,
1877, when his book was out, and then, to his relief,
he found that Hering's theory was very similar to his
own, so that, instead of having something sprung upon
him which would have caused him to want to alter his
book, he was supported. He at once wrote to the
Athenæum, calling attention to Hering's lecture, and
then pursued his studies in evolution.

Life and Habit was followed in 1879 by *Evolution
Old and New*, wherein he compared the teleological
or purposive view of evolution taken by Buffon, Dr.
Erasmus Darwin, and Lamarck with the view taken by
Charles Darwin, and came to the conclusion that the
old was better. But while agreeing with the earlier
writers in thinking that the variations whose accumulation results in species were originally due to intelligence,
he could not take the view that the intelligence resided
in an external personal God. He had done with all
that when he gave up the Resurrection of Jesus Christ
from the dead. He proposed to place the intelligence
inside the creature ("The Deadlock in Darwinism"
post).

In 1880 he continued the subject by publishing
Unconscious Memory. Chapter IV of this book is
concerned with a personal quarrel between himself and
Charles Darwin which arose out of the publication by
Charles Darwin of Dr. Krause's *Life of Erasmus Darwin*.

We need not enter into particulars here, the matter is fully dealt with in a pamphlet, *Charles Darwin and Samuel Butler : A Step towards Reconciliation*, which I wrote in 1911, the result of a correspondence between Mr. Francis Darwin and myself. Before this correspondence took place Mr. Francis Darwin had made several public allusions to *Life and Habit;* and in September, 1908, in his inaugural address to the British Association at Dublin, he did Butler the posthumous honour of quoting from his translation of Hering's lecture " On Memory," which is in *Unconscious Memory*, and of mentioning Butler as having enunciated the theory contained in *Life and Habit*.

In 1886 Butler published his last book on evolution, *Luck or Cunning as the Main Means of Organic Modification ?* His other contributions to the subject are some essays, written for the *Examiner* in 1879, " God the Known and God the Unknown," which were republished by Mr. Fifield in 1909, and the articles " The Deadlock in Darwinism" which appeared in the *Universal Review* in 1890 and are contained in this volume ; some further notes on evolution will be found in *The Note-Books of Samuel Butler* (1912).

It was while he was writing *Life and Habit* that I first met him. For several years he had been in the habit of spending six or eight weeks of the summer in Italy and the Canton Ticino, generally making Faido his headquarters. Many a page of his books was written while resting by the fountain of some subalpine village or waiting in the shade of the chestnuts till the light came so that he could continue a sketch. Every year he returned home by a different route, and thus gradually became acquainted with every part of the Canton and North Italy. There is scarcely a town or village, a point of view, a building, statue or picture in all this country with which he was not familiar. In 1878 he happened to be on the Sacro Monte above Varese at the time I took my holiday ; there I joined him, and nearly every year afterwards we were in Italy together.

He was always a delightful companion, and perhaps at his gayest on these occasions. " A man's holiday," he would say, " is his garden," and he set out to enjoy himself and to make everyone about him enjoy themselves too. I told him the old schoolboy muddle about Sir Walter Raleigh introducing tobacco and saying : " We shall this day light up such a fire in England as I trust shall never be put out." He had not heard it before and, though amused, appeared preoccupied, and perhaps a little jealous, during the rest of the evening. Next morning, while he was pouring out his coffee, his eyes twinkled and he said, with assumed carelessness :

" By the by, do you remember ?—wasn't it Columbus who bashed the egg down on the table and said ' Eppur non si muove ' ? "

He was welcome wherever he went, full of fun and ready to play while doing the honours of the country. Many of the peasants were old friends, and every day we were sure to meet someone who remembered him. Perhaps it would be an old woman labouring along under a burden ; she would smile and stop, take his hand and tell him how happy she was to meet him again and repeat her thanks for the empty wine bottle he had given her after an out-of-door luncheon in her neighbourhood four or five years before. There was another who had rowed him many times across the Lago di Orta and had never been in a train but once in her life, when she went to Novara to her son's wedding. He always remembered all about these people and asked how the potatoes were doing this year and whether the grandchildren were growing up into fine boys and girls, and he never forgot to inquire after the son who had gone to be a waiter in New York. At Civiasco there is a restaurant which used to be kept by a jolly old lady, known for miles round as La Martina ; we always lunched with her on our way over the Colma to and from Varallo-Sesia. On one occasion we were accompanied by two English ladies and, one being a teetotaller, Butler maliciously instructed La Martina to make the *sabbaglione* so that it should be *forte* and *abbondante*, and to say that the Marsala, with which it was more than flavoured, was nothing but vinegar. La Martina never forgot that when she looked in to see how things were going, he was pretending to lick the dish clean. These journeys provided the material for a book which he thought of calling "Verdi Prati," after one of Handel's most beautiful songs ; but he changed his mind, and it appeared at the end of 1881 as *Alps and Sanctuaries of Piedmont and the Canton Ticino* with more than eighty illustrations, nearly all by Butler. Charles Gogin made an etching for the frontispiece, drew some of the pictures, and put figures into others ; half a dozen are mine. They were all redrawn in ink from sketches made on the spot, in oil, water-colour, and pencil. There were also many illustrations of another kind—extracts from Handel's music, each chosen because Butler thought it suitable to the spirit of the scene he wished to bring before the reader. The introduction concludes with these words : " I have chosen Italy as my second country, and would dedicate this book to her as a thank-offering for the happiness she has afforded me."

In the spring of 1883 he began to compose music, and in 1885 we published together an album of minuets, gavottes, and fugues. This led to our writing *Narcissus*, which is an Oratorio Buffo in the Handelian manner—that is as nearly so as we could make it. It is a mistake to suppose that all Handel's oratorios are upon sacred subjects ; some of them are secular. And not only so, but, whatever the subject, Handel was never at a loss in treating anything that came into his words by way of allusion or illustration. As Butler puts it in one of his sonnets :

> He who gave eyes to ears and showed in sound
> All thoughts and things in earth or heaven above—
> From fire and hailstones running along the ground
> To Galatea grieving for her love—
> He who could show to all unseeing eyes
> Glad shepherds watching o'er their flocks by night,
> Or Iphis angel-wafted to the skies,
> Or Jordan standing as an heap upright—

And so on. But there is one subject which Handel never treated—I mean the Money Market. Perhaps he avoided it intentionally ; he was twice bankrupt, and Mr. R. A. Streatfeild tells me that the British Museum possesses a MS. letter from him giving instructions as to the payment of the dividends on £500 South Sea Stock. Let us hope he sold out before the bubble burst ; if so, he was more fortunate than Butler, who was at this time of his life in great anxiety about his own financial affairs. It seemed a pity that Dr. Morell had never offered Handel some such words as these :

> The steadfast funds maintain their wonted state
> While all the other markets fluctuate.

Butler wondered whether Handel would have sent the steadfast funds up above par and maintained them on an inverted pedal with all the other markets fluctuating iniquitously round them like the sheep that turn every one to his own way in the *Messiah*. He thought something of the kind ought to have been done, and in the absence of Handel and Dr. Morell we determined to write an oratorio that should attempt to supply the want. In order to make our libretto as plausible as possible, we adopted the dictum of Monsieur Jourdain's Maître à danser: " Lorsqu'on a des personnes à faire parler en musique, il faut bien que, pour la vraisemblance, on donne dans la bergerie." Narcissus is accordingly a shepherd in love with Amaryllis ; they come to London with other shepherds and lose their money in imprudent speculations on the Stock Exchange. In the second part the aunt and godmother of Narcissus, having died at an advanced age worth one hundred thousand pounds, all of which she has bequeathed to her nephew and godson, the obstacle to his union with Amaryllis is removed. The money is invested in consols and all ends happily.

In December, 1886, Butler's father died, and his financial difficulties ceased. He engaged Alfred Emery Cathie as clerk, but made no other change, except that he bought a pair of new hair brushes and a larger wash-hand basin. Any change in his mode of life was an event. When in London he got up at 6.30 in the summer and 7.30 in the winter, went into his sitting-room, lighted the fire, put the kettle on and returned to bed. In half an hour he got up again, fetched the kettle of hot water, emptied it into the cold water that was already in his bath, refilled the kettle and put it back on the fire. After dressing, he came into his sitting-room, made tea and cooked, in his Dutch oven, something he had bought the day before. His laundress was an elderly woman, and he could not trouble her to come to his rooms so early in the morning ; on the other hand, he could not stay in bed until he thought it right for her to go out ; so it ended in his doing a great deal for himself. He then got his breakfast and read the *Times*. At 9.30 Alfred came, with whom he discussed anything requiring attention, and soon afterwards his laundress arrived. Then he started to walk to the British Museum, where he arrived about 10.30, every alternate morning calling at the butcher's in Fetter Lane to order his meat. In the Reading Room at the Museum he sat at Block B (" B for Butler ") and spent an hour " posting his notes "—that is reconsidering, rewriting, amplifying, shortening, and indexing the contents of the little note-book he always carried in his pocket. After the notes he went on till 1.30 with whatever book he happened to be writing.

On three days of the week he dined in a restaurant on his way home, and on the other days he dined in his chambers where his laundress had cooked his dinner. At two o'clock Alfred returned (having been home to dinner with his wife and children) and got tea ready for him. He then wrote letters and attended to his accounts till 3.45, when he smoked his first cigarette. He used to smoke a great deal, but, believing it to be bad for him, took to cigarettes instead of pipes, and gradually smoked less and less, making it a rule not to begin till some particular hour, and pushing this hour later and later in the day, till it settled itself at 3.45. There was no water laid on in his rooms, and every day he fetched one can full from the tap in the court, Alfred fetching the rest. When anyone expostulated with him about cooking his own breakfast and fetching his own water, he replied that it was good for him to have a change of occupation. This was partly the fact, but the real reason, which he could not tell everyone, was that he shrank from inconveniencing anybody ; he always paid more than was necessary when anything was done for him, and was not happy then unless he did some of the work himself.

At 5.30 he got his evening meal, he called it his tea, and it was little more than a facsimile of breakfast. Alfred left in time to post the letters before six. Butler then wrote music till about 8, when he came to see me in Staple Inn, returning to Clifford's Inn by about 10. After a light supper, latterly not more than a piece of toast and a glass of milk, he played one game of his own particular kind of Patience, prepared his breakfast things and fire ready for the next morning, smoked his seventh and last cigarette, and went to bed at eleven o'clock.

He was fond of the theatre, but avoided serious pieces. He preferred to take his Shakespeare from the book, finding that the spirit of the plays rather evaporated under modern theatrical treatment. In one of his books he brightens up the old illustration of *Hamlet* without the Prince of Denmark by putting it thus : " If the character of Hamlet be entirely omitted, the play must suffer, even though Henry Irving himself be cast for the title-rôle." Anyone going to the theatre in this spirit would be likely to be less disappointed by performances that were comic or even frankly farcical. Latterly, when he grew slightly deaf, listening to any kind of piece became too much of an effort ; nevertheless, he continued to the last the habit of going to one pantomime every winter.

There were about twenty houses where he visited, but he seldom accepted an invitation to dinner—it upset the regularity of his life ; besides, he belonged to no club and had no means of returning hospitality. When two colonial friends called unexpectedly about noon one day, soon after he settled in London, he went to the nearest cook-shop in Fetter Lane and returned carrying a dish of hot roast pork and greens. This was all very well once in a way, but not the sort of thing to be repeated indefinitely.

On Thursdays, instead of going to the Museum, he often took a day off, going into the country sketching or walking, and on Sundays, whatever the weather, he nearly always went into the country walking ; his map of the district for thirty miles round London is covered all over with red lines showing where he had been. He sometimes went out of town from Saturday to Monday, and for over twenty years spent Christmas at Boulogne-sur-Mer.

There is a Sacro Monte at Varallo-Sesia with many chapels, each containing life-sized statues and frescoes illustrating the life of Christ. Butler had visited this sanctuary repeatedly, and was a great favourite with the townspeople, who knew that he was studying the statues and frescoes in the chapels, and who remembered that in the preface to *Alps and Sanctuaries* he had declared his intention of writing about them. In August, 1887, the Varallesi brought matters to a head by giving him a civic dinner on the Mountain. Everyone was present, there were several speeches and, when we were coming down the slippery mountain path after it was all over, he said to me :

" You know, there's nothing for it now but to write

that book about the Sacro Monte at once. It must be the next thing I do."

Accordingly, on returning home, he took up photography and, immediately after Christmas, went back to Varallo to photograph the statues and collect material. Much research was necessary and many visits to out-of-the-way sanctuaries which might have contained work by the sculptor Tabachetti, whom he was rescuing from oblivion and identifying with the Flemish Jean de Wespin. One of these visits, made after his book was published, forms the subject of " The Sanctuary of Montrigone," reproduced in this volume. *Ex Voto*, the book about Varallo, appeared in 1888, and an Italian translation by Cavaliere Angelo Rizzetti was published at Novara in 1894.

" Quis Desiderio . . . ? " the second essay in this volume, was developed in 1888 from something in a letter from Miss Savage nearly ten years earlier. On the 15th of December, 1878, in acknowledging this letter, Butler wrote :

I am sure that any tree or flower nursed by Miss Cobbe would be the *very* first to fade away and that her gazelles would die long before they ever came to know her *well*. The sight of the brass buttons on her pea-jacket would settle them out of hand.

There was an enclosure in Miss Savage's letter, but it is unfortunately lost ; I suppose it must have been a newspaper cutting with an allusion to Moore's poem and perhaps a portrait of Miss Frances Power Cobbe— pea-jacket, brass buttons, and all.

On the 10th November, 1879, Miss Savage, having been ill, wrote to Butler :

I have been dipping into the books of Moses, being sometimes at a loss for something to read while shut up in my apartment. You know that I have never read the Bible much, consequently there is generally something of a novelty that I hit on As you do know your Bible well, perhaps you can tell me what became of Aaron. The account given of his end in Numbers xx is extremely ambiguous and unsatisfactory. Evidently he did not come by his death fairly, but whether he was murdered secretly for the furtherance of some private ends, or publicly in a State sacrifice, I can't make out. I myself rather incline to the former opinion, but I should like to know what the experts say about it. A very nice, exciting little tale might be made out of it in the style of the police stories in *All the Year Round* called " The Mystery of Mount Hor or What became of Aaron ? " Don't forget to write to me.

Butler's people had been suggesting that he should try to earn money by writing in magazines, and Miss Savage was falling in with the idea and offering a practical suggestion. I do not find that he had anything to tell her about the death of Aaron. On 23rd March, 1880, she wrote :

Dear Mr. Butler : Read the subjoined poem of Wordsworth and let me know what you understand its meaning, to be. Of course I have my opinion, which I think of communicating to the Wordsworth Society. You can belong to that Society for the small sum of 2/6 per annum. I think of joining because it is cheap.

" The subjoined poem " was the one beginning : " She dwelt among the untrodden ways," and Butler made this note on the letter :

To the foregoing letter I answered that I concluded Miss Savage meant to imply that Wordsworth had murdered Lucy in order to escape a prosecution for breach of promise.

Miss Savage to Butler.

2nd April, 1880: My dear Mr. Butler : I don't think you see all that I do in the poem, and I am afraid that the

suggestion of a DARK SECRET in the poet's life is not so
very obvious after all. I was hoping you would propose to
devote yourself for a few months to reading the *Excursion*,
his letters, &c., with a view to following up the clue, and
I am disappointed though, to say the truth, the idea of a
crime had not flashed upon me when I wrote to you. How
well the works of *great* men repay attention and study !
But you, who know your Bible so well, how was it that you
did not detect the plagiarism in the last verse ? Just refer
to the account of the disappearance of Aaron (I have not a
Bible at hand, we want one sadly in the club) but I am
sure that the words are identical [I cannot see what Miss
Savage meant. 1901. S. B.] *Cassell's Magazine* have
offered a prize for setting the poem to music, and I fell to
thinking how it could be treated musically, and so came
to a right comprehension of it.

Although Butler, when editing Miss Savage's letters
in 1901, could not see the resemblance between
Wordsworth's poem and Numbers xx., he at once
saw a strong likeness between Lucy and Moore's
heroine whom he had been keeping in an accessible
pigeon-hole of his memory ever since his letter about
Miss Frances Power Cobbe. He now sent Lucy to keep
her company and often spoke of the pair of them as
probably the two most disagreeable young women in
English literature—an opinion which he must have
expressed to Miss Savage and with which I have no
doubt she agreed.

In the spring of 1888, on his return from photo-
graphing the statues at Varallo, he found, to his disgust,
that the authorities of the British Museum had
removed Frost's *Lives of Eminent Christians* from its
accustomed shelf in the Reading Room. Soon afterwards Harry Quilter asked him to write for the
Universal Review and he responded with " Quis
Desiderio . . . ? " In this essay he compares himself

to Wordsworth and dwells on the points of resemblance between Lucy and the book of whose assistance he had now been deprived in a passage which echoes the opening of Chapter V of *Ex Voto*, where he points out the resemblances between Varallo and Jerusalem.

Early in 1888 the leading members of the Shrewsbury Archæological Society asked Butler to write a memoir of his grandfather and of his father for their Quarterly Journal. This he undertook to do when he should have finished *Ex Voto*. In December, 1888, his sisters, with the idea of helping him to write the memoir, gave him his grandfather's correspondence, which extended from 1790 to 1839. On looking over these very voluminous papers he became penetrated with an almost Chinese reverence for his ancestor and, after getting the Archæological Society to absolve him from his promise to write the memoir, set about a full life of Dr. Butler, which was not published till 1896. The delay was caused partly by the immense quantity of documents he had to sift and digest, the number of people he had to consult and the many letters he had to write, and partly by something that arose out of *Narcissus*, which we published in June, 1888.

Butler was not satisfied with having written only half of this work ; he wanted it to have a successor, so that by adding his two halves together, he could say he had written a whole Handelian oratorio. While staying with his sisters at Shrewsbury with this idea in his mind, he casually took up a book by Alfred Ainger about Charles Lamb and therein stumbled upon something about the *Odyssey*. It was years since he had looked at the poem, but, from what he remembered, he thought it might provide a suitable subject for musical treatment. He did not, however, want to put Dr. Butler aside, so I undertook to investigate. It is stated on the title-page of both *Narcissus* and *Ulysses* that the words were written and the music composed by both of us. As to the music, each piece bears the initials of the one who actually composed it. As to the words, it was necessary first to settle some general scheme and this, in the case of *Narcissus*, grew in the course of conversation. The scheme of *Ulysses* was constructed in a more formal way and Butler had perhaps rather less to do with it. We were bound by the *Odyssey*, which is, of course, too long to be treated fully, and I selected incidents that attracted me and settled the order of the songs and choruses. For this purpose, as I out-Shakespeare Shakespeare in the smallness of my Greek, I used *The Adventures of Ulysses* by Charles Lamb, which we should have known nothing about but for Ainger's book. Butler acquiesced in my proposals, but, when it came to the words themselves, he wrote practically all the libretto, as he had done in the case of *Narcissus;* I did no more than suggest a few phrases and a few lines here and there.

We had sent *Narcissus* for review to the papers, and, as a consequence, about this time, made the acquaintance of Mr. J. A. Fuller Maitland, then musical critic of the *Times;* he introduced us to that learned musician William Smith Rockstro, under whom we studied medieval counterpoint while composing *Ulysses*. We had already made some progress with it when it occurred to Butler that it would not take long and might, perhaps, be safer if he were to look at the original poem, just to make sure that Lamb had not misled me. Not having forgotten all his Greek, he bought a copy of the *Odyssey* and was so fascinated

D

by it that he could not put it down. When he came
to the Phœacian episode of Ulysses at Scheria he felt
he must be reading the description of a real place and
that something in the personality of the author was
eluding him. For months he was puzzled, and, to help
in clearing up the mystery, set about translating the
poem. In August, 1891, he had preceded me to
Chiavenna and on a letter I wrote him, telling him
when to expect me, he made this note :

It was during the few days I was at Chiavenna (at the
Hotel Grotta Crimée) that I hit upon the feminine authorship of the *Odyssey*. I did not find out its having been
written at Trapani till January, 1892.

He suspected that the authoress in describing both
Scheria and Ithaca was drawing from her native
country and searched on the Admiralty charts for the
features enumerated in the poem ; this led him to the
conclusion that the country could only be Trapani,
Mount Eryx, and the Ægadean Islands. As soon as he
could after this discovery he went to Sicily to study
the locality and found it in all respects suitable for
his theory ; indeed, it was astonishing how things kept
turning up to support his view. It is all in his book
The Authoress of the Odyssey, published in 1897 and
dedicated to his friend Cavaliere Biagio Ingroja of
Calatafimi.

His first visit to Sicily was in 1892, in August—a hot
time of the year, but it was his custom to go abroad
in the autumn. He returned to Sicily every year
(except one), but latterly went in the spring. He made
many friends all over the island, and after his death
the people of Calatafimi called a street by his name,
the Via Samuel Butler, " thus," as Ingroja wrote
when he announced the event to me, " honouring a

great man's memory, handing down his name to posterity, and doing homage to the friendly English nation." Besides showing that the *Odyssey* was written by a woman in Sicily and translating the poem into English prose, he also translated the *Iliad*, and, in March, 1895, went to Greece and the Troad to see the country therein described, where he found nothing to cause him to disagree with the received theories.

It has been said of him in a general way that the fact of an opinion being commonly held was enough to make him profess the opposite. It was enough to make him examine the opinion for himself, when it affected any of the many subjects which interested him, and if, after giving it his best attention, he found it did not hold water, then no weight of authority could make him say that it did. This matter of the geography of the *Iliad* is only one among many commonly received opinions which he examined for himself and found no reason to dispute ; on these he considered it un-necessary to write.

It is characteristic of his passion for doing things thoroughly that he learnt nearly the whole of the *Odyssey* and the *Iliad* by heart. He had a Pickering copy of each poem, which he carried in his pocket and referred to in railway trains, both in England and 'Italy, when saying the poems over to himself. These two little books are now in the library of St. John's College, Cambridge. He was, however, disappointed to find that he could not retain more than a book or two at a time and that, on learning more, he forgot what he had learnt first ; but he was about sixty at the time. Shakespeare's Sonnets, on which he published a book in 1899, gave him less trouble in this respect ; he knew them all by heart, and also their order, and one consequence of this was that he wrote some sonnets in the Shakespearian form. He found this intimate knowledge of the poet's work more useful for his purpose than reading commentaries by those who were less familiar with it. " A commentary on a poem," he would say, " may be useful as material on which to form an estimate of the commentator, but the poem itself is the most important document you can consult, and it is impossible to know it too intimately if you want to form an opinion about it and its author."

It was always the author, the work of God, that interested him more than the book—the work of man ; the painter more than the picture ; the composer more than the music. " If a writer, a painter, or a musician makes me feel that he held those things to be lovable which I myself hold to be lovable I am satisfied ; art is only interesting in so far as it reveals the personality of the artist." Handel was, of course, " the greatest of all musicians." Among the painters, he chiefly loved Giovanni Bellini, Carpaccio, Gaudenzio Ferrari, Rembrandt, Holbein, Velasquez, and De Hooghe ; in poetry Shakespeare, Homer, and the Authoress of the *Odyssey ;* and in architecture the man, whoever he was, who designed the Temple of Neptune at Paestum. Life being short, he did not see why he should waste any of it in the company of inferior people when he had these. And he treated those he met in daily life in the same spirit : it was what he found them to be that attracted or repelled him ; what others thought about them was of little or no consequence.

And now, at the end of his life, his thoughts reverted to the two subjects which had occupied him more than thirty years previously—namely, *Erewhon* and the evidence for the death and resurrection of Jesus Christ. The idea of what might follow from belief in one single supposed miracle had been slumbering during all those years and at last rose again in the form of a sequel to *Erewhon*. In *Erewhon Revisited* Mr. Higgs returns to find that the Erewhonians now believe in him as a god in consequence of the supposed miracle of his going up in a balloon to induce his heavenly father to send the rain. Mr. Higgs and the reader know that there was no miracle in the case, but Butler wanted to show that whether it was a miracle or not did not signify provided that the people believed it to be one. And so Mr. Higgs is present in the temple which is being dedicated to him and his worship.

The existence of his son George was an after-thought and gave occasion for the second leading idea of the book—the story of a father trying to win the love of a hitherto unknown son by risking his life in order to show himself worthy of it—and succeeding.

Butler's health had already begun to fail, and when he started for Sicily on Good Friday, 1902, it was for the last time : he knew he was unfit to travel, but was determined to go, and was looking forward to meeting Mr. and Mrs. J. A. Fuller Maitland, whom he was to accompany over the Odyssean scenes at Trapani and Mount Eryx. But he did not get beyond Palermo ; there he was so much worse that he could not leave his room. In a few weeks he was well enough to be removed to Naples, and Alfred went out and brought him home to London. He was taken to a nursing home in St. John's Wood where he lay for a month, attended by his old friend Dr. Dudgeon, and where he died on the 18th June, 1902.

There was a great deal he still wanted to do. He had intended to revise *The Way of All Flesh*, to write a book about Tabachetti, and to publish a new edition of *Ex Voto* with the mistakes corrected. Also he wished to reconsider the articles reprinted in this volume and was looking forward to painting more sketches and composing more music. While lying ill and very feeble within a few days of the end, and not knowing whether it was to be the end or not, he said to me :

" I am much better to-day. I don't feel at all as though I were going to die. Of course, it will be all wrong if I do get well, for there is my literary position to be considered. First I write *Erewhon*—that is my opening subject ; then, after modulating freely through all my other books and the music and so on, I return gracefully to my original key and write *Erewhon Revisited*. Obviously, now is the proper moment to come to a full close, make my bow and retire ; but I believe I am getting well after all. It's very inartistic, but I cannot help it."

Some of his readers complain that they often do not know whether he is serious or jesting. He wrote of Lord Beaconsfield : " Earnestness was his greatest danger, but if he did not quite overcome it (as indeed who can ? it is the last enemy that shall be subdued), he managed to veil it with a fair amount of success."' To veil his own earnestness he turned most naturally to humour, employing it in a spirit of reverence, as all the great humorists have done, to express his deepest and most serious convictions. He was aware that he ran the risk of being misunderstood by some but he also knew that it is useless to try to please all, and, like Mozart, he wrote to please himself and a few intimate friends.

I cannot speak at length of his kindness, consideration, and sympathy ; nor of his generosity, the extent
of which was very great and can never be known—it
was sometimes exercised in unexpected ways, as when
he gave my laundress a shilling because it was " such
a beastly foggy morning " ; nor of his slightly archaic
courtliness—unless among people he knew well he
usually left the room backwards, bowing to the company ; nor of his punctiliousness, industry, and pains-
taking attention to detail—he kept accurate accounts
not only of all his property by double entry but also of
his daily expenditure, which he balanced to a halfpenny
every evening, and his handwriting, always beautiful
and legible, was more so at sixty-six than at twenty-
six ; nor of his patience and cheerfulness during years
of anxiety when he had few to sympathize with him ;
nor of the strange mixture of simplicity and shrewdness
that caused one who knew him well to say : " Il sait
tout ; il ne sait rien ; il est poète."

Epitaphs always fascinated him, and formerly he
used to say he should like to be buried at Langar and
to have on his tombstone the subject of the last of
Handel's *Six Great Fugues*. He called this " The Old
Man Fugue," and said it was like an epitaph composed
for himself by one who was very old and tired and
sorry for things ; and he made young Ernest Pontifex
in *The Way of all Flesh* offer it to Edward Overton as
an epitaph for his Aunt Alethea. Butler, however, left
off wanting any tombstone long before he died. In
accordance with his wish his body was cremated, and
a week later Alfred and I returned to Woking and
buried his ashes under the shrubs in the garden of
the crematorium, with nothing to mark the spot.

The Humour of Homer
and other Essays

By Samuel Butler

The Humour of Homer[1]

THE first of the two great poems commonly
ascribed to Homer is called the *Iliad*—a title
which we may be sure was not given it by the author.
It professes to treat of a quarrel between Agamemnon
and Achilles that broke out while the Greeks were
besieging the city of Troy, and it does, indeed, deal
largely with the consequences of this quarrel ; whether,
however, the ostensible subject did not conceal another
that was nearer the poet's heart—I mean the last
days, death, and burial of Hector—is a point that I
cannot determine. Nor yet can I determine how much
of the *Iliad* as we now have it is by Homer, and how
much by a later writer or writers. This is a very vexed
question, but I myself believe the *Iliad* to be entirely
by a single poet.

The second poem commonly ascribed to the same
author is called the *Odyssey*. It deals with the adventures of Ulysses during his ten years of wandering after
Troy had fallen. These two works have of late years
been believed to be by different authors. The *Iliad* is
now generally held to be the older work by some one
or two hundred years.

The leading ideas of the *Iliad* are love, war, and
plunder, though this last is less insisted on than the
other two. The key-note is struck with a woman's

[1] A lecture delivered at the Working Men's College, Great Ormond
Street, 30th January, 1892.

charms, and a quarrel among men for their possession. It is a woman who is at the bottom of the Trojan war itself. Woman throughout the *Iliad* is a being to be loved, teased, laughed at, and if necessary carried off. We are told in one place of a fine bronze cauldron for heating water which was worth twenty oxen, whereas a few lines lower down a good serviceable maid-of-all-work is valued at four oxen. I think there is a spice of malicious humour in this valuation, and am confirmed in this opinion by noting that though woman in the *Iliad* is on one occasion depicted as a wife so faithful and affectionate that nothing more perfect can be found either in real life or fiction, yet as a general rule she is drawn as teasing, scolding, thwarting, contradicting, and hoodwinking the sex that has the effrontery to deem itself her lord and master. Whether or no this view may have arisen from any domestic difficulties between Homer and his wife is a point which again I find it impossible to determine.

We cannot refrain from contemplating such possibilities. If we are to be at home with Homer there must be no sitting on the edge of one's chair dazzled by the splendour of his reputation. He was after all only a literary man, and those who occupy themselves with letters must approach him as a very honoured member of their own fraternity, but still as one who must have felt, thought, and acted much as themselves. He struck oil, while we for the most part succeed in boring only ; still we are his literary brethren, and if we would read his lines intelligently we must also read between them. That one so shrewd, and yet a dreamer of such dreams as have been vouchsafed to few indeed besides himself—that one so genially sceptical, and so given to looking into the heart of a matter, should have

been in such perfect harmony with his surroundings
as to think himself in the best of all possible worlds—
this is not believable. The world is always more or
less out of joint to the poet—generally more so ; and
unfortunately he always thinks it more or less his
business to set it right—generally more so. We are all
of us more or less poets—generally, indeed, less so ;
still we feel and think, and to think at all is to be out
of harmony with much that we think about. We may
be sure, then, that Homer had his full share of troubles,
and also that traces of these abound up and down his
work if we could only identify them, for everything
that everyone does is in some measure a portrait of
himself ; but here comes the difficulty—not to read
between the lines, not to try and detect the hidden
features of the writer—this is to be a dull, unsym-
pathetic, incurious reader ; and on the other hand to
try and read between them is to be in danger of running
after every Will o' the Wisp that conceit may raise
for our delusion.

I believe it will help you better to understand the
broad humour of the *Iliad*, which we shall presently
reach, if you will allow me to say a little more about
the general characteristics of the poem. Over and
above the love and war that are his main themes, there
is another which the author never loses sight of—I
mean distrust and dislike of the ideas of his time as
regards the gods and omens. No poet ever made gods
in his own image more defiantly than the author of
the *Iliad*. In the likeness of man created he them, and
the only excuse for him is that he obviously desired
his readers not to take them seriously. This at least
is the impression he leaves upon his reader, and when
so great a man as Homer leaves an impression it must

be presumed that he does so intentionally. It may be almost said that he has made the gods take the worse, not the better, side of man's nature upon them, and to be in all respects as we ourselves—yet without virtue. It should be noted, however, that the gods on the Trojan side are treated far more leniently than those who help the Greeks.

The chief gods on the Grecian side are Juno, Minerva, and Neptune. Juno, as you will shortly see, is a scolding wife, who in spite of all Jove's bluster wears the breeches, or tries exceedingly hard to do so. Minerva is an angry termagant—mean, mischief-making, and vindictive. She begins by pulling Achilles' hair, and later on she knocks the helmet from off the head of Mars. She hates Venus, and tells the Grecian hero Diomede that he had better not wound any of the other gods, but that he is to hit Venus if he can, which he presently does ' because he sees that she is feeble and not like Minerva or Bellona.' Neptune is a bitter hater.

Apollo, Mars, Venus, Diana, and Jove, so far as his wife will let him, are on the Trojan side. These, as I have said, meet with better, though still somewhat contemptuous, treatment at the poet's hand. Jove, however, is being mocked and laughed at from first to last, and if one moral can be drawn from the *Iliad* more clearly than another, it is that he is only to be trusted to a very limited extent. Homer's position, in fact, as regards divine interference is the very opposite of David's. David writes, " Put not your trust in princes nor in any child of man ; there is no sure help but from the Lord." With Homer it is, " Put not your trust in Jove neither in any omen from heaven ; there is but one good omen—to fight for one's

country. Fortune favours the brave ; heaven helps
those who help themselves."

The god who comes off best is Vulcan, the lame,
hobbling, old blacksmith, who is the laughing-stock
of all the others, and whose exquisitely graceful skilful
workmanship forms such an effective contrast to the
uncouth exterior of the workman. Him, as a man of
genius and an artist, and furthermore as a somewhat
despised artist, Homer treats, if with playfulness, still
with respect, in spite of the fact that circumstances
have thrown him more on the side of the Greeks than
of the Trojans, with whom I understand Homer's
sympathies mainly to lie.

The poet either dislikes music or is at best insensible
to it. Great poets very commonly are so. Achilles,
indeed, does on one occasion sing to his own accompaniment on the lyre, but we are not told that it was
any pleasure to hear him, and Patroclus, who was in
the tent at the time, was not enjoying it ; he was only
waiting for Achilles to leave off. But though not fond
of music, Homer has a very keen sense of the beauties
of nature, and is constantly referring both in and out
of season to all manner of homely incidents that are as
familiar to us as to himself. Sparks in the train of a
shooting-star ; a cloud of dust upon a high road ;
foresters going out to cut wood in a forest ; the shrill
cry of the cicale ; children making walls of sand on
the sea-shore, or teasing wasps when they have found
a wasps' nest ; a poor but very honest woman who
gains a pittance for her children by selling wool, and
weighs it very carefully ; a child clinging to its mother's
dress and crying to be taken up and carried—none of
these things escape him. Neither in the *Iliad* nor the
Odyssey do we ever receive so much as a hint as to the

time of year at which any of the events described are happening ; but on one occasion the author of the *Iliad* really has told us that it was a very fine day, and this not from a business point of view, but out of pure regard to the weather for its own sake.

With one more observation I will conclude my preliminary remarks about the *Iliad*. I cannot find its author within the four corners of the work itself. I believe the writer of the *Odyssey* to appear in the poem as a prominent and very fascinating character whom we shall presently meet, but there is no one in the *Iliad* on whom I can put my finger with even a passing idea that he may be the author. Still, if under some severe penalty I were compelled to find him, I should say it was just possible that he might consider his own lot to have been more or less like that which he forecasts for Astyanax, the infant son of Hector. At any rate his intimate acquaintance with the topography of Troy, which is now well ascertained, and still more his obvious attempt to excuse the non-existence of a great wall which, according to his story, ought to be there and which he knew had never existed, so that no trace could remain, while there were abundant traces of all the other features he describes—these facts convince me that he was in all probability a native of the Troad, or country round Troy. His plausibly concealed Trojan sympathies, and more particularly the aggravated exaggeration with which the flight of Hector is described, suggest to me, coming as they do from an astute and humorous writer, that he may have been a Trojan, at any rate by the mother's side, made captive, enslaved, compelled to sing the glories of his captors, and determined so to overdo them that if his masters cannot see through the irony others

sooner or later shall. This, however, is highly specu-
lative, and there are other views that are perhaps more
true, but which I cannot now consider.

I will now ask you to form your own opinions as
to whether Homer is or is not a shrewd and humorous
writer.

Achilles, whose quarrel with Agamemnon is the
ostensible subject of the poem, is son to a marine
goddess named Thetis, who had rendered Jove an
important service at a time when he was in great
difficulties. Achilles, therefore, begs his mother Thetis
to go up to Jove and ask him to let the Trojans dis-
comfit the Greeks for a time, so that Agamemnon may
find he cannot get on without Achilles' help, and may
thus be brought to reason.

Thetis tells her son that for the moment there is
nothing to be done, inasmuch as the gods are all of
them away from home. They are gone to pay a visit
to Oceanus in Central Africa, and will not be back for
another ten or twelve days ; she will see what can be
done, however, as soon as ever they return. This in
due course she does, going up to Olympus and laying
hold of Jove by the knee and by the chin. I may say
in passing that it is still a common Italian form of
salutation to catch people by the chin. Twice during
the last summer I have been so seized in token of
affectionate greeting, once by a lady and once by a
gentleman.

Thetis tells her tale to Jove, and concludes by saying
that he is to say straight out ' yes ' or ' no ' whether
he will do what she asks. Of course he can please
himself, but she should like to know how she stands.

" It will be a plaguy business," answers Jove, " for
me to offend Juno and put up with all the bitter tongue

E

she will give me. As it is, she is always nagging at me
and saying I help the Trojans, still, go away now at
once before she finds out that you have been here, and
leave the rest to me. See, I nod my head to you, and
this is the most solemn form of covenant into which I
can enter. I never go back upon it, nor shilly-shally
with anybody when I have once nodded my head."
Which, by the way, amounts to an admission that he
does shilly-shally sometimes.

Then he frowns and nods, shaking the hair on his
immortal head till Olympus rocks again. Thetis goes
off under the sea and Jove returns to his own palace.
All the other gods stand up when they see him coming,
for they do not dare to remain sitting while he passes,
but Juno knows he has been hatching mischief against
the Greeks with Thetis, so she attacks him in the
following words :

" You traitorous scoundrel," she exclaims, " which
of the gods have you been taking into your counsel
now ? You are always trying to settle matters behind
my back, and never tell me, if you can help it, a single
word about your designs."

" ' Juno,' replied the father of gods and men, ' you
must not expect to be told everything that I am
thinking about : you are my wife, it is true, but you
might not be able always to understand my meaning ;
in so far as it is proper for you to know of my inten-
tions you are the first person to whom I communicate
them either among the gods or among mankind, but
there are certain points which I reserve entirely for
myself, and the less you try to pry into these, or meddle
with them, the better for you.' "

" ' Dread son of Saturn,' answered Juno, ' what in
the world are you talking about ? *I* meddle and pry ?

No one, I am sure, can have his own way in everything more absolutely than you have. Still I have a strong misgiving that the old merman's daughter Thetis has been talking you over. I saw her hugging your knees this very self-same morning, and I suspect you have been promising her to kill any number of people down at the Grecian ships, in order to gratify Achilles.' "

" ' Wife,' replied Jove, ' I can do nothing but you suspect me. You will not do yourself any good, for the more you go on like that the more I dislike you, and it may fare badly with you. If I mean to have it so, I mean to have it so, you had better therefore sit still and hold your tongue as I tell you, for if I once begin to lay my hands about you, there is not a god in heaven who will be of the smallest use to you.'

" When Juno heard this she thought it better to submit, so she sat down without a word, but all the gods throughout Jove's mansion were very much perturbed. Presently the cunning workman Vulcan tried to pacify his mother Juno, and said, ' It will never do for you two to go on quarrelling and setting heaven in an uproar about a pack of mortals. The thing will not bear talking about. If such counsels are to prevail a god will not be able to get his dinner in peace. Let me then advise my mother (and I am sure it is her own opinion) to make her peace with my dear father, lest he should scold her still further, and spoil our banquet ; for if he does wish to turn us all out there can be no question about his being perfectly able to do so. Say something civil to him, therefore, and then perhaps he will not hurt us.'

" As he spoke he took a large cup of nectar and put it into his mother's hands, saying, ' Bear it, my dear mother, and make the best of it. I love you dearly and should be very sorry to see you get a thrashing. I should not be able to help you, for my father Jove is not a safe person to differ from. You know once before when I was trying to help you he caught me by the foot and chucked me from the heavenly threshold. I was all day long falling from morn to eve, but at sunset I came to ground on the island of Lemnos, and there was very little life left in me, till the Sintians came and tended me.'

" On this Juno smiled, and with a laugh took the cup from her son's hand. Then Vulcan went about among all other gods drawing nectar for them from his goblet, and they laughed immoderately as they saw him bustling about the heavenly mansion."

Then presently the gods go home to bed, each one in his own house that Vulcan had cunningly built for him or her. Finally Jove himself went to the bed which he generally occupied ; and Jove his wife went with him.

There is another quarrel between Jove and Juno at the beginning of the fourth book.

The gods are sitting on the golden floor of Jove's palace and drinking one another's health in the nectar with which Hebe from time to time supplies them. Jove begins to tease Juno, and to provoke her with some sarcastic remarks that are pointed at her though not addressed to her directly.

" ' Menelaus,' he exclaimed, ' has two good friends among the goddesses, Juno and Minerva, but they only sit still and look on, while Venus on the other hand takes much better care of Paris, and defends him when he is in danger. She has only just this moment been rescuing him when he made sure he was at death's door, for the victory really did lie with Menelaus.

We must think what we are to do about all this. Shall we renew strife between the combatants or shall we make them friends again ? I think the best plan would be for the City of Priam to remain unpillaged, but for Menelaus to have his wife Helen sent back to him.'

" Minerva and Juno groaned in spirit when they heard this. They were sitting side by side, and thinking what mischief they could do to the Trojans. Minerva for her part said not one word, but sat scowling at her father, for she was in a furious passion with him, but Juno could not contain herself, so she said—

" ' What, pray, son of Saturn, is all this about ? Is my trouble then to go for nothing, and all the pains that I have taken, to say nothing of my horses, and the way we have sweated and toiled to get the people together against Priam and his children ? You can do as you please, but you must not expect all of us to agree with you.'

" And Jove answered, ' Wife, what harm have Priam and Priam's children done you that you rage so furiously against them, and want to sack their city ? Will nothing do for you but you must eat Priam with his sons and all the Trojans into the bargain ? Have it your own way then, for I will not quarrel with you—only remember what I tell you : if at any time I want to sack a city that belongs to any friend of yours, it will be no use your trying to hinder me, you will have to let me do it, for I only yield to you now with the greatest reluctance. If there was one city under the sun which I respected more than another it was Troy with its king and people. My altars there have never been without the savour of fat or of burnt sacrifice and all my dues were paid.'

" ' My own favourite cities,' answered Juno, ' are
Argos, Sparta, and Mycenæ. Sack them whenever you
may be displeased with them. I shall not make the
smallest protest against your doing so. It would be
no use if I did, for you are much stronger than I am,
only I will not submit to seeing my own work wasted.
I am a goddess of the same race as yourself. I am
Saturn's eldest daughter and am not only nearly
related to you in blood, but I am wife to yourself,
and you are king over the gods. Let it be a case, then,
of give and take between us, and the other gods will
follow our lead. Tell Minerva, therefore, to go down
at once and set the Greeks and Trojans by the ears
again, and let her so manage it that the Trojans shall
break their oaths and be the aggressors.' "

This is the very thing to suit Minerva, so she goes at
once and persuades the Trojans to break their oath.

In a later book we are told that Jove has positively
forbidden the gods to interfere further in the struggle.
Juno therefore determines to hoodwink him. First she
bolted herself inside her own room on the top of Mount
Ida and had a thorough good wash. Then she scented
herself, brushed her golden hair, put on her very best
dress and all her jewels. When she had done this, she
went to Venus and besought her for the loan of her
charms.

" ' You must not be angry with me, Venus,' she
began, ' for being on the Grecian side while you are
yourself on the Trojan ; but you know every one falls
in love with you at once, and I want you to lend me
some of your attractions. I have to pay a visit at the
world's end to Oceanus and Mother Tethys. They took
me in and were very good to me when Jove turned
Saturn out of heaven and shut him up under the sea.

They have been quarrelling this long time past and
will not speak to one another. So I must go and see
them, for if I can only make them friends again I am
sure that they will be grateful to me for ever afterwards.' "

Venus thought this reasonable, so she took off her
girdle and lent it to Juno, an act by the way which
argues more good nature than prudence on her part.
Then Juno goes down to Thrace, and in search of Sleep
the brother of Death. She finds him and shakes hands
with him. Then she tells him she is going up to
Olympus to make love to Jove, and that while she is
occupying his attention Sleep is to send him off into
a deep slumber.

Sleep says he dares not do it. He would lull any of
the other gods, but Juno must remember that she had
got him into a great scrape once before in this way,
and Jove hurled the gods about all over the palace,
and would have made an end of him once for all, if he
had not fled under the protection of Night, whom Jove
did not venture to offend.

Juno bribes him, however, with a promise that if he
will consent she will marry him to the youngest of the
Graces, Pasithea. On this he yields ; the pair then
go up to the top of Mount Ida, and Sleep gets into a
high pine tree just in front of Jove.

As soon as Jove sees Juno, armed as she for the
moment was with all the attractions of Venus, he falls
desperately in love with her, and says she is the only
goddess he ever really loved. True, there had been
the wife of Ixion and Danae, and Europa and Semele,
and Alcmena, and Latona, not to mention herself in
days gone by, but he never loved any of these as he
now loved her, in spite of his having been married

to her for so many years. What then does she want ?

Juno tells him the same rigmarole about Oceanus and Mother Tethys that she had told Venus, and when she has done Jove tries to embrace her.

" What," exclaims Juno, " kiss me in such a public place as the top of Mount Ida ! Impossible ! I could never show my face in Olympus again, but I have a private room of my own and "—" What nonsense, my love ! " exclaims the sire of gods and men as he catches her in his arms. On this Sleep sends him into a deep slumber, and Juno then sends Sleep to bid Neptune go off to help the Greeks at once.

When Jove awakes and finds the trick that has been played upon him, he is very angry and blusters a good deal as usual, but somehow or another it turns out that he has got to stand it and make the best of it.

In an earlier book he has said that he is not surprised at anything Juno may do, for she always has crossed him and always will ; but he cannot put up with such disobedience from his own daughter Minerva. Somehow or another, however, here too as usual it turns out that he has got to stand it. " And then," Minerva exclaims in yet another place (VIII. 373), " I suppose he will be calling me his grey-eyed darling again, presently."

Towards the end of the poem the gods have a set-to among themselves. Minerva sends Mars sprawling, Venus comes to his assistance, but Minerva knocks her down and leaves her. Neptune challenges Apollo, but Apollo says it is not proper for a god to fight his own uncle, and declines the contest. His sister Diana taunts him with cowardice, so Juno grips her by the wrist and boxes her ears till she writhes again. Latona,

the mother of Apollo and Diana, then challenges
Mercury, but Mercury says that he is not going to fight
with any of Jove's wives, so if she chooses to say she
has beaten him she is welcome to do so. Then Latona
picks up poor Diana's bow and arrows that have fallen
from her during her encounter with Juno, and Diana
meanwhile flies up to the knees of her father Jove,
sobbing and sighing till her ambrosial robe trembles all
around her.

" Jove drew her towards him, and smiling pleasantly
exclaimed, ' My dear child, which of the heavenly
beings has been wicked enough to behave in this way
to you, as though you had been doing something
naughty ? '

" ' Your wife, Juno,' answered Diana, ' has been ill-
treating me ; all our quarrels always begin with her.' "

The above extracts must suffice as examples of the
kind of divine comedy in which Homer brings the gods
and goddesses upon the scene. Among mortals the
humour, what there is of it, is confined mainly to the
grim taunts which the heroes fling at one another when
they are fighting, and more especially to crowing over
a fallen foe. The most subtle passage is the one in
which Briseis, the captive woman about whom Achilles
and Agamemnon have quarrelled, is restored by Agamemnon to Achilles. Briseis on her return to the tent
of Achilles finds that while she has been with Agamemnon, Patroclus has been killed by Hector, and his
dead body is now lying in state. She flings herself
upon the corpse and exclaims—

" How one misfortune does keep falling upon me
after another ! I saw the man to whom my father and
mother had married me killed before my eyes, and my

three own dear brothers perished along with him ; but you, Patroclus, even when Achilles was sacking our city and killing my husband, told me that I was not to cry ; for you said that Achilles himself should marry me, and take me back with him to Phthia, where we should have a wedding feast among the Myrmidons. You were always kind to me, and I should never cease to grieve for you."

This may of course be seriously intended, but Homer was an acute writer, and if we had met with such a passage in Thackeray we should have taken him to mean that so long as a woman can get a new husband, she does not much care about losing the old one—a sentiment which I hope no one will imagine that I for one moment endorse or approve of, and which I can only explain as a piece of sarcasm aimed possibly at Mrs. Homer.

And now let us turn to the *Odyssey*, a work which I myself think of as the *Iliad's* better half or wife. Here we have a poem of more varied interest, instinct with not less genius, and on the whole I should say, if less robust, nevertheless of still greater fascination— one, moreover, the irony of which is pointed neither at gods nor woman, but with one single and perhaps intercalated exception, at man. Gods and women may sometimes do wrong things, but, except as regards the intrigue between Mars and Venus just referred to, they are never laughed at. The scepticism of the *Iliad* is that of Hume or Gibbon ; that of the *Odyssey* (if any) is like the occasional mild irreverence of the Vicar's daughter. When Jove says he will do a thing, there is no uncertainty about his doing it. Juno hardly appears at all, and when she does she never quarrels with her husband. Minerva has more to do than any of the other gods or goddesses, but she has nothing in common with the Minerva whom we have already seen in the *Iliad*. In the *Odyssey* she is the fairy god-mother who seems to have no object in life but to protect Ulysses and Telemachus, and keep them straight at any touch and turn of difficulty. If she has any other function, it is to be patroness of the arts and of all intellectual development. The Minerva of the *Odyssey* may indeed sit on a rafter like a swallow and hold up her ægis to strike panic into the suitors while Ulysses kills them ; but she is a perfect lady, and would no more knock Mars and Venus down one after the other than she would stand on her head. She is, in fact, a distinct person in all respects from the Minerva of the *Iliad*. Of the remaining gods Neptune, as the persecutor of the hero, comes worst off ; but even he is treated as though he were a very important person.

In the *Odyssey* the gods no longer live in houses and sleep in four-post bedsteads, but the conception of their abode, like that of their existence altogether, is far more spiritual. Nobody knows exactly where they live, but they say it is in Olympus, where there is neither rain nor hail nor snow, and the wind never beats roughly ; but it abides in everlasting sunshine, and in great peacefulness of light wherein the blessed gods are illumined for ever and ever. It is hardly possible to conceive anything more different from the Olympus of the *Iliad*.

Another very material point of difference between the *Iliad* and the *Odyssey* lies in the fact that the Homer of the *Iliad* always knows what he is talking about, while the supposed Homer of the *Odyssey* often makes mistakes that betray an almost incredible ignorance of detail. Thus the giant Polyphemus drives in his ewes home from their pasture, and milks them. The lambs of course have not been running with them ; they have been left in the yards, so they have had nothing to eat. When he has milked the ewes, the giant lets each one of them have her lamb—to get, I suppose, what strippings it can, and beyond this what milk the ewe may yield during the night. In the morning, however, Polyphemus milks the ewes again. Hence it is plain either that he expected his lambs to thrive on one pull *per diem* at a milked ewe, and to be kind enough not to suck their mothers, though left with them all night through, or else that the writer of the *Odyssey* had very hazy notions about the relations between lambs and ewes, and of the ordinary methods of procedure on an upland dairy-farm.

In nautical matters the same inexperience is betrayed. The writer knows all about the corn and wine that must be put on board ; the store-room in which these are kept and the getting of them are described inimitably, but there the knowledge ends ; the other things put on board are " the things that are generally taken on board ships." So on a voyage we are told that the sailors do whatever is wanted doing, but we have no details. There is a shipwreck, which does duty more than once without the alteration of a word. I have seen such a shipwreck at Drury Lane. Anyone, moreover, who reads any authentic account of actual adventures will perceive at once that those of the *Odyssey* are the creation of one who has had no history. Ulysses has to make a raft ; he makes it about as broad as they generally make a good big ship, but we do not seem to have been at the pains to measure a good big ship.

I will add no more however on this head. The leading characteristics of the *Iliad*, as we saw, were love, war, and plunder. The leading idea of the *Odyssey* is the infatuation of man, and the key-note is struck in the opening paragraph, where we are told how the sailors of Ulysses must needs, in spite of every warning, kill and eat the cattle of the sun-god, and perished accordingly.

A few lines lower down the same note is struck with even greater emphasis. The gods have met in council, and Jove happens at the moment to be thinking of Ægisthus, who had met his death at the hand of Agamemnon's son Orestes, in spite of the solemn warning that Jove had sent him through the mouth of Mercury. It does not seem necessary for Jove to turn his attention to Clytemnestra, the partner of Ægisthus's guilt. Of this lady we are presently told that she was naturally of an excellent disposition, and would never have gone wrong but for the loss of the protector in whose charge Agamemnon had left her. When she was left alone without an adviser—well, if a base designing man took to flattering and misleading her— what else could be expected? The infatuation of man, with its corollary, the superior excellence of woman, is the leading theme ; next to this come art, religion, and, I am almost ashamed to add, money. There is no love-business in the *Odyssey* except the return of a bald elderly married man to his elderly wife and grown-up son after an absence of t venty years, and furious at having been robbed of so much money in the mean-time. But this can hardly be called love-business ; it is at the utmost domesticity. There is a charming young princess, Nausicaa, but though she affects a passing tenderness for the elderly hero of her creation as soon as Minerva has curled his bald old hair for him and tittivated him up all over, she makes it abundantly plain that she will not look at a single one of her actual flesh and blood admirers. There is a leading young gentleman, Telemachus, who is nothing if he is not πεπνυμένος, or canny, well-principled, and discreet ; he has an amiable and most sensible young male friend who says that he does not like crying at meal times— he will cry in the forenoon on an empty stomach as much as anyone pleases, but he cannot attend properly to his dinner and cry at the same time. Well, there is no lady provided either for this nice young man or for Telemachus. They are left high and dry as bachelors. Two goddesses indeed, Circe and Calypso, do one after the other take possession of Ulysses, but the way in which he accepts a situation which after all was none of his seeking, and which it is plain he does not care two straws about, is, I believe, dictated solely by a desire to exhibit the easy infidelity of Ulysses himself in contrast with the unswerving constancy and fidelity of his wife Penelope. Throughout the *Odyssey* the men do not really care for women, nor the women for men ; they have to pretend to do so now and again, but it is a got-up thing, and the general attitude of the sexes towards one another is very much that of Helen, who says that her husband Menelaus is really not deficient in person or understanding : or again of Penelope herself, who, on being asked by Ulysses on his return what she thought of him, said that she did not think very much of him nor very little of him ; in fact, she did not think much about him one way or the other. True, later on she relents and becomes more effusive ; in fact, when she and Ulysses sat up talking in bed and Ulysses told her the story of his adventures, she never went to sleep once. Ulysses never had to nudge her with his elbow and say, " Come, wake up, Penelope, you are not listening " ; but, in spite of the devotion exhibited here, the love-business in the *Odyssey* is artificial and described by one who had never felt it, whereas in the *Iliad* it is spontaneous and obviously genuine, as by one who knows all about it perfectly well. The love-business in fact of the *Odyssey* is turned on as we turn on the gas—when we cannot get on without it, but not otherwise.

A fascinating brilliant girl, who naturally adopts for her patroness the blue-stocking Minerva ; a man-hatress, as clever girls so often are, and determined to pay the author of the *Iliad* out for his treatment of her sex by insisting on its superior moral, not to say intellectual, capacity, and on the self-sufficient imbecility of man unless he has a woman always at his elbow to keep him tolerably straight and in his proper place— this, and not the musty fusty old bust we see in libraries, is the kind of person who I believe wrote the *Odyssey*. Of course in reality the work must be written by a man, because they say so at Oxford and Cambridge, and they know everything down in Oxford and Cambridge ; but I venture to say that if the *Odyssey* were to appear anonymously for the first time now, and to be sent round to the papers for review, there is not even a professional critic who would not see that it is a woman's writing and not a man's. But letting this pass, I can hardly doubt, for reasons which I gave in yesterday's *Athenæum*, and for others that I cannot now insist upon, that the poem was written by a native of Trapani on the coast of Sicily, near Marsala. Fancy what the position of a young, ardent, brilliant woman must have been in a small Sicilian sea-port, say some

eight or nine hundred years before the birth of Christ.
It makes one shudder to think of it. Night after night
she hears the dreary blind old bard Demodocus drawl
out his interminable recitals taken from our present
Iliad, or from some other of the many poems now lost
that dealt with the adventures of the Greeks before
Troy or on their homeward journey. Man and his
doings ! always the same old story, and woman always
to be treated either as a toy or as a beast of burden,
or at any rate as an incubus. Why not sing of woman
also as she is when she is unattached and free from
the trammels and persecutions of this tiresome tyrant,
this insufferably self-conceited bore and booby, man ?

" I wish, my dear," exclaims her mother Arete, after
one of these little outbreaks, " that you would do it
yourself. I am sure you could do it beautifully if you
would only give your mind to it."

" Very well, mother," she replies, " and I will bring
in all about you and father, and how I go out for a
washing-day with the maids,"—and she kept her word,
as I will presently show you.

I should tell you that Ulysses, having got away from
the goddess Calypso, with whom he had been living
for some seven or eight years on a lonely and very
distant island in mid-ocean, is shipwrecked on the
coast of Phæacia, the chief town of which is Scheria.
After swimming some forty-eight hours in the water
he effects a landing at the mouth of a stream, and, not
having a rag of clothes on his back, covers himself up
under a heap of dried leaves and goes to sleep. I will
now translate from the *Odyssey* itself.

" So here Ulysses slept, worn out with labour and
sorrow ; but Minerva went off to the chief town of
the Phæacians, a people who used to live in Hypereia

near the wicked Cyclopes. Now the Cyclopes were stronger than they and plundered them, so Nausithous settled them in Scheria far from those who would loot them. He ran a wall round about the city, built houses and temples, and allotted the lands among his people ; but he was gathered to his fathers, and the good king Alcinous was now reigning. To his palace then Minerva hastened that she might help Ulysses to get home.

" She went straight to the painted bedroom of Nausicaa, who was daughter to King Alcinous, and lovely as a goddess. Near her there slept two maids-in-waiting, both very pretty, one on either side of the doorway, which was closed with a beautifully made door. She took the form of the famous Captain Dumas's daughter, who was a bosom friend of Nausicaa and just her own age ; then coming into the room like a breath of wind she stood near the head of the bed and said—

" ' Nausicaa, what could your mother have been about to have such a lazy daughter ? Here are your clothes all lying in disorder, yet you are going to be married almost directly, and should not only be well-dressed yourself, but should see that those about you look clean and tidy also. This is the way to make people speak well of you, and it will please your father and mother, so suppose we make to-morrow a washing day, and begin the first thing in the morning. I will come and help you, for all the best young men among your own people are courting you, and you are not going to remain a maid much longer. Ask your father, then, to have a horse and cart ready for us at daybreak to take the linen and baskets, and you can ride too, which will be much pleasanter for you than walking, for the washing ground is a long way out of the town.'

F

" When she had thus spoken Minerva went back to Olympus. By and by morning came, and as soon as Nausicaa woke she began thinking about her dream. She went to the other end of the house to tell her father and mother all about it, and found them in their own room. Her mother was sitting by the fireside spinning with her maids-in-waiting all around her, and she happened to catch her father just as he was going out to attend a meeting of the Town Council which the Phæacian aldermen had convened. So she stopped him and said, ' Papa, dear, could you manage to let me have a good big waggon ? I want to take all our dirty clothes to the river and wash them. You are the chief man here, so you ought to have a clean shirt on when you attend meetings of the Council. Moreover, you have five sons at home, two of them married and the other three are good-looking young bachelors ; you know they always like to have clean linen when they go out to a dance, and I have been thinking about all this.' "

You will observe that though Nausicaa dreams that she is going to be married shortly, and that all the best young men of Scheria are in love with her, she does not dream that she has fallen in love with any one of them in particular, and that thus every preparation is made for her getting married except the selection of the bridegroom.

You will also note that Nausicaa has to keep her father up to putting a clean shirt on when he ought to have one, whereas her young brothers appear to keep herself up to having a clean shirt ready for them when they want one. These little touches are so lifelike and so feminine that they suggest drawing from life by a female member of Alcinous's own family who knew his character from behind the scenes.

I would also say before proceeding further that in some parts of France and Germany it is still the custom to have but one or at most two great washing days in the year. Each household is provided with an enormous quantity of linen, which when dirty is just soaked and rinsed, and then put aside till the great washing day of the year. This is why Nausicaa wants a waggon, and has to go so far afield. If it was only a few collars and a pocket-handkerchief or two she could no doubt have found water enough near at hand. The big spring or autumn wash, however, is evidently intended.

Returning now to the *Odyssey*, when he had heard what Nausicaa wanted Alcinous said :

" ' You shall have the mules, my love, and whatever else you have a mind for, so be off with you.'

" Then he told the servants, and they got the waggon out and harnessed the mules, while the princess brought the clothes down from the linen room and placed them on the waggon. Her mother got ready a nice basket of provisions with all sorts of good things, and a goatskin full of wine. The princess now got into the waggon, and her mother gave her a golden cruse of oil that she and her maids might anoint themselves.

" Then Nausicaa took the whip and reins and gave the mules a touch which sent them off at a good pace. They pulled without flagging, and carried not only Nausicaa and her wash of clothes, but the women also who were with her.

" When they got to the river they went to the washing pools, through which even in summer there ran enough pure water to wash any quantity of linen, no matter how dirty. Here they unharnessed the mules and turned them out to feed in the sweet juicy grass that grew by the river-side. They got the clothes out of the waggon, brought them to the water, and vied with one another in treading upon them and banging them about to get the dirt out of them When they had got them quite clean, they laid them out by the seaside where the waves had raised a high beach of shingle, and set about washing and anointing themselves with olive oil. Then they got their dinner by the side of the river, and waited for the sun to finish drying the clothes. By and by, after dinner, they took off their head-dresses and began to play at ball, and Nausicaa sang to them."

I think you will agree with me that there is no haziness—no milking of ewes that have had a lamb with them all night—here. The writer is at home and on her own ground.

" When they had done folding the clothes and were putting the mules to the waggon before starting home again, Minerva thought it was time Ulysses should wake up and see the handsome girl who was to take him to the city of the Phæacians. So the princess threw a ball at one of the maids, which missed the maid and fell into the water. On this they all shouted, and the noise they made woke up Ulysses, who sat up in his bed of leaves and wondered where in the world he could have got to.

" Then he crept from under the bush beneath which he had slept, broke off a thick bough so as to cover his nakedness, and advanced towards Nausicaa and her maids ; these last all ran away, but Nausicaa stood her ground, for Minerva had put courage into her heart, so she kept quite still, and Ulysses could not make up his mind whether it would be better to go up to her, throw himself at her feet, and embrace her knees as a suppliant—[in which case, of course, he would have to drop the bough] or whether it would be better for him to make an apology to her at a reasonable distance, and ask her to be good enough to give him some clothes and show him the way to the town. On the whole he thought it would be better to keep at arm's length, in case the princess should take offence at his coming too near her."

Let me say in passing that this is one of many passages which have led me to conclude that the *Odyssey* is written by a woman. A girl, such as Nausicaa describes herself, young, unmarried, unattached, and hence, after all, knowing little of what men feel on these matters, having by a cruel freak of inspiration got her hero into such an awkward predicament, might conceivably imagine that he would argue as she represents him, but no man, except such a woman's tailor as could never have written such a masterpiece as the *Odyssey*, would ever get his hero into such an undignified scrape at all, much less represent him as arguing as Ulysses does. I suppose Minerva was so busy making Nausicaa brave that she had no time to put a little sense into Ulysses' head, and remind him that he was nothing if not full of sagacity and resource. To return—

Ulysses now begins with the most judicious apology that his unaided imagination can suggest. " I beg your ladyship's pardon," he exclaims, " but are you goddess or are you a mortal woman ? If you are a goddess and live in heaven, there can be no doubt but you are Jove's daughter Diana, for your face and figure are exactly like hers," and so on in a long speech which I need not further quote from.

" Stranger," replied Nausicaa, as soon as the speech

was ended, " you seem to be a very sensible well-disposed person. There is no accounting for luck ; Jove gives good or ill to every man, just as he chooses, so you must take your lot, and make the best of it." She then tells him she will give him clothes and everything else that a foreigner in distress can reasonably expect. She calls back her maids, scolds them for running away, and tells them to take Ulysses and wash him in the river after giving him something to eat and drink. So the maids give him the little gold cruse of oil and tell him to go and wash himself, and as they seem to have completely recovered from their alarm, Ulysses is compelled to say, " Young ladies, please stand a little on one side, that I may wash the brine from off my shoulders and anoint myself with oil ; for it is long enough since my skin has had a drop of oil upon it. I cannot wash as long as you keep standing there. I have no clothes on, and it makes me very uncomfortable."

So they stood aside and went and told Nausicaa. Meanwhile (I am translating closely), " Minerva made him look taller and stronger than before ; she gave him some more hair on the top of his head, and made it flow down in curls most beautifully ; in fact she glorified him about the head and shoulders as a cunning workman who has studied under Vulcan or Minerva enriches a fine piece of plate by gilding it."

Again I argue that I am reading a description of as it were a prehistoric Mr. Knightley by a not less prehistoric Jane Austen—with this difference that I believe Nausicaa is quietly laughing at her hero and sees through him, whereas Jane Austen takes Mr. Knightley seriously.

" Hush, my pretty maids," exclaimed Nausicaa as

soon as she saw Ulysses coming back with his hair curled, " hush, for I want to say something. I believe the gods in heaven have sent this man here. There is something very remarkable about him. When I first saw him I thought him quite plain and common-place, and now I consider him one of the handsomest men I ever saw in my life. I should like my future husband [who, it is plain, then, is not yet decided upon] to be just such another as he is, if he would only stay here, and not want to go away. However, give him something to eat and drink."

Nausicaa now says they must be starting home-ward ; so she tells Ulysses that she will drive on first herself, but that he is to follow after her with the maids. She does not want to be seen coming into the town with him ; and then follows another passage which clearly shows that for all the talk she has made about getting married she has no present intention of changing her name.

" ' I am afraid,' she says, ' of the gossip and scandal which may be set on foot about me behind my back, for there are some very ill-natured people in the town, and some low fellow, if he met us, might say, ' Who is this fine-looking stranger who is going about with Nausicaa ? Where did she pick him up ? I suppose she is going to marry him, or perhaps he is some ship-wrecked sailor from foreign parts ; or has some god come down from heaven in answer to her prayers, and she is going to live with him ? It would be a good thing if she would take herself off and find a husband somewhere else, for she will not look at one of the many excellent young Phæacians who are in love with her ' ; and I could not complain, for I should myself think ill of any girl whom I saw going about with men unknown to her father and mother, and without having been married to him in the face of all the world.' "

This passage could never have been written by the local bard, who was in great measure dependent on Nausicaa's family ; he would never speak thus of his patron's daughter ; either the passage is Nausicaa's apology for herself, written by herself, or it is pure invention, and this last, considering the close adherence to the actual topography of Trapani on the Sicilian Coast, and a great deal else that I cannot lay before you here, appears to me improbable.

Nausicaa then gives Ulysses directions by which he can find her father's house. " When you have got past the courtyard," she says, " go straight through the main hall, till you come to my mother's room. You will find her sitting by the fire and spinning her purple wool by firelight. She will make a lovely picture as she leans back against a column with her maids ranged behind her. Facing her stands my father's seat in which he sits and topes like an immortal god. Never mind him, but go up to my mother and lay your hands upon her knees, if you would be forwarded on your homeward voyage." From which I conclude that Arete ruled Alcinous, and Nausicaa ruled Arete.

Ulysses follows his instructions aided by Minerva, who makes him invisible as he passes through the town and through the crowds of Phæacian guests who are feasting in the king's palace. When he has reached the queen, the cloak of thick darkness falls off, and he is revealed to all present, kneeling at the feet of Queen Arete, to whom he makes his appeal. It has already been made apparent in a passage extolling her virtue at some length, but which I have not been able to quote, that Queen Arete is, in the eyes of the writer,

a much more important person than her husband
Alcinous.

Every one, of course, is very much surprised at seeing
Ulysses, but after a little discussion, from which it
appears that the writer considers Alcinous to be a
person who requires a good deal of keeping straight
in other matters besides clean linen, it is settled that
Ulysses shall be fêted on the following day and then
escorted home. Ulysses now has supper and remains
with Alcinous and Arete after the other guests are
gone away for the night. So the three sit by the fire
while the servants take away the things, and Arete is
the first to speak. She has been uneasy for some time
about Ulysses' clothes, which she recognized as her
own make, and at last she says, " Stranger, there is a
question or two that I should like to put to you myself.
Who in the world are you ? And who gave you those
clothes ? Did you not say you had come here from
beyond the seas ? "

Ulysses explains matters, but still withholds his
name, nevertheless Alcinous (who seems to have
shared in the general opinion that it was high time his
daughter got married, and that, provided she married
somebody, it did not much matter who the bridegroom
might be) exclaimed, " By Father Jove, Minerva, and
Apollo, now that I see what kind of a person you are
and how exactly our opinions coincide upon every
subject, I should so like it if you would stay with us
always, marry Nausicaa, and become my son-in-law."

Ulysses turns the conversation immediately, and
meanwhile Queen Arete told her maids to put a bed
in the corridor, and make it with red blankets, and it
was to have at least one counterpane. They were also
to put a woollen nightgown for Ulysses. " The maids

took a torch, and made the bed as fast as they could :
when they had done so they came up to Ulysses and
said, ' This way, sir, if you please, your room is quite
ready ' ; and Ulysses was very glad to hear them say
so."

On the following day Alcinous holds a meeting of
the Phæacians and proposes that Ulysses should have
a ship got ready to take him home at once : this being
settled he invites all the leading people, and the fifty-
two sailors who are to man Ulysses' ship, to come up
to his own house, and he will give them a banquet—
for which he kills a dozen sheep, eight pigs, and two
oxen. Immediately after gorging themselves at the
banquet they have a series of athletic competitions,
and from this I gather the poem to have been written
by one who saw nothing very odd in letting people
compete in sports requiring very violent exercise
immediately after a heavy meal. Such a course may
have been usual in those days, but certainly is not
generally adopted in our own.

At the games Alcinous makes himself as ridiculous
as he always does, and Ulysses behaves much as the
hero of the preceding afternoon might be expected to
do—but on his praising the Phæacians towards the
close of the proceedings Alcinous says he is a person of
such singular judgment that they really must all of
them make him a very handsome present. " Twelve
of you," he exclaims, " are magistrates, and there is
myself—that makes thirteen ; suppose we give him
each one of us a clean cloak, a tunic, and a talent of
gold,"—which in those days was worth about two
hundred and fifty pounds.

This is unanimously agreed to, and in the evening,
towards sundown, the presents began to make their

appearance at the palace of King Alcinous, and the king's sons, perhaps prudently as you will presently see, place them in the keeping of their mother Arete.

When the presents have all arrived, Alcinous says to Arete, " Wife, go and fetch the best chest we have, and put a clean cloak and a tunic in it. In the meantime Ulysses will take a bath."

Arete orders the maids to heat a bath, brings the chest, packs up the raiment and gold which the Phæacians have brought, and adds a cloak and a good tunic as King Alcinous's own contribution.

Yes, but where—and that is what we are never told —is the £250 which he ought to have contributed as well as the cloak and tunic ? And where is the beautiful gold goblet which he had also promised ?

" See to the fastening yourself," says Queen Arete to Ulysses, " for fear anyone should rob you while you are asleep in the ship."

Ulysses, we may be sure, was well aware that Alcinous's £250 was not in the box, nor yet the goblet, but he took the hint at once and made the chest fast without the delay of a moment, with a bond which the cunning goddess Circe had taught him.

He does not seem to have thought his chance of getting the £250 and the goblet, and having to unpack his box again, was so great as his chance of having his box tampered with before he got it away, if he neglected to double-lock it at once and put the key in his pocket. He has always a keen eye to money ; indeed the whole *Odyssey* turns on what is substantially a money quarrel, so this time without the prompting of Minerva he does one of the very few sensible things which he does, on his own account, throughout the whole poem.

Supper is now served, and when it is over, Ulysses, pressed by Alcinous, announces his name and begins the story of his adventures.

It is with profound regret that I find myself unable to quote any of the fascinating episodes with which his narrative abounds, but I have said I was going to lecture on the humour of Homer—that is to say of the *Iliad* and the *Odyssey*—and must not be diverted from my subject. I cannot, however, resist the account which Ulysses gives of his meeting with his mother in Hades, the place of departed spirits, which he has visited by the advice of Circe. His mother comes up to him and asks him how he managed to get into Hades, being still alive. I will translate freely, but quite closely, from Ulysses' own words, as spoken to the Phæacians.

" And I said, ' Mother, I had to come here to consult the ghost of the old Theban prophet Teiresias, I have never yet been near Greece, nor set foot on my native land, and have had nothing but one long run of ill luck from the day I set out with Agamemnon to fight at Troy. But tell me how you came here yourself ? Did you have a long and painful illness or did heaven vouchsafe you a gentle easy passage to eternity ? Tell me also about my father and my son ? Is my property still in their hands, or has someone else got hold of it who thinks that I shall not return to claim it ? How, again, is my wife conducting herself ? Does she live with her son and make a home for him, or has she married again ? '

" My mother answered, ' Your wife is still mistress of your house, but she is in very great straits and spends the greater part of her time in tears. No one has actually taken possession of your property, and

Telemachus still holds it. He has to accept a great
many invitations, and gives much the sort of enter-
tainments in return that may be expected from one in
his position. Your father remains in the old place,
and never goes near the town ; he is very badly off,
and has neither bed nor bedding, nor a stick of furni-
ture of any kind. In winter he sleeps on the floor in
front of the fire with the men, and his clothes are in a
shocking state, but in summer, when the warm weather
comes on again, he sleeps out in the vineyard on a bed
of vine leaves. He takes on very much about your
not having returned, and suffers more and more as he
grows older : as for me I died of nothing whatever in
the world but grief about yourself. There was not a
thing the matter with me, but my prolonged anxiety
on your account was too much for me, and in the end
it just wore me out.' "

In the course of time Ulysses comes to a pause
in his narrative and Queen Arete makes a little
speech.

" ' What do you think,' she said to the Phæacians,
' of such a guest as this ? Did you ever see anyone
at once so good-looking and so clever ? It is true,
indeed, that his visit is paid more particularly to myself,
but you all participate in the honour conferred upon
us by a visitor of such distinction. Do not be in a
hurry to send him off, nor stingy in the presents you
make to one in so great need ; for you are all of you
very well off.' "

You will note that the queen does not say " we are
all of us very well off."

" Then the hero Echeneus, who was the oldest man
among them, added a few words of his own. ' My
friends,' he said, ' there cannot be two opinions about

the graciousness and sagacity of the remarks that have just fallen from Her Majesty ; nevertheless it is with His Majesty King Alcinous that the decision must ultimately rest.'

" ' The thing shall be done,' exclaimed Alcinous, ' if I am still king over the Phæacians. As for our guest, I know he is anxious to resume his journey, still we must persuade him if we can to stay with us until to-morrow, by which time I shall be able to get together the balance of the sum which I mean to press on his acceptance.' "

So here we have it straight out that the monarch knew he had only contributed the coat and waistcoat, and did not know exactly how he was to lay his hands on the £250. What with piracy—for we have been told of at least one case in which Alcinous had looted a town and stolen his housemaid Eurymedusa—what with insufficient changes of linen, toping like an immortal god, swaggering at large, and open-handed hospitality, it is plain and by no means surprising that Alcinous is out at elbows ; nor can there be a better example of the difference between the occasional broad comedy of the *Iliad* and the delicate but very bitter satire of the *Odyssey* than the way in which the fact that Alcinous is in money difficulties is allowed to steal upon us, as contrasted with the obvious humour of the quarrels between Jove and Juno. At any rate we can hardly wonder at Ulysses having felt that to a monarch of such mixed character the unfastened box might prove a temptation greater than he could resist. To return, however, to the story—

" If it please your Majesty," said he, in answer to King Alcinous, " I should be delighted to stay here for another twelve months, and to accept from your hands the vast treasures and the escort which you are so generous as to promise me. I should obviously gain by doing so, for I should return fuller-handed to my own people and should thus be both more respected and more loved by my acquaintance. Still to receive such presents——"

The king perceived his embarrassment, and at once relieved him. " No one," he exclaimed, " who looks at you can for one moment take you for a charlatan or a swindler. I know there are many of these unscrupulous persons going about just now with such plausible stories that it is very hard to disbelieve them ; there is, however, a finish about your style which convinces me of your good disposition," and so on for more than I have space to quote ; after which Ulysses again proceeds with his adventures.

When he had finished them Alcinous insists that the leading Phæacians should each one of them give Ulysses a still further present of a large kitchen copper and a three-legged stand to set it on, " but," he continues, " as the expense of all these presents is really too heavy for the purse of any private individual, I shall charge the whole of them on the rates " : literally, " We will repay ourselves by getting it in from among the people, for this is too heavy a present for the purse of a private individual." And what this can mean except charging it on the rates I do not know.

Of course everyone else sends up his tripod and his cauldron, but we hear nothing about any, either tripod or cauldron, from King Alcinous. He is very fussy next morning stowing them under the ship's benches, but his time and trouble seem to be the extent of his contribution. It is hardly necessary to say that Ulysses had to go away without the £250, and that we never hear of the promised goblet being presented. Still he had done pretty well.

I have not quoted anything like all the absurd remarks made by Alcinous, nor shown you nearly as completely as I could do if I had more time how obviously the writer is quietly laughing at him in her sleeve. She understands his little ways as she understands those of Menelaus, who tells Telemachus and Pisistratus that if they like he will take them a personally conducted tour round the Peloponnese, and that they can make a good thing out of it, for everyone will give them something—fancy Helen or Queen Arete making such a proposal as this. They are never laughed at, but then they are women, whereas Alcinous and Menelaus are men, and this makes all the difference.

And now in conclusion let me point out the irony of literature in connection with this astonishing work. Here is a poem in which the hero and heroine have already been married many years before it begins : it is marked by a total absence of love-business in such sense as we understand it : its interest centres mainly in the fact of a bald elderly gentleman, whose little remaining hair is red, being eaten out of house and home during his absence by a number of young men who are courting the supposed widow—a widow who, if she be fair and fat, can hardly also be less than forty. Can any subject seem more hopeless ? Moreover, this subject so initially faulty is treated with a carelessness in respect of consistency, ignorance of commonly known details, and disregard of ordinary canons, that can hardly be surpassed, and yet I cannot think that in the whole range of literature there is a work which can be decisively placed above it. I am afraid you will hardly accept this ; I do not see how you can be expected to do so, for in the first place there is no even tolerable prose translation, and in the second, the *Odyssey*, like the *Iliad*, has been a school book for over two thousand five hundred years, and what more cruel revenge than this can dullness take on genius? The *Iliad* and *Odyssey* have been used as text-books for education during at least two thousand five hundred years, and yet it is only during the last forty or fifty that people have begun to see that they are by different authors. There was, indeed, so I learn from Colonel Mure's valuable work, a band of scholars some few hundreds of years before the birth of Christ, who refused to see the *Iliad* and *Odyssey* as by the same author, but they were snubbed and snuffed out, and for more than two thousand years were considered to have been finally refuted. Can there be any more scathing satire upon the value of literary criticism? It would seem as though Minerva had shed the same thick darkness over both the poems as she shed over Ulysses, so that they might go in and out among the dons of Oxford and Cambridge from generation to generation, and none should see them. If I am right, as I believe I am, in holding the *Odyssey* to have been written by a young woman, was ever sleeping beauty more effectually concealed behind a more impenetrable hedge of dulness? —and she will have to sleep a good many years yet before anyone wakes her effectually. But what else can one expect from people, not one of whom has been at the very slight exertion of noting a few of the writer's main topographical indications, and then looking for them in an Admiralty chart or two? Can any step be more obvious and easy—indeed, it is so simple that I am ashamed of myself for not having taken it forty years ago. Students of the *Odyssey* for the most part

G

are so engrossed with the force of the zeugma, and
of the enclitic particle γε ; they take so much more
interest in the digamma and in the Æolic dialect, than
they do in the living spirit that sits behind all these
things and alone gives them their importance, that,
naturally enough, not caring about the personality, it
remains and always must remain invisible to them.

If I have helped to make it any less invisible to
yourselves, let me ask you to pardon the somewhat
querulous tone of my concluding remarks.

Quis Desiderio . . .?[1]

LIKE Mr. Wilkie Collins, I, too, have been asked to lay some of my literary experiences before the readers of the *Universal Review*. It occurred to me that the *Review* must be indeed universal before it could open its pages to one so obscure as myself; but, nothing daunted by the distinguished company among which I was for the first time asked to move, I resolved to do as I was told, and went to the British Museum to see what books I had written. Having refreshed my memory by a glance at the catalogue, I was about to try and diminish the large and ever-increasing circle of my non-readers when I became aware of a calamity that brought me to a standstill, and indeed bids fair, so far as I can see at present, to put an end to my literary existence altogether.

I should explain that I cannot write unless I have a sloping desk, and the reading-room of the British Museum, where alone I can compose freely, is un-provided with sloping desks. Like every other organism, if I cannot get exactly what I want I make shift with the next thing to it; true, there are no desks in the reading-room, but, as I once heard a visitor from the country say, " it contains a large number of very interesting works." I know it was not right, and hope the Museum authorities will not

---

[1] Published in the *Universal Review*, July, 1888.

be severe upon me if any of them reads this confession ;
but I wanted a desk, and set myself to consider which
of the many very interesting works which a grateful
nation places at the disposal of its would-be authors
was best suited for my purpose.

For mere reading I suppose one book is pretty
much as good as another ; but the choice of a desk-
book is a more serious matter. It must be neither too
thick nor too thin ; it must be large enough to make
a substantial support ; it must be strongly bound so
as not to yield or give ; it must not be too troublesome to carry backwards and forwards ; and it must
live on shelf C, D, or E, so that there need be no
stooping or reaching too high. These are the conditions which a really good book must fulfil ; simple,
however, as they are, it is surprising how few volumes
comply with them satisfactorily ; moreover, being
perhaps too sensitively conscientious, I allowed
another consideration to influence me, and was sincerely
anxious not to take a book which would be in constant
use for reference by readers, more especially as, if I
did this, I might find myself disturbed by the officials.

For weeks I made experiments upon sundry poetical
and philosophical works, whose names I have forgotten,
but could not succeed in finding my ideal desk, until
at length, more by luck than cunning, I happened to
light upon Frost's *Lives of Eminent Christians*, which
I had no sooner tried than I discovered it to be the
very perfection and *ne plus ultra* of everything that a
book should be. It lived in Case No. 2008, and I
accordingly took at once to sitting in Row B, where for
the last dozen years or so I have sat ever since.

The first thing I have done whenever I went to the
Museum has been to take down Frost's *Lives of*

Eminent Christians and carry it to my seat. It is not the custom of modern writers to refer to the works to which they are most deeply indebted, and I have never, that I remember, mentioned it by name before ; but it is to this book alone that I have looked for support during many years of literary labour, and it is round this to me invaluable volume that all my own have page by page grown up. There is none in the Museum to which I have been under anything like such constant obligation, none which I can so ill spare, and none which I would choose so readily if I were allowed to select one single volume and keep it for my own.

On finding myself asked for a contribution to the *Universal Review*, I went, as I have explained, to the Museum, and presently repaired to bookcase No. 2008 to get my favourite volume. Alas! it was in the room no longer. It was not in use, for its place was filled up already ; besides, no one ever used it but myself. Whether the ghost of the late Mr. Frost has been so eminently unchristian as to interfere, or whether the authorities have removed the book in ignorance of the steady demand which there has been for it on the part of at least one reader, are points I cannot determine. All I know is that the book is gone, and I feel as Wordsworth is generally supposed to have felt when he became aware that Lucy was in her grave, and exclaimed so emphatically that this would make a considerable difference to him, or words to that effect.

Now I think of it, Frost's *Lives of Eminent Christians* was very like Lucy. The one resided at Dovedale in Derbyshire, the other in Great Russell Street, Bloomsbury. I admit that I do not see the resemblance here

at this moment, but if I try to develop my perception
I shall doubtless ere long find a marvellously striking
one.   In other respects, however, than mere local
habitat the likeness is obvious.   Lucy was not particularly attractive either inside or out—no more was
Frost's *Lives of Eminent Christians ;* there were few
to praise her, and of those few still fewer could bring
themselves to like her ; indeed, Wordsworth himself
seems to have been the only person who thought much
about her one way or the other.   In like manner, I
believe I was the only reader who thought much one
way or the other about Frost's *Lives of Eminent
Christians,* but this in itself was one of the attractions of
the book ; and as for the grief we respectively felt
and feel, I believe my own to be as deep as Wordsworth's, if not more so.

I said above, " as Wordsworth is generally supposed
to have felt " ; for anyone imbued with the spirit of
modern science will read Wordsworth's poem with
different eyes from those of a mere literary critic.   He
will note that Wordsworth is most careful not to
explain the nature of the difference which the death of
Lucy will occasion to him.   He tells us that there will
be a difference ; but there the matter ends.   The
superficial reader takes it that he was very sorry she
was dead ; it is, of course, possible that he may have
actually been so, but he has not said this.   On the
contrary, he has hinted plainly that she was ugly, and
generally disliked ; she was only like a violet when she
was half-hidden from the view, and only fair as a star
when there were so few stars out that it was practically
impossible to make an invidious comparison.   If there
were as many as even two stars the likeness was felt
to be at an end.   If Wordsworth had imprudently

promised to marry this young person during a time
when he had been unusually long in keeping to good
resolutions, and had afterwards seen someone whom
he liked better, then Lucy's death would undoubtedly
have made a considerable difference to him, and this
is all that he has ever said that it would do. What right
have we to put glosses upon the masterly reticence of a
poet, and credit him with feelings possibly the very
reverse of those he actually entertained ?

Sometimes, indeed, I have been inclined to think
that a mystery is being hinted at more dark than any
critic has suspected. I do not happen to possess a
copy of the poem, but the writer, if I am not mistaken,
says that " few could know when Lucy ceased to be."
" Ceased to be " is a suspiciously euphemistic expression, and the words " few could know " are not
applicable to the ordinary peaceful death of a domestic
servant such as Lucy appears to have been. No
matter how obscure the deceased, any number of
people commonly can know the day and hour of his
or her demise, whereas in this case we are expressly
told it would be impossible for them to do so. Wordsworth was nothing if not accurate, and would not have
said that few could know, but that few actually did
know, unless he was aware of circumstances that
precluded all but those implicated in the crime of her
death from knowing the precise moment of its occur-
rence. If Lucy was the kind of person not obscurely
portrayed in the poem ; if Wordsworth had murdered
her, either by cutting her throat or smothering her,
in concert, perhaps, with his friends Southey and
Coleridge ; and if he had thus found himself released
from an engagement which had become irksome to
him, or possibly from the threat of an action for breach

of promise, then there is not a syllable in the poem with which he crowns his crime that is not alive with meaning. On any other supposition to the general reader it is unintelligible.

We cannot be too guarded in the interpretations we put upon the words of great poets. Take the young lady who never loved the dear gazelle—and I don't believe she did ; we are apt to think that Moore intended us to see in this creation of his fancy a sweet, amiable, but most unfortunate young woman, whereas all he has told us about her points to an exactly opposite conclusion. In reality, he wished us to see a young lady who had been a habitual complainer from her earliest childhood ; whose plants had always died as soon as she bought them, while those belonging to her neighbours had flourished. The inference is obvious, nor can we reasonably doubt that Moore intended us to draw it ; if her plants were the very first to fade away, she was evidently the very first to neglect or otherwise maltreat them. She did not give them enough water, or left the door of her fern-case open when she was cooking her dinner at the gas stove, or kept them too near the paraffin oil, or other like folly ; and as for her temper, see what the gazelles did ; as long as they did not know her " well," they could just manage to exist, but when they got to understand her real character, one after another felt that death was the only course open to it, and accordingly died rather than live with such a mistress. True, the young lady herself said the gazelles loved her ; but disagreeable people are apt to think themselves amiable, and in view of the course invariably taken by the gazelles themselves anyone accustomed to weigh evidence will hold that she was probably mistaken.

I must, however, return to Frost's *Lives of Eminent Christians*. I will leave none of the ambiguity about my words in which Moore and Wordsworth seem to have delighted. I am very sorry the book is gone, and know not where to turn for its successor. Till I have found a substitute I can write no more, and I do not know how to find even a tolerable one. I should try a volume of Migne's *Complete Course of Patrology*, but I do not like books in more than one volume, for the volumes vary in thickness, and one never can remember which one took ; the four volumes, however, of Bede in Giles's *Anglican Fathers* are not open to this objection, and I have reserved them for favourable consideration. Mather's *Magnalia* might do, but the binding does not please me ; Cureton's *Corpus Ignatianum* might also do if it were not too thin. I do not like taking Norton's *Genuineness of the Gospels*, as it is just possible someone may be wanting to know whether the Gospels are genuine or not, and be unable to find out because I have got Mr. Norton's book. Baxter's *Church History of England*, Lingard's *Anglo-Saxon Church*, and Cardwell's *Documentary Annals*, though none of them as good as Frost, are works of considerable merit ; but on the whole I think Arvine's *Cyclopedia of Moral and Religious Anecdote* is perhaps the one book in the room which comes within measurable distance of Frost. I should probably try this book first, but it has a fatal objection in its too seductive title. " I am not curious," as Miss Lottie Venne says in one of her parts, " but I like to know," and I might be tempted to pervert the book from its natural uses and open it, so as to find out what kind of a thing a moral and religious anecdote is. I know, of course, that there are a great many anecdotes in the Bible, but no one thinks of calling them either moral or religious, though some of them certainly seem as if they might fairly find a place in Mr. Arvine's work. There are some things, however, which it is better not to know, and take it all round I do not think I should be wise in putting myself in the way of temptation, and adopting Arvine as the successor to my beloved and lamented Frost.

Some successor I must find, or I must give up writing altogether, and this I should be sorry to do. I have only as yet written about a third, or from that —counting works written but not published—to a half of the books which I have set myself to write. It would not so much matter if old age was not staring me in the face. Dr. Parr said it was " a beastly shame for an old man not to have laid down a good cellar of port in his youth " ; I, like the greater number, I suppose, of those who write books at all, write in order that I may have something to read in my old age when I can write no longer. I know what I shall like better than anyone can tell me, and write accordingly ; if my career is nipped in the bud, as seems only too likely, I really do not know where else I can turn for present agreeable occupation, nor yet how to make suitable provision for my later years. Other writers can, of course, make excellent provision for their own old ages, but they cannot do so for mine, any more than I should succeed if I were to try to cater for theirs. It is one of those cases in which no man can make agreement for his brother.

I have no heart for continuing this article, and if I had, I have nothing of interest to say. No one's literary career can have been smoother or more unchequered than mine. I have published all my books at my own expense, and paid for them in due course. What can be conceivably more unromantic? For some years I had a little literary grievance against the authorities of the British Museum because they would insist on saying in their catalogue that I had published three sermons on Infidelity in the year 1820. I thought I had not, and got them out to see. They were rather funny, but they were not mine. Now, however, this grievance has been removed. I had another little quarrel with them because they would describe me as " of St. John's College, Cambridge," an establishment for which I have the most profound veneration, but with which I have not had the honour to be connected for some quarter of a century. At last they said they would change this description if I would only tell them what I was, for, though they had done their best to find out, they had themselves failed. I replied with modest pride that I was a Bachelor of Arts. I keep all my other letters inside my name, not outside. They mused and said it was unfortunate that I was not a Master of Arts. Could I not get myself made a Master? I said I understood that a Mastership was an article the University could not do under about five pounds, and that I was not disposed to go sixpence higher than three ten. They again said it was a pity, for it would be very inconvenient to them if I did not keep to something between a bishop and a poet. I might be anything I liked in reason, provided I showed proper respect for the alphabet; but they had got me between " Samuel Butler, bishop," and " Samuel Butler, poet." It would be very troublesome to shift me, and bachelor came before bishop. This was reasonable, so I replied that, under those circumstances, if they pleased, I thought

I would like to be a philosophical writer. They embraced the solution, and, no matter what I write now, I must remain a philosophical writer as long as I live, for the alphabet will hardly be altered in my time, and I must be something between " Bis " and " Poe." If I could get a volume of my excellent namesake's *Hudibras* out of the list of my works, I should be robbed of my last shred of literary grievance, so I say nothing about this, but keep it secret, lest some worse thing should happen to me. Besides, I have a great respect for my namesake, and always say that if *Erewhon* had been a racehorse it would have been got by *Hudibras* out of *Analogy*. Someone said this to me many years ago, and I felt so much flattered that I have been repeating the remark as my own ever since.

But how small are these grievances as compared with those endured without a murmur by hundreds of writers far more deserving than myself. When I see the scores and hundreds of workers in the reading-room who have done so much more than I have, but whose work is absolutely fruitless to themselves, and when I think of the prompt recognition obtained by my own work, I ask myself what I have done to be thus rewarded. On the other hand, the feeling that I have succeeded far beyond my deserts hitherto, makes it all the harder for me to acquiesce without complaint in the extinction of a career which I honestly believe to be a promising one ; and once more I repeat that, unless the Museum authorities give me back my Frost, or put a locked clasp on Arvine, my career must be extinguished. Give me back Frost, and, if life and health are spared, I will write another dozen of volumes yet before I hang up my fiddle—if so

serious a confusion of metaphors may be pardoned. I
know from long experience how kind and considerate
both the late and present superintendents of the
reading-room were and are, but I doubt how far either
of them would be disposed to help me on this occasion ;
continue, however, to rob me of my Frost, and,
whatever else I may do, I will write no more books.

Note by Dr. Garnett, British Museum.—The frost
has broken up. Mr. Butler is restored to literature.
Mr. Mudie may make himself easy. England will still
boast a humorist ; and the late Mr. Darwin (to
whose posthumous machinations the removal of the
book was owing) will continue to be confounded.—
R. Garnett.

Ramblings in Cheapside[1]

WALKING the other day in Cheapside I saw some turtles in Mr. Sweeting's window, and was tempted to stay and look at them. As I did so I was struck not more by the defences with which they were hedged about, than by the fatuousness of trying to hedge that in at all which, if hedged thoroughly, must die of its own defencefulness. The holes for the head and feet through which the turtle leaks out, as it were, on to the exterior world, and through which it again absorbs the exterior world into itself—" catching on " through them to things that are thus both turtle and not turtle at one and the same time—these holes stultify the armour, and show it to have been designed by a creature with more of faithfulness to a fixed idea, and hence onesidedness, than of that quick sense of relative importances and their changes, which is the main factor of good living.

The turtle obviously had no sense of proportion ; it differed so widely from myself that I could not comprehend it ; and as this word occurred to me, it occurred also that until my body comprehended its body in a physical material sense, neither would my mind be able to comprehend its mind with any thoroughness. For unity of mind can only be consummated by unity of body ; everything, therefore,

---

[1] Published in the *Universal Review*, December, 1890.

must be in some respects both knave and fool to all
that which has not eaten it, or by which it has not been
eaten. As long as the turtle was in the window and I
in the street outside, there was no chance of our
comprehending one another.

Nevertheless, I knew that I could get it to agree
with me if I could so effectually buttonhole and fasten
on to it as to eat it. Most men have an easy method
with turtle soup, and I had no misgiving but that if
I could bring my first premise to bear I should prove
the better reasoner. My difficulty lay in this initial
process, for I had not with me the argument that would
alone compel Mr. Sweeting to think that I ought to be
allowed to convert the turtles—I mean I had no money
in my pocket. No missionary enterprise can be
carried on without any money at all, but even so
small a sum as half a crown would, I suppose, have
enabled me to bring the turtle partly round, and with
many half-crowns I could in time no doubt convert
the lot, for the turtle needs must go where the money
drives. If, as is alleged, the world stands on a turtle,
the turtle stands on money. No money no turtle.
As for money, that stands on opinion, credit, trust,
faith—things that, though highly material in connection with money, are still of immaterial essence.

The steps are perfectly plain. The men who caught
the turtles brought a fairly strong and definite opinion
to bear upon them, that passed into action, and later
on into money. They thought the turtles would come
that way, and verified their opinion ; on this, will
and action were generated, with the result that the men
turned the turtles on their backs and carried them
off. Mr. Sweeting touched these men with money,
which is the outward and visible sign of verified

opinion. The customer touches Mr. Sweeting with money, Mr. Sweeting touches the waiter and the cook with money. They touch the turtle with skill and verified opinion. Finally, the customer applies the clinching argument that brushes all sophisms aside, and bids the turtle stand protoplasm to protoplasm with himself, to know even as it is known.

But it must be all touch, touch, touch ; skill, opinion, power, and money, passing in and out with one another in any order we like, but still link to link and touch to touch. If there is failure anywhere in respect of opinion, skill, power, or money, either as regards quantity or quality, the chain can be no stronger than its weakest link, and the turtle and the clinching argument will fly asunder. Of course, if there is an initial failure in connection, through defect in any member of the chain, or of connection between the links, it will no more be attempted to bring the turtle and the clinching argument together, than it will to chain up a dog with two pieces of broken chain that are disconnected. The contact throughout must be conceived as absolute ; and yet perfect contact is inconceivable by us, for on becoming perfect it ceases to be contact, and becomes essential, once for all inseverable, identity. The most absolute contact short of this is still contact by courtesy only. So here, as everywhere else, Eurydice glides off as we are about to grasp her. We can see nothing face to face ; our utmost seeing is but a fumbling of blind finger-ends in an over-crowded pocket.

Presently my own blind finger-ends fished up the conclusion, that as I had neither time nor money to spend on perfecting the chain that would put me in

full spiritual contact with Mr. Sweeting's turtles, I
had better leave them to complete their education at
someone else's expense rather than mine, so I walked
on towards the Bank. As I did so it struck me how
continually we are met by this melting of one existence
into another. The limits of the body seem well
defined enough as definitions go, but definitions
seldom go far. What, for example, can seem more
distinct from a man than his banker or his solicitor ?
Yet these are commonly so much parts of him that
he can no more cut them off and grow new ones, than
he can grow new legs or arms ; neither must he wound
his solicitor ; a wound in the solicitor is a very serious
thing. As for his bank—failure of his bank's action may
be as fatal to a man as failure of his heart. I have said
nothing about the medical or spiritual adviser, but most
men grow into the society that surrounds them by the
help of these four main tap-roots, and not only into the
world of humanity, but into the universe at large. We
can, indeed, grow butchers, bakers, and greengrocers,
almost *ad libitum*, but these are low developments,
and correspond to skin, hair, or finger-nails. Those
of us again who are not highly enough organized to
have grown a solicitor or banker can generally repair
the loss of whatever social organization they may
possess as freely as lizards are said to grow new tails ;
but this with the higher social, as well as organic,
developments is only possible to a very limited extent.

The doctrine of metempsychosis, or transmigration
of souls—a doctrine to which the foregoing considerations are for the most part easy corollaries—crops up
no matter in what direction we allow our thoughts to
wander. And we meet instances of transmigration of
body as well as of soul. I do not mean that both body

H

and soul have transmigrated together, far from it ; but that, as we can often recognize a transmigrated mind in an alien body, so we not less often see a body that is clearly only a transmigration, linked on to someone else's new and alien soul. We meet people every day whose bodies are evidently those of men and women long dead, but whose appearance we know through their portraits. We see them going about in omnibuses, railway carriages, and in all public places. The cards have been shuffled, and they have drawn fresh lots in life and nationalities, but anyone fairly well up in medieval and last-century portraiture knows them at a glance.

Going down once towards Italy I saw a young man in the train whom I recognized, only he seemed to have got younger. He was with a friend, and his face was in continual play, but for some little time I puzzled in vain to recollect where it was that I had seen him before. All of a sudden I remembered he was King Francis I of France. I had hitherto thought the face of this king impossible, but when I saw it in play I understood it. His great contemporary Henry VIII keeps a restaurant in Oxford Street. Falstaff drove one of the St. Gothard diligences for many years, and only retired when the railway was opened. Titian once made me a pair of boots at Vicenza, and not very good ones. At Modena I had my hair cut by a young man whom I perceived to be Raffaelle. The model who sat to him for his celebrated Madonnas is first lady in a confectionery establishment at Montreal. She has a little motherly pimple on the left side of her nose that is misleading at first, but on examination she is readily recognized ; probably Raffaelle's model had the pimple too, but Raffaelle left it out—as he would.

Handel, of course, is Madame Patey. Give Madame Patey Handel's wig and clothes, and there would be no telling her from Handel. It is not only that the features and the shape of the head are the same, but there is a certain imperiousness of expression and attitude about Handel which he hardly attempts to conceal in Madame Patey. It is a curious coincidence that he should continue to be such an incomparable renderer of his own music. Pope Julius II was the late Mr. Darwin. Rameses II is a blind woman now, and stands in Holborn, holding a tin mug. I never could understand why I always found myself humming " They oppressed them with burthens " when I passed her, till one day I was looking in Mr. Spooner's window in the Strand, and saw a photograph of Rameses II. Mary Queen of Scots wears surgical boots and is subject to fits, near the Horse Shoe in Tottenham Court Road.

Michael Angelo is a commissionaire ; I saw him on board the *Glen Rosa,* which used to run every day from London to Clacton-on-Sea and back. It gave me quite a turn when I saw him coming down the stairs from the upper deck, with his bronzed face, flattened nose, and with the familiar bar upon his forehead. I never liked Michael Angelo, and never shall, but I am afraid of him, and was near trying to hide when I saw him coming towards me. He had not got his commissionaire's uniform on, and I did not know he was one till I met him a month or so later in the Strand. When we got to Blackwall the music struck up and people began to dance. I never saw a man dance so much in my life. He did not miss a dance all the way to Clacton, nor all the way back again, and when not dancing he was flirting and cracking jokes. I could hardly believe my eyes when I reflected that this man had painted the famous " Last Judgment," and had made all those statues.

Dante is, or was a year or two ago, a waiter at Brissago on the Lago Maggiore, only he is better-tempered-looking, and has a more intellectual expression. He gave me his ideas upon beauty : " Tutto ch' è vero è bello," he exclaimed, with all his old self-confidence. I am not afraid of Dante. I know people by their friends, and he went about with Virgil, so I said with some severity, " No, Dante, il naso della Signora Robinson è vero, ma non è bello " ; and he admitted I was right. Beatrice's name is Towler ; she is waitress at a small inn in German Switzerland. I used to sit at my window and hear people call " Towler, Towler, Towler," fifty times in a forenoon. She was the exact antithesis to Abra ; Abra, if I remember, used to come before they called her name, but no matter how often they called Towler, everyone came before she did. I suppose they spelt her name Taula, but to me it sounded Towler ; I never, however, met anyone else with this name. She was a sweet, artless little hussy, who made me play the piano to her, and she said it was lovely. Of course I only played my own compositions ; so I believed her, and it all went off very nicely. I thought it might save trouble if I did not tell her who she really was, so I said nothing about it.

I met Socrates once. He was my muleteer on an excursion which I will not name, for fear it should identify the man. The moment I saw my guide I knew he was somebody, but for the life of me I could not remember who. All of a sudden it flashed across me that he was Socrates. He talked enough for six, but it was all in *dialetto*, so I could not understand him, nor, when I had discovered who he was, did I much try to do so. He was a good creature, a trifle given to stealing fruit and vegetables, but an amiable man enough. He had had a long day with his mule and me, and he only asked me five francs. I gave him ten, for I pitied his poor old patched boots, and there was a meekness about him that touched me. "And now, Socrates," said I at parting, "we go on our several ways, you to steal tomatoes, I to filch ideas from other people ; for the rest—which of these two roads will be the better going, our father which is in heaven knows, but we know not."

I have never seen Mendelssohn, but there is a fresco of him on the terrace, or open-air dining-room, of an inn at Chiavenna. He is not called Mendelssohn, but I knew him by his legs. He is in the costume of a dandy of some five-and-forty years ago, is smoking a cigar, and appears to be making an offer of marriage to his cook. Beethoven both my friend Mr. H. Festing Jones and I have had the good fortune to meet ; he is an engineer now, and does not know one note from another ; he has quite lost his deafness, is married, and is, of course, a little squat man with the same refractory hair that he always had. It was very interesting to watch him, and Jones remarked that before the end of dinner he had become positively posthumous. One morning I was told the Beethovens were going away, and before long I met their two heavy boxes being carried down the stairs. The boxes were so squab and like their owners, that I half thought for a moment that they were inside, and should hardly have been surprised to see them spring up like a couple of Jacks-in-the-box. "Sono indentro ? " said I, with a frown of wonder, pointing to the boxes. The porters knew what I meant, and laughed. But there is no end to the list of people whom I have been able to recognize, and before I had got through it myself, I found I had walked some distance, and had involuntarily paused in front of a second-hand bookstall.

I do not like books. I believe I have the smallest library of any literary man in London, and I have no wish to increase it. I keep my books at the British Museum and at Mudie's, and it makes me very angry if anyone gives me one for my private library. I once heard two ladies disputing in a railway carriage as to whether one of them had or had not been wasting money. " I spent it in books," said the accused, " and it's not wasting money to buy books." " Indeed, my dear, I think it is," was the rejoinder, and in practice I agree with it. Webster's Dictionary, Whitaker's Almanack, and Bradshaw's Railway Guide should be sufficient for any ordinary library ; it will be time enough to go beyond these when the mass of useful and entertaining matter which they provide has been mastered. Nevertheless, I admit that sometimes, if not particularly busy, I stop at a second-hand bookstall and turn over a book or two from mere force of habit.

I know not what made me pick up a copy of Æschylus—of course in an English version—or rather I know not what made Æschylus take up with me, for he took me rather than I him ; but no sooner had he got me than he began puzzling me, as he has done any time this forty years, to know wherein his transcendent merit can be supposed to lie. To me he is, like the greater number of classics in all ages and countries, a literary Struldbrug, rather than a true ambrosia-fed immortal. There are true immortals, but they are few and far between ; most classics are as great impostors dead as they were when living, and while posing as gods are, five-sevenths of them, only Struldbrugs. It comforts me to remember that Aristophanes liked Æschylus no better than I do. True, he praises him by comparison with Sophocles and Euripides, but he only does so that he may run down these last more effectively. Aristophanes is a safe man to follow, nor do I see why it should not be as correct to laugh with him as to pull a long face with the Greek Professors ; but this is neither here nor there, for no one really cares about Æschylus ; the more interesting question is how he contrived to make so many people for so many years pretend to care about him.

Perhaps he married somebody's daughter. If a man would get hold of the public ear, he must pay, marry, or fight. I have never understood that Æschylus was a man of means, and the fighters do not write poetry, so I suppose he must have married a theatrical manager's daughter, and got his plays brought out that way. The ear of any age or country is like its land, air, and water ; it seems limitless but is really limited, and is already in the keeping of those who naturally enough will have no squatting on such valuable property. It is written and talked up to as closely as the means of subsistence are bred up to by a teeming population. There is not a square inch of it but is in private hands, and he who would freehold any part of it must do so by purchase, marriage, or fighting, in the usual way—and fighting gives the longest, safest tenure. The public itself has hardly more voice in the question who shall have its ear, than the land has in choosing its owners. It is farmed as those who own it think most profitable to themselves, and small blame to them ; nevertheless, it has a residuum of mulishness

which the land has not, and does sometimes dispossess
its tenants. It is in this residuum that those who fight
place their hope and trust.

Or perhaps Æschylus squared the leading critics of
his time. When one comes to think of it, he must
have done so, for how is it conceivable that such plays
should have had such runs if he had not ? I met a lady
one year in Switzerland who had some parrots that
always travelled with her and were the idols of her life.
These parrots would not let anyone read aloud in their
presence, unless they heard their own names introduced
from time to time. If these were freely interpolated
into the text they would remain as still as stones, for
they thought the reading was about themselves. If
it was not about them it could not be allowed. The
leaders of literature are like these parrots ; they do
not look at what a man writes, nor if they did would
they understand it much better than the parrots do ;
but they like the sound of their own names, and if
these are freely interpolated in a tone they take as
friendly, they may even give ear to an outsider.
Otherwise they will scream him off if they can.

I should not advise anyone with ordinary indepen-
dence of mind to attempt the public ear unless he is confident that he can out-lung and out-last his own generation ; for if he has any force, people will and ought to
be on their guard against him, inasmuch as there is no
knowing where he may not take them. Besides, they
have staked their money on the wrong men so often
without suspecting it, that when there comes one whom
they do suspect it would be madness not to bet against
him. True, he may die before he has outscreamed his
opponents, but that has nothing to do with it. If
his scream was well pitched it will sound clearer when

he is dead. We do not know what death is. If we know so little about life which we have experienced, how shall we know about death which we have not—and in the nature of things never can ? Everyone, as I said years ago in *Alps and Sanctuaries*, is an immortal to himself, for he cannot know that he is dead until he is dead, and when dead how can he know anything about anything ? All we know is, that even the humblest dead may live long after all trace of the body has disappeared ; we see them doing it in the bodies and memories of those that come after them ; and not a few live so much longer and more effectually than is desirable, that it has been necessary to get rid of them by Act of Parliament. It is love that alone gives life, and the truest life is that which we live not in ourselves but vicariously in others, and with which we have no concern. Our concern is so to order ourselves that we may be of the number of them that enter into life—although we know it not.

Æschylus did so order himself ; but his life is not of that inspiriting kind that can be won through fighting the good fight only—or being believed to have fought it. His voice is the echo of a drone, drone-begotten and drone-sustained. It is not a tone that a man must utter or die—nay, even though he die ; and likely enough half the allusions and hard passages in Æschylus of which we can make neither head nor tail are in reality only puffs of some of the literary leaders of his time.

The lady above referred to told me more about her parrots. She was like a Nasmyth's hammer going slow—very gentle, but irresistible. She always read the newspaper to them. What was the use of having a newspaper if one did not read it to one's parrots ?

" And have you divined," I asked, " to which side
they incline in politics ? "

" They do not like Mr. Gladstone," was the somewhat freezing answer ; " this is the only point on
which we disagree, for I adore him. Don't ask more
about this, it is a great grief to me. I tell them everything," she continued, " and hide no secret from
them."

" But can any parrot be trusted to keep a secret ? "

" Mine can."

" And on Sundays do you give them the same
course of reading as on a week-day, or do you make
a difference ? "

" On Sundays I always read them a genealogical
chapter from the Old or New Testament, for I can
thus introduce their names without profanity. I
always keep tea by me in case they should ask for it
in the night, and I have an Etna to warm it for them ;
they take milk and sugar. The old white-headed
clergyman came to see them last night ; it was very
painful, for Jocko reminded him so strongly of his
late . . . "

I thought she was going to say " wife," but it
proved to have been only of a parrot that he had once
known and loved.

One evening she was in difficulties about the quarantine, which was enforced that year on the Italian
frontier. The local doctor had gone down that morning
to see the Italian doctor and arrange some details.
" Then, perhaps, my dear," she said to her husband,
" he is the quarantine." " No, my love," replied her
husband. " The quarantine is not a person, it is a
place where they put people " , but she would not be
comforted, and suspected the quarantine as an enemy

that might at any moment pounce out upon her and her parrots. So a lady told me once that she had been in like trouble about the anthem. She read in her Prayer Book that in choirs and places where they sing "here followeth the anthem," yet the person with this most mysteriously sounding name never did follow. They had a choir, and no one could say the church was not a place where they sang, for they did sing—both chants and hymns. Why, then, this persistent slackness on the part of the anthem, who at this juncture should follow her papa, the rector, into the reading-desk? No doubt he would come some day, and then what would he be like? Fair or dark? Tall or short? Would he be bald and wear spectacles like papa, would he be young and good-looking? Anyhow, there was something wrong, for it was announced that he would follow, and he never did follow; therefore there was no knowing what he might not do next.

I heard of the parrots a year or two later as giving lessons in Italian to an English maid. I do not know what their terms were. Alas! since then both they and their mistress have joined the majority. When the poor lady felt her end was near she desired (and the responsibility for this must rest with her, not me) that the birds might be destroyed, as fearing that they might come to be neglected, and knowing that they could never be loved again as she had loved them. On being told that all was over, she said, "Thank you," and immediately expired.

Reflecting in such random fashion, and strolling with no greater method, I worked my way back through Cheapside and found myself once more in front of Sweeting's window. Again the turtles attracted me. They were alive, and so far at any rate they agreed with me. Nay, they had eyes, mouths, legs, if not arms, and feet, so there was much in which we were both of a mind, but surely they must be mistaken in arming themselves so very heavily. Any creature on getting what the turtle aimed at would overreach itself and be landed not in safety but annihilation. It should have no communion with the outside world at all, for death could creep in wherever the creature could creep out ; and it must creep out somewhere if it was to hook on to outside things. What death can be more absolute than such absolute isolation ? Perfect death, indeed, if it were attainable (which it is not), is as near perfect security as we can reach, but it is not the kind of security aimed at by any animal that is at the pains of defending itself. For such want to have things both ways, desiring the livingness of life without its perils, and the safety of death without its deadness, and some of us do actually get this for a considerable time, but we do not get it by plating ourselves with armour as the turtle does. We tried this in the Middle Ages, and no longer mock ourselves with the weight of armour that our forefathers carried in battle. Indeed the more deadly the weapons of attack become the more we go into the fight slug-wise.

Slugs have ridden their contempt for defensive armour as much to death as the turtles their pursuit of it. They have hardly more than skin enough to hold themselves together ; they court death every time they cross the road. Yet death comes not to them more than to the turtle, whose defences are so great that there is little left inside to be defended. Moreover, the slugs fare best in the long run, for turtles are dying out, while slugs are not, and there must be millions of slugs all the world over for every single turtle. Of the two vanities, therefore, that of the slug seems most substantial.

In either case the creature thinks itself safe, but is sure to be found out sooner or later ; nor is it easy to explain this mockery save by reflecting that everything must have its meat in due season, and that meat can only be found for such a multitude of mouths by giving everything as meat in due season to something else. This is like the Kilkenny cats, or robbing Peter to pay Paul ; but it is the way of the world, and as every animal must contribute in kind to the picnic of the universe, one does not see what better arrangement could be made than the providing each race with a hereditary fallacy, which shall in the end get it into a scrape, but which shall generally stand the wear and tear of life for some time. " *Do ut des* " is the writing on all flesh to him that eats it ; and no creature is dearer to itself than it is to some other that would devour it.

Nor is there any statement or proposition more invulnerable than living forms are. Propositions prey upon and are grounded upon one another just like living forms. They support one another as plants and animals do ; they are based ultimately on credit, or faith, rather than the cash of irrefragable conviction. The whole universe is carried on on the credit system, and if the mutual confidence on which it is based were to collapse, it must itself collapse immediately. Just or unjust, it lives by faith ; it is based on vague and impalpable opinion that by some inscrutable process passes into will and action, and is made manifest in matter and in flesh : it is meteoric—suspended in mid-air ; it is the baseless fabric of a vision so vast, so vivid, and so gorgeous that no base can seem more broad than such stupendous baselessness, and yet any man can bring it about his ears by being over-curious ; when faith fails, a system based on faith fails also.

Whether the universe is really a paying concern, or whether it is an inflated bubble that must burst sooner or later, this is another matter. If people were to demand cash payment in irrefragable certainty for everything that they have taken hitherto as paper money on the credit of the bank of public opinion, is there money enough behind it all to stand so great a drain even on so great a reserve ? Probably there is not, but happily there can be no such panic, for even though the cultured classes may do so, the uncultured are too dull to have brains enough to commit such stupendous folly. It takes a long course of academic training to educate a man up to the standard which he must reach before he can entertain such questions seriously, and by a merciful dispensation of Providence university training is almost as costly as it is unprofitable. The majority will thus be always unable to afford it, and will base their opinions on mother wit and current opinion rather than on demonstration.

So I turned my steps homewards ; I saw a good many more things on my way home, but I was told that I was not to see more this time than I could get into twelve pages of the *Universal Review ;* I must therefore reserve any remark which I think might perhaps entertain the reader for another occasion.

The Aunt, the Nieces, and the Dog[1]

WHEN a thing is old, broken, and useless we throw it on the dust-heap, but when it is sufficiently old, sufficiently broken, and sufficiently useless we give money for it, put it into a museum, and read papers over it which people come long distances to hear. By and by, when the whirligig of time has brought on another revenge, the museum itself becomes a dust-heap, and remains so till after long ages it is rediscovered, and valued as belonging to a neo-rubbish age—containing, perhaps, traces of a still older paleo-rubbish civilization. So when people are old, indigent, and in all respects incapable, we hold them in greater and greater contempt as their poverty and impotence increase, till they reach the pitch when they are actually at the point to die, whereon they become sublime. Then we place every resource our hospitals can command at their disposal, and show no stint in our consideration for them.

It is the same with all our interests. We care most about extremes of importance and of unimportance ; but extremes of importance are tainted with fear,

---

[1] Published in the *Universal Review*, May, 1889. As I have several times been asked if the letters here reprinted were not fabricated by Butler himself, I take this opportunity of stating that they are authentic in every particular, and that the originals are now in my possession.—R. A. S.

and a very imperfect fear casteth out love. Extremes
of unimportance cannot hurt us, therefore we are well
disposed towards them ; the means may come to do so,
therefore we do not love them. Hence we pick a fly out
of a milk-jug and watch with pleasure over its recovery,
for we are confident that under no conceivable circumstances will it want to borrow money from us ; but we
feel less sure about a mouse, so we show it no quarter.
The compilers of our almanacs well know this
tendency of our natures, so they tell us, not when
Noah went into the ark, nor when the temple of
Jerusalem was dedicated, but that Lindley Murray,
grammarian, died January 16th, 1826. This is not
because they could not find so many as three hundred
and sixty-five events of considerable interest since the
creation of the world, but because they well know we
would rather hear of something less interesting. We
care most about what concerns us either very closely,
or so little that practically we have nothing whatever
to do with it.

I once asked a young Italian, who professed to have
a considerable knowledge of English literature, which
of all our poems pleased him best. He replied without
a moment's hesitation :

> " Hey diddle diddle, the cat and the fiddle,
> The cow jumped over the moon ;
> The little dog laughed to see such sport,
> And the dish ran away with the spoon."

He said this was better than anything in Italian.
They had Dante and Tasso, and ever so many more
great poets, but they had nothing comparable to
" Hey diddle diddle," nor had he been able to conceive
how anyone could have written it. Did I know the
author's name, and had we given him a statue ? On

this I told him of the young lady of Harrow who would go to church in a barrow, and plied him with whatever rhyming nonsense I could call to mind, but it was no use ; all of these things had an element of reality that robbed them of half their charm, whereas " Hey diddle diddle " had nothing in it that could conceivably concern him.

So again it is with the things that gall us most. What is it that rises up against us at odd times and smites us in the face again and again for years after it has happened ? That we spent all the best years of our life in learning what we have found to be a swindle, and to have been known to be a swindle by those who took money for misleading us ? That those on whom we most leaned most betrayed us ? That we have only come to feel our strength when there is little strength left of any kind to feel ? These things will hardly much disturb a man of ordinary good temper. But that he should have said this or that little unkind and wanton saying ; that he should have gone away from this or that hotel and given a shilling too little to the waiter ; that his clothes were shabby at such or such a garden-party—these things gall us as a corn will sometimes do, though the loss of a limb may not be seriously felt.

I have been reminded lately of these considerations with more than common force by reading the very voluminous correspondence left by my grandfather, Dr. Butler, of Shrewsbury, whose memoirs I am engaged in writing. I have found a large number of interesting letters on subjects of serious import, but must confess that it is to the hardly less numerous lighter letters that I have been most attracted, nor do I feel sure that my eminent namesake did not share my

predilection. Among other letters in my possession I
have one bundle that has been kept apart, and has
evidently no connection with Dr. Butler's own life. I
cannot use these letters, therefore, for my book, but
over and above the charm of their inspired spelling, I
find them of such an extremely trivial nature that I
incline to hope the reader may derive as much amusement from them as I have done myself, and venture
to give them the publicity here which I must refuse
them in my book. The dates and signatures have, with
the exception of Mrs. Newton's, been carefully erased,
but I have collected that they were written by the
two servants of a single lady who resided at no great
distance from London, to two nieces of the said lady
who lived in London itself. The aunt never writes, but
always gets one of the servants to do so for her. She
appears either as " your aunt " or as " She " ; her
name is not given, but she is evidently looked upon
with a good deal of awe by all who had to do with her.

The letters almost all of them relate to visits either
of the aunt to London, or of the nieces to the aunt's
home, which, from occasional allusions to hopping, I
gather to have been in Kent, Sussex, or Surrey. I have
arranged them to the best of my power, and take the
following to be the earliest. It has no signature, but is
not in the handwriting of the servant who styles herself
Elizabeth, or Mrs. Newton. It runs :—

" MADAM,—Your Aunt Wishes me to inform you
she will be glad if you will let hir know if you think of
coming To hir House thiss month or Next as she
cannot have you in September on a kount of the Hoping
If you ar coming she thinkes she had batter Go to
London on the Day you com to hir House she says you

shall have everry Thing raddy for you at hir House
and Mrs. Newton to meet you and stay with you till
She returnes a gann.

" if you arnot Coming thiss Summer She will be in
London before thiss Month is out and will Sleep on the
Sofy As She willnot be in London more thann two nits.
and She Says she willnot truble you on anny a kount
as She Will returne the Same Day before She will plage
you anny more. but She thanks you for asking hir to
London. but She says She cannot leve the house at
prassant She sayhir Survants ar to do for you as she
cannot lodge yours nor she willnot have thim in at
the house anny more to brake and destroy hir thinks
and beslive hir and make up Lies by hir and Skandel
as your too did She says she mens to pay fore 2 Nits
and one day, She says the Pepelwill let hir have it if you
ask thim to let hir : you Will be so good as to let hir
know sun : wish She is to do, as She says She dos not
care anny thing a bout it. which way tiss she is
batter than She was and desirs hir Love to bouth
bouth.

" Your aunt wises to know how the silk Clocks ar
madup [how the silk cloaks are made up] with a Cape
or a wood as she is a goin to have one madeup to rideout
in in hir littel shas [chaise].

" Charles is a butty and so good.

" Mr & Mrs Newton ar quite wall & desires to be
remembered to you."

I can throw no light on the meaning of the verb to
" beslive." Each letter in the MS. is so admirably
formed that there can be no question about the word
being as I have given it. Nor have I been able to
discover what is referred to by the words " Charles is a

butty and so good." We shall presently meet with a Charles who " flies in the Fier," but that Charles appears to have been in London, whereas this one is evidently in Kent, or wherever the aunt lived.

The next letter is from Mrs. Newton :—

" DER MISS ——, I Receve your Letter your Aunt is vary Ill and Lowspireted I Donte think your Aunt wood Git up all Day if My Sister Wasnot to Persage her We all Think hir lif is two monopolous. you Wish to know Who Was Liveing With your Aunt. that is My Sister and Willian —— and Cariline —— as Cock and Old Poll Pepper is Come to Stay With her a Littel Wile and I hoped [hopped] for Your Aunt, and Harry has Worked for your Aunt all the Summer. Your Aunt and Harry Whent to the Wells Races and Spent a very Pleasant Day your Aunt has Lost Old Fanney Sow She Died about a Week a Go Harry he Wanted your Aunt to have her killed and send her to London and Shee Wold Fech her £11 the Farmers have Lost a Great Deal of Cattel such as Hogs and Cows What theay call the Plage I Whent to your Aunt as you Wish Mee to Do But She Told Mee She Did not wont aney Boddy She Told Mee She Should Like to Come up to see you But She Cant Come know for she is Boddyley ill and Harry Donte Work there know But he Go up there Once in Two or Three Day Harry Offered is self to Go up to Live With your Aunt But She Made him know Ancer. I hav Been up to your Aunt at Work for 5 Weeks Hopping and Ragluting Your Aunt Donte Eat nor Drink But vary Littel indeed.

" I am Happy to Say We are Both Quite Well and I am Glad no hear you are Both Quite Well

" MRS NEWTON."

This seems to have made the nieces propose to pay a visit to their aunt, perhaps to try and relieve the monopoly of her existence and cheer her up a little. In their letter, doubtless, the dog motive is introduced that is so finely developed presently by Mrs. Newton. I should like to have been able to give the theme as enounced by the nieces themselves, but their letters are not before me. Mrs. Newton writes :—

" MY DEAR GIRLS,—Your Aunt receiv your Letter your Aunt will Be vary glad to see you as it quite a greeable if it tis to you and Shce is Quite Willing to Eair the beds and the Rooms if you Like to Trust to hir and the Servantes ; if not I may Go up there as you Wish. My Sister Sleeps in the Best Room as she allways Did and the Coock in the garret and you Can have the Rooms the same as you allways Did as your Aunt Donte set in the Parlour She Continlery Sets in the Ciching. your Aunt says she Cannot Part from the dog know hows and She Says he will not hurt you for he is Like a Child and I can safeley say My Self he wonte hurt you as She Cannot Sleep in the Room With out him as he allWay Sleep in the Same Room as She Dose. your Aunt is agreeable to Git in What Coles and Wood you Wish for I am know happy to say your Aunt is in as Good health as ever She Was and She is happy to hear you are Both Well your Aunt Wishes for Ancer By Return of Post."

The nieces replied that their aunt must choose between the dog and them, and Mrs. Newton sends a second letter which brings her development to a climax. It runs :—

" DEAR MISS ——, I have Receve your Letter and
i Whent up to your Aunt as you Wish me and i Try to
Perveal With her about the Dog But she Wold not
Put the Dog away nor it alow him to Be Tied up But
She Still Wishes you to Come as Shee says the Dog
Shall not interrup you for She Donte alow the Dog
nor it the Cats to Go in the Parlour never sence She
has had it Donup ferfere of Spoiling the Paint your
Aunt think it vary Strange you Should Be so vary
Much afraid of a Dog and She says you Cant Go out
in London But What you are up a gance one and She
says She Wonte Trust the Dog in know one hands But
her Owne for She is afraid theay Will not fill is Belley
as he Lives upon Rost Beeff and Rost and Boil Moutten
Wich he Eats More then the Servantes in the House
there is not aney One Wold Beable to Give Sattefack-
tion upon that account Harry offerd to Take the Dog
But She Wood not Trust him in our hands so I Cold
not Do aney thing With her your Aunt youse to Tell
Me When we was at your House in London She Did
not know how to make you amens and i Told her know
it was the Time to Do it But i Consider She sets the
Dog Before you your Aunt keep know Beer know
Sprits know Wines in the House of aney Sort Oneley a
Little Barl of Wine I made her in the Summer the
Workmen and servantes are a Blige to Drink wauter
Morning Noon and Night your Aunt the Same She
Donte Low her Self aney Tee nor Coffee But is Loocking
Wonderful Well

" I Still Remane your Humble Servant Mrs Newton

" I am vary sorry to think the Dog Perventes your
Comeing

" I am Glad to hear you are Both Well and we are
the same."

The nieces remained firm, and from the following letter it is plain the aunt gave way. The dog motive is repeated *pianissimo*, and is not returned to—not at least by Mrs. Newton.

" DEAR MISS ——, I Receve your Letter on Thursday i Whent to your Aunt and i see her and She is a Greable to everry thing i asked her and seme so vary Much Please to see you Both Next Tuseday and she has sent for the Faggots to Day and she Will Send for the Coles to Morrow and i will Go up there to Morrow Morning and Make the Fiers and Tend to the Beds and sleep in it Till you Come Down your Aunt sends her Love to you Both and she is Quite well your Aunt Wishes you wold Write againe Before you Come as she ma Expeckye and the Dog is not to Gointo the Parlor a Tall
" your Aunt kind Love to you Both & hopes you Wonte Fail in Coming according to Prommis
" MRS NEWTON."

From a later letter it appears that the nieces did not pay their visit after all, and what is worse a letter had miscarried, and the aunt sat up expecting them from seven till twelve at night, and Harry had paid for " Faggots and Coles quarter of Hund. Faggots Half tun of Coles 1*l*. 1*s*. 3*d*." Shortly afterwards, however, " She " again talks of coming up to London herself and writes through her servant :—

" My Dear girls i Receve your kind letter & I am happy to hear you ar both Well and I Was in hopes of seeing of you Both Down at My House this spring to stay a Wile I am Quite well my self in Helth But vary

Low Spireted I am vary sorry to hear the Misforting of Poor charles & how he cum to flie in the Fier I cannot think. I should like to know if he is dead or a Live, and I shall come to London in August & stay three or four daies if it is agreable to you. Mrs. Newton has lost her mother in Law 4 day March & I hope you send me word Wather charles is Dead or a Live as soon as possible, and will you send me word what Little Betty is for I cannot make her out.''

The next letter is a new handwriting, and tells the nieces of their aunt's death in the following terms :—

" DEAR MISS ——, It is my most painful duty to inform you that your dear aunt expired this morning comparatively easy as Hannah informs me and in so doing restored her soul to the custody of him whom she considered to be alone worthy of its care.

" The doctor had visited her about five minutes previously and had applied a blister.

" You and your sister will I am sure excuse further details at present and believe me with kindest remembrances to remain   " Yours truly, &c."

After a few days a lawyer's letter informs the nieces that their aunt had left them the bulk of her not very considerable property, but had charged them with an annuity of £1 a week to be paid to Harry and Mrs. Newton so long as the dog lived.

The only other letters by Mrs. Newton are written on paper of a different and more modern size ; they leave an impression of having been written a good many years later. I take them as they come. The first is very short :—

" DEAR MISS ——, i write to say i cannot possiblely come on Wednesday as we have killed a pig.   your's truely,
           " ELIZABETH NEWTON."

The second runs :—

" DEAR MISS ——, i hope you are both quite well in health & your Leg much better i am happy to say i am getting quite well again i hope Amandy has reached you safe by this time i sent a small parcle by Amandy, there was half a dozen Pats of butter & the Cakes was very homely and not so light as i could wish i hope by this time Sarah Ann has promised she will stay untill next monday as i think a few daies longer will not make much diferance and as her young man has been very considerate to wait so long as he has i think he would for a few days Longer dear Miss —— I wash for William and i have not got his clothes yet as it has been delayed by the carrier & i cannot possiblely get it done before Sunday and i do not Like traviling on a Sunday but to oblige you i would come but to come sooner i cannot possiblely but i hope Sarah Ann will be prevailed on once more as She has so many times i feel sure if she tells her young man he will have patient for he is a very kind young man
         " i remain your sincerely
            " ELIZABETH NEWTON."

The last letter in my collection seems written almost within measurable distance of the Christmas-card era. The sheet is headed by a beautifully embossed device of some holly in red and green, wishing the recipient of the letter a merry Xmas and a happy new year, while the border is crimped and edged with blue. I know not what it is, but there is something in the writer's highly finished style that reminds me of Mendelssohn. It would almost do for the words of one of his celebrated " Lieder ohne Worte " :—

" DEAR MISS MARIA,—I hasten to acknowledge the receipt of your kind note with the inclosure for which I return my best thanks. I need scarcely say how glad I was to know that the volumes secured your approval, and that the announcement of the improvement in the condition of your Sister's legs afforded me infinite pleasure. The gratifying news encouraged me in the hope that now the nature of the disorder is comprehended her legs will—notwithstanding the process may be gradual—ultimately get quite well. The pretty Robin Redbreast which lay ensconced in your epistle, conveyed to me, in terms more eloquent than words, how much you desired me those Compliments which the little missive he bore in his bill expressed ; the emblem is sweetly pretty, and now that we are again allowed to felicitate each other on another recurrence of the season of the Christian's rejoicing, permit me to tender to yourself, and by you to your Sister, mine and my Wife's heartfelt congratulations and warmest wishes with respect to the coming year. It is a common belief that if we take a retrospective view of each departing year, as it behoves us annually to do, we shall find the blessings which we have received to immeasurably outnumber our causes of sorrow. Speaking for myself I can fully subscribe to that sentiment, and doubtless neither Miss —— nor yourself are exceptions. Miss ——'s illness and consequent confinement to the house has been a severe trial, but in that trouble an opportunity was afforded you to prove a Sister's devotion and she has been enabled to realise a larger (if possible) display of sisterly affection.

" A happy Christmas to you both, and may the new year prove a Cornucopia from which still greater blessings than even those we have hitherto received, shall issue, to benefit us all by contributing to our temporal happiness and, what is of higher importance, conducing to our felicity hereafter.

" I was sorry to hear that you were so annoyed with mice and rats, and if I should have an opportunity to obtain a nice cat I will do so and send my boy to your house with it.

" I remain,
" Yours truly."

How little what is commonly called education can do after all towards the formation of a good style, and what a delightful volume might not be entitled " Half Hours with the Worst Authors." Why, the finest word I know of in the English language was coined, not by my poor old grandfather, whose education had left little to desire, nor by any of the admirable scholars whom he in his turn educated, but by an old matron who presided over one of the halls, or houses of his school. This good lady, whose name by the way was Bromfield, had a fine high temper of her own, or thought it politic to affect one. One night when the boys were particularly noisy she burst like a hurricane into the hall, collared a youngster, and told him he was the " rampingest-scampingest-rackety-tackety-tow-row-roaringest boy in the whole school." Would Mrs. Newton have been able to set the aunt and the dog before us so vividly if she had been more

highly educated ? Would Mrs. Bromfield have been
able to forge and hurl her thunderbolt of a word if she
had been taught how to do so, or indeed been at much
pains to create it at all ? It came. It was her χάρισμα.
She did not probably know that she had done what
the greatest scholar would have had to rack his brains
over for many an hour before he could even approach.
Tradition says that having brought down her boy she
looked round the hall in triumph, and then after a
moment's lull said, " Young gentlemen, prayers are
excused," and left them.

I have sometimes thought that, after all, the main
use of a classical education consists in the check it
gives to originality, and the way in which it prevents
an inconvenient number of people from using their
own eyes. That we will not be at the trouble of
looking at things for ourselves if we can get anyone
to tell us what we ought to see goes without saying,
and it is the business of schools and universities to
assist us in this respect. The theory of evolution
teaches that any power not worked at pretty high
pressure will deteriorate : originality and freedom
from affectation are all very well in their way, but we
can easily have too much of them, and it is better that
none should be either original or free from cant but
those who insist on being so, no matter what hindrances
obstruct, nor what incentives are offered them to see
things through the regulation medium. To insist on
seeing things for oneself is to be an ἰδιώτης, or in
plain English, an idiot ; nor do I see any safer check
against general vigour and clearness of thought, with
consequent terseness of expression, than that provided
by the curricula of our universities and schools of
public instruction. If a young man, in spite of every

effort to fit him with blinkers, will insist on getting rid of them, he must do so at his own risk. He will not be long in finding out his mistake. Our public schools and universities play the beneficent part in our social scheme that cattle do in forests : they browse the seedlings down and prevent the growth of all but the luckiest and sturdiest. Of course, if there are too many either cattle or schools, they browse so effectually that they find no more food, and starve till equilibrium is restored ; but it seems to be a provision of nature that there should always be these alternate periods, during which either the cattle or the trees are getting the best of it ; and, indeed, without such provision we should have neither the one nor the other. At this moment the cattle, doubtless, are in the ascendant, and if university extension proceeds much farther, we shall assuredly have no more Mrs. Newtons and Mrs. Bromfields; but whatever is is best, and, on the whole, I should propose to let things find pretty much their own level.

However this may be, who can question that the treasures hidden in many a country house contain sleeping beauties even fairer than those that I have endeavoured to waken from long sleep in the foregoing article ? How many Mrs. Quicklys are there not living in London at this present moment ? For that Mrs. Quickly was an invention of Shakespeare's I will not believe. The old woman from whom he drew said every word that he put into Mrs. Quickly's mouth, and a great deal more which he did not and perhaps could not make use of. This question, however, would again lead me far from my subject, which I should mar were I to dwell upon it longer, and therefore leave with the hope that it may give my readers absolutely no food whatever for reflection.

How to Make the Best
of Life [1]

I HAVE been asked to speak on the question how
to make the best of life, but may as well confess at
once that I know nothing about it. I cannot think that
I have made the best of my own life, nor is it likely that
I shall make much better of what may or may not
remain to me. I do not even know how to make the
best of the twenty minutes that your committee has
placed at my disposal, and as for life as a whole, who
ever yet made the best of such a colossal opportunity
by conscious effort and deliberation? In little things
no doubt deliberate and conscious effort will help us,
but we are speaking of large issues, and such kingdoms
of heaven as the making the best of these come not by
observation.

The question, therefore, on which I have undertaken
to address you is, as you must all know, fatuous, if it
be faced seriously. Life is like playing a violin solo in
public and learning the instrument as one goes on. One
cannot make the best of such impossibilities, and the
question is doubly fatuous until we are told which of
our two lives—the conscious or the unconscious—is
held by the asker to be the truer life. Which does the
question contemplate—the life we know, or the life
which others may know, but which we know not?

[1] An address delivered at the Somerville Club, February 27th, 1895.

Death gives a life to some men and women compared with which their so-called existence here is as nothing. Which is the truer life of Shakespeare, Handel, that divine woman who wrote the *Odyssey*, and of Jane Austen—the life which palpitated with sensible warm motion within their own bodies, or that in virtue of which they are still palpitating in ours ? In whose consciousness does their truest life consist— their own, or ours ? Can Shakespeare be said to have begun his true life till a hundred years or so after he was dead and buried ? His physical life was but as an embryonic stage, a coming up out of darkness, a twilight and dawn before the sunrise of that life of the world to come which he was to enjoy hereafter. We all live for a while after we are gone hence, but we are for the most part stillborn, or at any rate die in infancy, as regards that life which every age and country has recognized as higher and truer than the one of which we are now sentient. As the life of the race is larger, longer, and in all respects more to be considered than that of the individual, so is the life we live in others larger and more important than the one we live in ourselves. This appears nowhere perhaps more plainly than in the case of great teachers, who often in the lives of their pupils produce an effect that reaches far beyond anything produced while their single lives were yet unsupplemented by those other lives into which they infused their own.

Death to such people is the ending of a short life, but it does not touch the life they are already living in those whom they have taught ; and happily, as none can know when he shall die, so none can make sure that he too shall not live long beyond the grave ; for the life after death is like money before

it—no one can be sure that it may not fall to him or her
even at the eleventh hour.   Money and immortality
come in such odd unaccountable ways that no one is cut
off from hope.   We may not have made either of them
for ourselves, but yet another may give them to us in
virtue of his or her love, which shall illumine us for
ever, and establish us in some heavenly mansion where-
of we neither dreamed nor shall ever dream.   Look at
the Doge Loredano Loredani, the old man's smile upon
whose face has been reproduced so faithfully in so
many lands that it can never henceforth be forgotten—
would he have had one hundredth part of the life he now
lives had he not been linked awhile with one of those
heaven-sent men who know *che cosa è amor ?*   Look
at Rembrandt's old woman in our National Gallery ;
had she died before she was eighty-three years old she
would not have been living now.   Then, when she was
eighty-three, immortality perched upon her as a bird
on a withered bough.

I seem to hear someone say that this is a mockery,
a piece of special pleading, a giving of stones to those
that ask for bread.   Life is not life unless we can feel it,
and a life limited to a knowledge of such fraction of our
work as may happen to survive us is no true life in
other people ; salve it as we may, death is not life any
more than black is white.

The objection is not so true as it sounds.   I do not
deny that we had rather not die, nor do I pretend that
much even in the case of the most favoured few can
survive them beyond the grave.   It is only because
this is so that our own life is possible ; others have
made room for us, and we should make room for others
in our turn without undue repining.   What I maintain
is that a not inconsiderable number of people do

actually attain to a life beyond the grave which we can
all feel forcibly enough, whether they can do so or not—
that this life tends with increasing civilization to
become more and more potent, and that it is better
worth considering, in spite of its being unfelt by ourselves, than any which we have felt or can ever feel in
our own persons.

Take an extreme case. A group of people are photographed by Edison's new process—say Titiens, Tre-
belli, and Jenny Lind, with any two of the finest men
singers the age has known—let them be photographed
incessantly for half an hour while they perform a scene
in *Lohengrin ;* let all be done stereoscopically. Let
them be phonographed at the same time so that their
minutest shades of intonation are preserved, let the
slides be coloured by a competent artist, and then let
the scene be called suddenly into sight and sound, say a
hundred years hence. Are those people dead or alive ?
Dead to themselves they are, but while they live so
powerfully and so livingly in us, which is the greater
paradox—to say that they are alive or that they are
dead ? To myself it seems that their life in others
would be more truly life than their death to themselves
is death. Granted that they do not present all the
phenomena of life—who ever does so even when he is
held to be alive ? We are held to be alive because we
present a sufficient number of living phenomena to let
the others go without saying ; those who see us take the
part for the whole here as in everything else, and surely,
in the case supposed above, the phenomena of life pre-
dominate so powerfully over those of death, that the
people themselves must be held to be more alive than
dead. Our living personality is, as the word implies,
only our mask, and those who still own such a mask as

K

I have supposed have a living personality. Granted again that the case just put is an extreme one ; still many a man and many a woman has so stamped him or herself on his work that, though we would gladly have the aid of such accessories as we doubtless presently shall have to the livingness of our great dead, we can see them very sufficiently through the master-pieces they have left us.

As for their own unconsciousness I do not deny it. The life of the embryo was unconscious before birth, and so is the life—I am speaking only of the life revealed to us by natural religion—after death. But as the embryonic and infant life of which we were unconscious was the most potent factor in our after life of consciousness, so the effect which we may un-consciously produce in others after death, and it may be even before it on those who have never seen us, is in all sober seriousness our truer and more abiding life, and the one which those who would make the best of their sojourn here will take most into their consideration.

Unconsciousness is no bar to livingness. Our con-scious actions are a drop in the sea as compared with our unconscious ones. Could we know all the life that is in us by way of circulation, nutrition, breathing, waste and repair, we should learn what an infinitesi-mally small part consciousness plays in our present existence ; yet our unconscious life is as truly life as our conscious life, and though it is unconscious to itself it emerges into an indirect and vicarious con-sciousness in our other and conscious self, which exists but in virtue of our unconscious self. So we have also a vicarious consciousness in others. The unconscious life of those that have gone before us has in great part moulded us into such men and women as we are, and our own unconscious lives will in like manner have a vicarious consciousness in others, though we be dead enough to it in ourselves.

If it is again urged that it matters not to us how much we may be alive in others, if we are to know nothing about it, I reply that the common instinct of all who are worth considering gives the lie to such cynicism. I see here present some who have achieved, and others who no doubt will achieve, success in literature. Will one of them hesitate to admit that it is a lively pleasure to her to feel that on the other side of the world someone may be smiling happily over her work, and that she is thus living in that person though she knows nothing about it ? Here it seems to me that true faith comes in. Faith does not consist, as the Sunday School pupil said, " in the power of believing that which we know to be untrue." It consists in holding fast that which the healthiest and most kindly instincts of the best and most sensible men and women are intuitively possessed of, without caring to require much evidence further than the fact that such people are so convinced ; and for my own part I find the best men and women I know unanimous in feeling that life in others, even though we know nothing about it, is nevertheless a thing to be desired and gratefully accepted if we can get it either before death or after. I observe also that a large number of men and women do actually attain to such life, and in some cases continue so to live, if not for ever, yet to what is practically much the same thing. Our life then in this world is, to natural religion as much as to revealed, a period of probation. The use we make of it is to settle how far we are to enter into another, and whether that other is to be a heaven of just affection or a hell of righteous condemnation.

Who, then, are the most likely so to run that they may obtain tnis veritable prize of our high calling ? Setting aside such lucky numbers, drawn as it were in the lottery of immortality, which I have referred to casually above, and setting aside also the chances and changes from which even immortality is not exempt, who on the whole are most likely to live anew in the affectionate thoughts of those who never so much as saw them in the flesh, and know not even their names ? There is a *nisus*, a straining in the dull dumb economy of things, in virtue of which some, whether they will it and know it or no, are more likely to live after death than others, and who are these ? Those who aimed at it as by some great thing that they would do to make them famous ? Those who have lived most in themselves and for themselves, or those who have been most ensouled consciously, but perhaps better unconsciously, directly but more often indirectly, by the most living souls past and present that have flitted near them ? Can we think of a man or woman who grips us firmly, at the thought of whom we kindle when we are alone in our honest daw's plumes, with none to admire or shrug his shoulders, can we think of one such, the secret of whose power does not lie in the charm of his or her personality—that is to say, in the wideness of his or her sympathy with, and therefore life in and communion with other people ? In the wreckage that comes ashore from the sea of time there is much tinsel stuff that we must preserve and study if we would know our own times and people ; granted that many a dead charlatan lives long and enters largely and necessarily into our own lives ; we use them and throw them away when we have done with them. I do not speak of these, I do not speak of the

Virgils and Alexander Popes, and who can say how
many more whose names I dare not mention for fear
of offending. They are as stuffed birds or beasts in a
museum ; serviceable no doubt from a scientific stand-
point, but with no vivid or vivifying hold upon us.
They seem to be alive, but are not. I am speaking of
those who do actually live in us, and move us to higher
achievements though they be long dead, whose life
thrusts out our own and overrides it. I speak of those
who draw us ever more towards them from youth to
age, and to think of whom is to feel at once that we are
in the hands of those we love, and whom we would
most wish to resemble. What is the secret of the hold
that these people have upon us ? Is it not that while,
conventionally speaking, alive, they most merged
their lives in, and were in fullest communion with
those among whom they lived ? They found their
lives in losing them. We never love the memory of
anyone unless we feel that he or she was himself or
herself a lover.

I have seen it urged, again, in querulous accents, that
the so-called immortality even of the most immortal
is not for ever. I see a passage to this effect in a book
that is making a stir as I write. I will quote it. The
writer says :—

" So, it seems to me, is the immortality we so glibly
predicate of departed artists. If they survive at all,
it is but a shadowy life they live, moving on through
the gradations of slow decay to distant but inevitable
death. They can no longer, as heretofore, speak
directly to the hearts of their fellow-men, evoking
their tears or laughter, and all the pleasures, be they
sad or merry, of which imagination holds the secret.

Driven from the market-place they become first the companions of the student, then the victims of the specialist. He who would still hold familiar intercourse with them must train himself to penetrate the veil which in ever-thickening folds conceals them from the ordinary gaze ; he must catch the tone of a vanished society, he must move in a circle of alien associations, he must think in a language not his own."[1]

This is crying for the moon, or rather pretending to cry for it, for the writer is obviously insincere. I see the *Saturday Review* says the passage I have just quoted " reaches almost to poetry," and indeed I find many blank verses in it, some of them very aggressive. No prose is free from an occasional blank verse, and a good writer will not go hunting over his work to rout them out, but nine or ten in little more than as many lines is indeed reaching too near to poetry for good prose. This, however, is a trifle, and might pass if the tone of the writer was not so obviously that of cheap pessimism. I know not which is cheapest, pessimism or optimism. One forces lights, the other darks ; both are equally untrue to good art, and equally sure of their effect with the groundlings. The one extenuates, the other sets down in malice. The first is the more amiable lie, but both are lies, and are known to be so by those who utter them. Talk about catching the tone of a vanished society to understand Rembrandt or Giovanni Bellini ! It is nonsense—the folds do not thicken in front of these men ; we understand them as well as those among whom they went about in the flesh, and perhaps better. Homer and Shakespeare

[1] The *Foundations of Belief*, by the Right Hon. A. J. Balfour. Longmans, 1895, p. 48.

speak to us probably far more effectually than they did to the men of their own time, and most likely we have them at their best. I cannot think that Shakespeare talked better than we hear him now in *Hamlet* or *Henry the Fourth ;* like enough he would have been found a very disappointing person in a drawing-room. People stamp themselves on their work ; if they have not done so they are naught, if they have we have them ; and for the most part they stamp themselves deeper on their work than on their talk. No doubt Shakespeare and Handel will be one day clean forgotten, as though they had never been born. The world will in the end die ; mortality therefore itself is not immortal, and when death dies the life of these men will die with it—but not sooner. It is enough that they should live within us and move us for many ages as they have and will. Such immortality, therefore, as some men and women are born to achieve, or have thrust upon them, is a practical if not a technical immortality, and he who would have more let him have nothing.

I see I have drifted into speaking rather of how to make the best of death than of life, but who can speak of life without his thoughts turning instantly to that which is beyond it ? He or she who has made the best of the life after death has made the best of the life before it ; who cares one straw for any such chances and changes as will commonly befall him here if he is upheld by the full and certain hope of everlasting life in the affections of those that shall come after ? If the life after death is happy in the hearts of others, it matters little how unhappy was the life before it.

And now I leave my subject, not without misgiving that I shall have disappointed you. But for the great

attention which is being paid to the work from which
I have quoted above, I should not have thought it well
to insist on points with which you are, I doubt not,
as fully impressed as I am: but that book weakens
the sanctions of natural religion, and minimizes the
comfort which it affords us, while it does more to
undermine than to support the foundations of what is
commonly called belief. Therefore I was glad to
embrace this opportunity of protesting. Otherwise I
should not have been so serious on a matter that
transcends all seriousness. Lord Beaconsfield cut it
shorter with more effect. When asked to give a rule of
life for the son of a friend he said, " Do not let him
try and find out who wrote the letters of Junius."
Pressed for further counsel, he added, " Nor yet who
was the man in the iron mask "—and he would say no
more. Don't bore people. And yet I am by no means
sure that a good many people do not think themselves
ill-used unless he who addresses them has thoroughly
well bored them—especially if they have paid any
money for hearing him. My great namesake said,
" Surely the pleasure is as great of being cheated as to
cheat," and great as the pleasure both of cheating and
boring undoubtedly is, I believe he was right. So
I remember a poem which came out some thirty years
ago in *Punch*, about a young lady who went forth in
quest to " Some burden make or burden bear, but
which she did not greatly care, oh Miserie." So, again,
all the holy men and women who in the Middle Ages
professed to have discovered how to make the best
of life took care that being bored, if not cheated, should
have a large place in their programme. Still there are
limits, and I close not without fear that I may have
exceeded them.

The Sanctuary of Montrigone[1]

THE only place in the Valsesia, except Varallo, where I at present suspect the presence of Tabachetti[2] is at Montrigone, a little-known sanctuary dedicated to St. Anne, about three-quarters of a mile south of Borgo-Sesia station. The situation is, of course, lovely, but the sanctuary does not offer any features of architectural interest. The sacristan told me it was founded in 1631 ; and in 1644 Giovanni d'Enrico, while engaged in superintending and completing the work undertaken here by himself and Giacomo Ferro, fell ill and died. I do not know whether or no there was an earlier sanctuary on the same site, but was told it was built on the demolition of a stronghold belonging to the Counts of Biandrate.

The incidents which it illustrates are treated with even more than the homeliness usual in works of this description when not dealing with such solemn events as the death and passion of Christ. Except when these subjects were being represented, something of the

[1] Published in the *Universal Review*, November, 1888.

[2] Since this essay was written it has been ascertained by Cavaliere Francesco Negri, of Casale Monferrato, that Tabachetti died in 1615. If, therefore, the Sanctuary of Montrigone was not founded until 1631, it is plain that Tabachetti cannot have worked there. All the latest discoveries about Tabachetti's career will be found in Cavaliere Negri's pamphlet *Il Santuario di Crea* (Alessandria, 1902). See also note on p. 195.—R. A. S.

latitude, and even humour, allowed in the old mystery plays was permitted, doubtless from a desire to render the work more attractive to the peasants, who were the most numerous and most important pilgrims. It is not until faith begins to be weak that it fears an occasionally lighter treatment of semi-sacred subjects, and it is impossible to convey an accurate idea of the spirit prevailing at this hamlet of sanctuary without attuning oneself somewhat to the more pagan character of the place. Of irreverence, in the sense of a desire to laugh at things that are of high and serious import, there is not a trace, but at the same time there is a certain unbending of the bow at Montrigone which is not perceivable at Varallo.

The first chapel to the left on entering the church is that of the Birth of the Virgin. St. Anne is sitting up in bed. She is not at all ill—in fact, considering that the Virgin has only been born about five minutes, she is wonderful; still the doctors think it may be perhaps better that she should keep her room for half an hour longer, so the bed has been festooned with red and white paper roses, and the counterpane is covered with bouquets in baskets and in vases of glass and china. These cannot have been there during the actual birth of the Virgin, so I suppose they had been in readiness, and were brought in from an adjoining room as soon as the baby had been born. A lady on her left is bringing in some more flowers, which St. Anne is receiving with a smile and most gracious gesture of the hands. The first thing she asked for, when the birth was over, was for her three silver hearts. These were immediately brought to her, and she has got them all on, tied round her neck with a piece of blue silk ribbon.

Dear mamma has come. We felt sure she would, and that any little misunderstandings between her and Joachim would ere long be forgotten and forgiven. They are both so good and sensible, if they would only understand one another. At any rate, here she is, in high state at the right hand of the bed. She is dressed in black, for she has lost her husband some few years previously, but I do not believe a smarter, sprier old lady for her years could be found in Palestine, nor yet that either Giovanni d'Enrico or Giacomo Ferro could have conceived or executed such a character. The sacristan wanted to have it that she was not a woman at all, but was a portrait of St. Joachim, the Virgin's father. "Sembra una donna," he pleaded more than once, "ma non è donna." Surely, however, in works of art even more than in other things, there is no "is" but seeming, and if a figure seems female it must be taken as such. Besides, I asked one of the leading doctors at Varallo whether the figure was man or woman. He said it was evident I was not married, for that if I had been I should have seen at once that she was not only a woman but a mother-in-law of the first magnitude, or, as he called it, "una suocera tremenda," and this without knowing that I wanted her to be a mother-in-law myself. Unfortunately she had no real drapery, so I could not settle the question as my friend Mr. H. F. Jones and I had been able to do at Varallo with the figure of Eve that had been turned into a Roman soldier assisting at the capture of Christ. I am not, however, disposed to waste more time upon anything so obvious, and will content myself with saying that we have here the Virgin's grandmother. I had never had the pleasure, so far as I remembered, of meeting this lady before, and was glad to have an opportunity of making her acquaintance.

Tradition says that it was she who chose the Virgin's name, and if so, what a debt of gratitude do we not owe her for her judicious selection ! It makes one shudder to think what might have happened if she had named the child Keren-Happuch, as poor Job's daughter was called. How could we have said, "Ave Keren-Happuch !" What would the musicians have done ? I forget whether Maher-Shalal-Hash-Baz was a man or a woman, but there were plenty of names quite as unmanageable at the Virgin's grandmother's option, and we cannot sufficiently thank her for having chosen one that is so euphonious in every language which we need take into account. For this reason alone we should not grudge her her portrait, but we should try to draw the line here. I do not think we ought to give the Virgin's great-grandmother a statue. Where is it to end ? It is like Mr. Crookes's ultimissimate atoms ; we used to draw the line at ultimate atoms, and now it seems we are to go a step farther back and have ultimissimate atoms. How long, I wonder, will it be before we feel that it will be a material help to us to have ultimissimissimate atoms ? Quavers stopped at demi-semi-demi, but there is no reason to suppose that either atoms or ancestresses of the Virgin will be so complacent.

I have said that on St. Anne's left hand there is a lady who is bringing in some flowers. St. Anne was always passionately fond of flowers. There is a pretty story told about her in one of the Fathers, I forget which, to the effect that when a child she was asked which she liked best—cakes or flowers ? She could not yet speak plainly and lisped out, " Oh fowses, pretty fowses " ; she added, however, with a sigh and as a kind of wistful corollary, " but cakes are very nice." She is not to have any cakes just now, but as soon as she has done thanking the lady for her beautiful nosegay, she is to have a couple of nice new-laid eggs, that are being brought her by another lady. Valsesian women immediately after their confinement always have eggs beaten up with wine and sugar, and one can tell a Valsesian Birth of the Virgin from a Venetian or a Florentine by the presence of the eggs. I learned this from an eminent Valsesian professor of medicine, who told me that, though not according to received rules, the eggs never seemed to do any harm. Here they are evidently to be beaten up, for there is neither spoon nor egg-cup, and we cannot suppose that they were hard-boiled. On the other hand, in the Middle Ages Italians never used egg-cups and spoons for boiled eggs. The medieval boiled egg was always eaten by dipping bread into the yolk.

Behind the lady who is bringing in the eggs is the under-under-nurse who is at the fire warming a towel. In the foreground we have the regulation midwife holding the regulation baby (who, by the way, was an astonishingly fine child for only five minutes old). Then comes the under-nurse—a good buxom creature, who, as usual, is feeling the water in the bath to see that it is of the right temperature. Next to her is the head-nurse, who is arranging the cradle. Behind the head-nurse is the under-under-nurse's drudge, who is just going out upon some errands. Lastly—for by this time we have got all round the chapel—we arrive at the Virgin's grandmother's body-guard, a stately, responsible-looking lady, standing in waiting upon her mistress. I put it to the reader—is it conceivable that St.

Joachim should have been allowed in such a room at such a time, or that he should have had the courage to avail himself of the permission, even though it had been extended to him ? At any rate, is it conceivable that he should have been allowed to sit on St. Anne's right hand, laying down the law with a " Marry, come up " here, and a " Marry, go down " there, and a couple of such unabashed collars as the old lady has put on for the occasion ?

Moreover (for I may as well demolish this mischievous confusion between St. Joachim and his mother-in-law once and for all), the merest tyro in hagiology knows that St. Joachim was not at home when the Virgin was born. He had been hustled out of the temple for having no children, and had fled desolate and dismayed into the wilderness. It shows how silly people are, for all the time he was going, if they had only waited a little, to be the father of the most remarkable person of purely human origin who had ever been born, and such a parent as this should surely not be hurried. The story is told in the frescoes of the chapel of Loreto, only a quarter of an hour's walk from Varallo, and no one can have known it better than D'Enrico. The frescoes are explained by written passages that tell us how, when Joachim was in the desert, an angel came to him in the guise of a fair, civil young gentleman, and told him the Virgin was to be born. Then, later on, the same young gentleman appeared to him again, and bade him " in God's name be comforted, and turn again to his content," for the Virgin had been actually born. On which St. Joachim, who seems to have been of opinion that marriage after all *was* rather a failure, said that, as things were going on so nicely without him, he would stay in the desert just a little longer, and offered up a lamb as a pretext to gain time. Perhaps he guessed about his mother-in-law, or he may have asked the angel. Of course, even in spite of such evidence as this, I may be mistaken about the Virgin's grandmother's sex, and the sacristan may be right ; but I can only say that if the lady sitting by St. Anne's bedside at Montrigone is the Virgin's father—well, in that case I must reconsider a good deal that I have been accustomed to believe was beyond question.

Taken singly, I suppose that none of the figures in the chapel, except the Virgin's grandmother, should be rated very highly. The under-nurse is the next best figure, and might very well be Tabachetti's, for neither Giovanni d'Enrico nor Giacomo Ferro was successful with his female characters. There is not a single really comfortable woman in any chapel by either of them on the Sacro Monte at Varallo. Tabachetti, on the other hand, delighted in women ; if they were young he made them comely and engaging, if they were old he gave them dignity and individual character, and the under-nurse is much more in accordance with Tabachetti's habitual mental attitude than with D'Enrico's or Giacomo Ferro's. Still there are only four figures out of the eleven that are mere otiose supers, and taking the work as a whole it leaves a pleasant impression as being throughout naïve and homely, and sometimes, which is of less importance, technically excellent.

Allowance must, of course, be made for tawdry accessories and repeated coats of shiny oleaginous paint—very disagreeable where it has peeled off and almost more so where it has not. What work could stand against such treatment as the Valsesian terra-

cotta figures have had to put up with ? Take the
Venus of Milo ; let her be done in terra-cotta, and have
run, not much, but still something, in the baking ;
paint her pink, two oils, all over, and then varnish
her—it will help to preserve the paint ; glue a lot of
horsehair on to her pate, half of which shall have come
off, leaving the glue still showing ; scrape her, not too
thoroughly, get the village drawing-master to paint
her again, and the drawing-master in the next provincial town to put a forest background behind her
with the brightest emerald-green leaves that he can do
for the money ; let this painting and scraping and
repainting be repeated several times over ; festoon
her with pink and white flowers made of tissue paper ;
surround her with the cheapest German imitations of
the cheapest decorations that Birmingham can produce ; let the night air and winter fogs get at her for
three hundred years, and how easy, I wonder, will it be
to see the goddess who will be still in great part there ?
True, in the case of the Birth of the Virgin chapel at
Montrigone, there is no real hair and no fresco background, but time has had abundant opportunities
without these. I will conclude my notice of this chapel
by saying that on the left, above the door through
which the under-under-nurse's drudge is about to pass,
there is a good painted terra-cotta bust, said—but I
believe on no authority—to be a portrait of Giovanni
d'Enrico. Others say that the Virgin's grandmother
is Giovanni d'Enrico, but this is even more absurd than
supposing her to be St. Joachim.

The next chapel to the Birth of the Virgin is that of
the *Sposalizio*. There is no figure here which suggests
Tabachetti, but still there are some very good ones.
The best have no taint of *barocco ;* the man who did

them, whoever he may have been, had evidently a good deal of life and go, was taking reasonable pains, and did not know too much. Where this is the case no work can fail to please. Some of the figures have real hair and some terra-cotta. There is no fresco background worth mentioning. A man sitting on the steps of the altar with a book on his lap, and holding up his hand to another, who is leaning over him and talking to him, is among the best figures ; some of the disappointed suitors who are breaking their wands are also very good.

The angel in the Annunciation chapel, which comes next in order, is a fine, burly, ship's-figurehead, commercial-hotel sort of being enough, but the Virgin is very ordinary. There is no real hair and no fresco background, only three dingy old blistered pictures of no interest whatever.

In the Visit of Mary to Elizabeth there are three pleasing subordinate lady attendants, two to the left and one to the right of the principal figures ; but these figures themselves are not satisfactory. There is no fresco background. Some of the figures have real hair and some terra-cotta.

In the Circumcision and Purification chapel—for both these events seem contemplated in the one that follows—there are doves, but there is neither dog nor knife. Still Simeon, who has the infant Saviour in his arms, is looking at him in a way which can only mean that, knife or no knife, the matter is not going to end here. At Varallo they have now got a dreadful knife for the Circumcision chapel. They had none last winter. What they have now got would do very well to kill a bullock with, but could not be used professionally with safety for any animal smaller than a

L

rhinoceros. I imagine that someone was sent to Novara to buy a knife, and that, thinking it was for the Massacre of the Innocents chapel, he got the biggest he could see. Then when he brought it back people said " chow " several times, and put it upon the table and went away.

Returning to Montrigone, the Simeon is an excellent figure, and the Virgin is fairly good, but the prophetess Anna, who stands just behind her, is by far the most interesting in the group, and is alone enough to make me feel sure that Tabachetti gave more or less help here, as he had done years before at Orta. She, too, like the Virgin's grandmother, is a widow lady, and wears collars of a cut that seems to have prevailed ever since the Virgin was born some twenty years previously. There is a largeness and simplicity of treatment about the figure to which none but an artist of the highest rank can reach, and D'Enrico was not more than a second or third-rate man. The hood is like Handel's Truth sailing upon the broad wings of Time, a prophetic strain that nothing but the old experience of a great poet can reach. The lips of the prophetess are for the moment closed, but she has been prophesying all the morning, and the people round the wall in the background are in ecstasies at the lucidity with which she has explained all sorts of difficulties that they had never been able to understand till now. They are putting their forefingers on their thumbs and their thumbs on their forefingers, and saying how clearly they see it all and what a wonderful woman Anna is. A prophet indeed is not generally without honour save in his own country, but then a country is generally not without honour save with its own prophet, and Anna has been glorifying her country rather than reviling it. Besides, the rule may not have applied to prophetesses.

The Death of the Virgin is the last of the six chapels inside the church itself. The Apostles, who of course are present, have all of them real hair, but, if I may say so, they want a wash and a brush-up so very badly that I cannot feel any confidence in writing about them. I should say that, take them all round, they are a good average sample of apostle as apostles generally go. Two or three of them are nervously anxious to find appropriate quotations in books that lie open before them, which they are searching with eager haste ; but I do not see one figure about which I should like to say positively that it is either good or bad. There is a good bust of a man, matching the one in the Birth of the Virgin chapel, which is said to be a portrait of Giovanni d'Enrico, but it is not known whom it represents.

Outside the church, in three contiguous cells that form part of the foundations, are :—

1. A dead Christ, the head of which is very impressive, while the rest of the figure is poor. I examined the treatment of the hair, which is terra-cotta, and compared it with all other like hair in the chapels above described ; I could find nothing like it, and think it most likely that Giacomo Ferro did the figure, and got Tabachetti to do the head, or that they brought the head from some unused figure by Tabachetti at Varallo, for I know no other artist of the time and neighbourhood who could have done it.

2. A Magdalene in the desert. The desert is a little coal-cellar of an arch, containing a skull and a profusion of pink and white paper bouquets, the two largest of which the Magdalene is hugging while she is saying her prayers. She is a very self-sufficient lady,

who we may be sure will not stay in the desert a day
longer than she can help, and while there will flirt even
with the skull if she can find nothing better to flirt with.
I cannot think that her repentance is as yet genuine,
and as for her praying there is no object in her doing
so, for she does not want anything.

3. In the next desert there is a very beautiful figure
of St. John the Baptist kneeling and looking upwards.
This figure puzzles me more than any other at Montrigone ; it appears to be of the fifteenth rather than the
sixteenth century ; it hardly reminds me of Gaudenzio,
and still less of any other Valsesian artist. It is a work
of unusual beauty, but I can form no idea as to its
authorship.

I wrote the foregoing pages in the church at Montrigone itself, having brought my camp-stool with me.
It was Sunday ; the church was open all day, but
there was no Mass said, and hardly anyone came. The
sacristan was a kind, gentle, little old man, who let me
do whatever I wanted. He sat on the doorstep of the
main door, mending vestments, and to this end was
cutting up a fine piece of figured silk from one to two
hundred years old, which, if I could have got it,
for half its value, I should much like to have bought.
I sat in the cool of the church while he sat in the doorway, which was still in shadow, snipping and snipping,
and then sewing, I am sure with admirable neatness.
He made a charming picture, with the arched portico
over his head, the green grass and low church wall
behind him, and then a lovely landscape of wood and
pasture and valleys and hillside. Every now and then
he would come and chirrup about Joachim, for he was
pained and shocked at my having said that his Joachim
was someone else and not Joachim at all. I said I was

very sorry, but I was afraid the figure was a woman. He asked me what he was to do. He had known it, man and boy, this sixty years, and had always shown it as St. Joachim ; he had never heard anyone but myself question his ascription, and could not suddenly change his mind about it at the bidding of a stranger. At the same time he felt it was a very serious thing to continue showing it as the Virgin's father if it was really her grandmother. I told him I thought this was a case for his spiritual director, and that if he felt uncomfortable about it he should consult his parish priest and do as he was told.

On leaving Montrigone, with a pleasant sense of having made acquaintance with a new and, in many respects, interesting work, I could not get the sacristan and our difference of opinion out of my head. What, I asked myself, are the differences that unhappily divide Christendom, and what are those that divide Christendom from modern schools of thought, but a seeing of Joachims as the Virgin's grandmothers on a larger scale ? True, we cannot call figures Joachim when we know perfectly well that they are nothing of the kind ; but I registered a vow that henceforward when I called Joachims the Virgin's grandmothers I would bear more in mind than I have perhaps always hitherto done, how hard it is for those who have been taught to see them as Joachims to think of them as something different. I trust that I have not been unfaithful to this vow in the preceding article. If the reader differs from me, let me ask him to remember how hard it is for one who has got a figure well into his head as the Virgin's grandmother to see it as Joachim.

A Medieval Girl School[1]

THIS last summer I revisited Oropa, near Biella,
to see what connection I could find between the
Oropa chapels and those at Varallo. I will take this
opportunity of describing the chapels at Oropa, and
more especially the remarkable fossil, or petrified girl
school, commonly known as the *Dimora*, or Sojourn of
the Virgin Mary in the Temple.

If I do not take these works so seriously as the reader
may expect, let me beg him, before he blames me, to go
to Oropa and see the originals for himself. Have the
good people of Oropa themselves taken them very
seriously ? Are we in an atmosphere where we need be
at much pains to speak with bated breath ? We, as is
well known, love to take even our pleasures sadly ; the
Italians take even their sadness *allegramente*, and
combine devotion with amusement in a manner that we
shall do well to study if not imitate. For this best
agrees with what we gather to have been the custom
of Christ himself, who, indeed, never speaks of austerity
but to condemn it. If Christianity is to be a living
faith, it must penetrate a man's whole life, so that he
can no more rid himself of it than he can of his flesh
and bones or of his breathing. The Christianity that
can be taken up and laid down as if it were a watch or a
book is Christianity in name only. The true Christian

[1] Published in the *Universal Review*, December, 1889.

166

can no more part from Christ in mirth than in sorrow. And, after all, what is the essence of Christianity ? What is the kernel of the nut ? Surely common sense and cheerfulness, with unflinching opposition to the charlatanisms and Pharisaisms of a man's own times. The essence of Christianity lies neither in dogma, nor yet in abnormally holy life, but in faith in an unseen world, in doing one's duty, in speaking the truth, in finding the true life rather in others than in oneself, and in the certain hope that he who loses his life on these behalfs finds more than he has lost. What can Agnosticism do against such Christianity as this ? I should be shocked if anything I had ever written or shall ever write should seem to make light of these things. I should be shocked also if I did not know how to be amused with things that amiable people obviously intended to be amusing.

The reader may need to be reminded that Oropa is among the somewhat infrequent sanctuaries at which the Madonna and infant Christ are not white, but black. I shall return to this peculiarity of Oropa later on, but will leave it for the present. For the general characteristics of the place I must refer the reader to my book *Alps and Sanctuaries*. I propose to confine myself here to the ten or a dozen chapels containing life-sized terra-cotta figures, painted up to nature, that form one of the main features of the place. At a first glance, perhaps, all these chapels will seem uninteresting ; I venture to think, however, that some, if not most of them, though falling a good deal short of the best work at Varallo and Crea, are still in their own way of considerable importance. The first chapel with which we need concern ourselves is numbered 4, and shows the Conception of the Virgin Mary. It represents St. Anne as kneeling before a terrific dragon or, as the Italians call it, " insect," about the size of a Crystal Palace pleiosaur. This " insect " is supposed to have just had its head badly crushed by St. Anne, who seems to be begging its pardon. The text " Ipsa conteret caput tuum " is written outside the chapel. The figures have no artistic interest. As regards dragons being called insects, the reader may perhaps remember that the island of S. Giulio, in the Lago d'Orta, was infested with *insetti*, which S. Giulio destroyed, and which appear, in a fresco underneath the church on the island, to have been monstrous and ferocious dragons ; but I cannot remember whether their bodies are divided into three sections, and whether or no they have exactly six legs—without which, I am told, they cannot be true insects.

The fifth chapel represents the Birth of the Virgin. Having obtained permission to go inside it, I found the date 1715 cut large and deep on the back of one figure before baking, and I imagine that this date covers the whole. There is a Queen Anne feeling throughout the composition, and if we were told that the sculptor and Francis Bird, sculptor of the statue in front of St. Paul's Cathedral, had studied under the same master, we could very well believe it. The apartment in which the Virgin was born is spacious, and in striking contrast to the one in which she herself gave birth to the Redeemer. St. Anne occupies the centre of the composition, in an enormous bed ; on her right there is a lady of the George Cruikshank style of beauty, and on the left an older person. Both are gesticulating and impressing upon St. Anne the enormous obligation she has just conferred upon mankind ; they seem also to be imploring her not to overtax her strength, but, strange to say, they are giving her neither flowers nor anything to eat and drink. I know no other birth of the Virgin in which St. Anne wants so little keeping up.

I have explained in my book *Ex Voto*, but should perhaps repeat here, that the distinguishing characteristic of the Birth of the Virgin, as rendered by Valsesian artists, is that St. Anne always has eggs immediately after the infant is born, and usually a good deal more, whereas the Madonna never has anything to eat or drink. The eggs are in accordance with a custom that still prevails among the peasant classes in the Valsesia, where women on giving birth to a child generally are given a *sabaglione*—an egg beaten up with a little wine, or rum, and sugar. East of Milan the Virgin's mother does not have eggs, and I suppose, from the absence of the eggs at Oropa, that the custom above referred to does not prevail in the Biellese district. The Virgin also is invariably washed. St. John the Baptist, when he is born at all, which is not very often, is also washed ; but I have not observed that St. Elizabeth has anything like the attention paid her that is given to St. Anne. What, however, is wanting here at Oropa in meat and drink is made up in Cupids ; they swarm like flies on the walls, clouds, cornices, and capitals of columns.

Against the right-hand wall are two lady-helps, each warming a towel at a glowing fire, to be ready against the baby should come out of its bath ; while in the right-hand foreground we have the *levatrice*, who having discharged her task, and being now so disposed, has removed the bottle from the chimney-piece, and put it near some bread, fruit and a chicken, over which she is about to discuss the confinement with two other gossips. The *levatrice* is a very characteristic figure, but the best in the chapel is the one of the head-nurse, near the middle of the composition ; she has now the infant in full charge, and is showing it to St. Joachim, with an expression as though she were telling him that her husband was a merry man. I am afraid Shakespeare was dead before the sculptor was born, otherwise I should have felt certain that he had drawn Juliet's nurse from this figure. As for the little Virgin herself, I believe her to be a fine boy of about ten months old. Viewing the work as a whole, if I only felt more sure what artistic merit really is, I should say that, though the chapel cannot be rated very highly from some standpoints, there are others from which it may be praised warmly enough. It is innocent of anatomy-worship, free from affectation or swagger, and not devoid of a good deal of homely *naïveté*. It can no more be compared with Tabachetti or Donatello than Hogarth can with Rembrandt or Giovanni Bellini ; but as it does not transcend the limitations of its age, so neither is it wanting in whatever merits that age possessed ; and there is no age without merits of some kind. There is no inscription saying who made the figures, but tradition gives them to Pietro Aureggio Termine, of Biella, commonly called Aureggio. This is confirmed by their strong resemblance to those in the *Dimora* Chapel, in which there is an inscription that names Aureggio as the sculptor.

The sixth chapel deals with the Presentation of the Virgin in the Temple. The Virgin is very small, but it must be remembered that she is only seven years old, and she is not nearly so small as she is at Crea, where, though a life-sized figure is intended, the head is hardly bigger than an apple. She is rushing up the steps with

open arms towards the High Priest, who is standing
at the top. For her it is nothing alarming ; it is the
High Priest who appears frightened ; but it will all
come right in time. The Virgin seems to be saying,
" Why, don't you know me ? I'm the Virgin Mary."
But the High Priest does not feel so sure about that,
and will make further inquiries. The scene, which
comprises some twenty figures, is animated enough,
and though it hardly kindles enthusiasm, still does not
fail to please. It looks as though of somewhat older
date than the Birth of the Virgin chapel, and I should
say shows more signs of direct Valsesian influence. In
Marocco's book about Oropa it is ascribed to Aureggio,
but I find it difficult to accept this.

The seventh, and in many respects most interesting
chapel at Oropa, shows what is in reality a medieval
Italian girl school, as nearly like the thing itself as
the artist could make it ; we are expected, however,
to see in this the high-class kind of Girton College for
young gentlewomen that was attached to the Temple
at Jerusalem, under the direction of the Chief Priest's
wife, or some one of his near female relatives. Here all
well-to-do Jewish young women completed their education, and here accordingly we find the Virgin, whose
parents desired she should shine in every accomplishment, and enjoy all the advantages their ample means
commanded.

I have met with no traces of the Virgin during the
years between her Presentation in the Temple and her
becoming head girl at Temple College. These years,
we may be assured, can hardly have been other than
eventful ; but incidents, or bits of life, are like living
forms—it is only here and there, as by rare chance,
that one of them gets arrested and fossilized ; the

greater number disappear like the greater number of antediluvian molluscs, and no one can say why one of these flies, as it were, of life should get preserved in amber more than another. Talk, indeed, about luck and cunning ; what a grain of sand as against a hundredweight is cunning's share here as against luck's. What moment could be more humdrum and unworthy of special record than the one chosen by the artist for the chapel we are considering ? Why should this one get arrested in its flight and made immortal when so many worthier ones have perished ? Yet preserved it assuredly is ; it is as though some fairy's wand had struck the medieval Miss Pinkerton, Amelia Sedley, and others who do duty instead of the Hebrew originals. It has locked them up as sleeping beauties, whose charms all may look upon. Surely the hours are like the women grinding at the mill—the one is taken and the other left, and none can give the reason more than he can say why Gallio should have won immortality by caring for none of " these things."

It seems to me, moreover, that fairies have changed their practice now in the matter of sleeping beauties, much as shopkeepers have done in Regent Street. Formerly the shopkeeper used to shut up his goods behind strong shutters, so that no one might see them after closing hours. Now he leaves everything open to the eye and turns the gas on. So the fairies, who used to lock up their sleeping beauties in impenetrable thickets, now leave them in the most public places they can find, as knowing that they will there most certainly escape notice. Look at De Hooghe ; look at *The Pilgrim's Progress*, or even Shakespeare himself— how long they slept unawakened, though they were in broad daylight and on the public thoroughfares all the

time. Look at Tabachetti, and the masterpieces he
left at Varallo. His figures there are exposed to the
gaze of every passer-by ; yet who heeds them ? Who,
save a very few, even know of their existence ? Look
again at Gaudenzio Ferrari, or the "Danse des Paysans,"
by Holbein, to which I ventured to call attention in the
Universal Review. No, no ; if a thing be in Central
Africa, it is the glory of this age to find it out ; so the
fairies think it safer to conceal their *protégés* under a
show of openness ; for the schoolmaster is much
abroad, and there is no hedge so thick or so thorny as
the dulness of culture.

It may be, again, that ever so many years hence,
when Mr. Darwin's earth-worms shall have buried
Oropa hundreds of feet deep, someone sinking a well
or making a railway-cutting will unearth these chapels,
and will believe them to have been houses, and to
contain the *exuviæ* of the living forms that tenanted
them. In the meantime, however, let us return to a
consideration of the chapel as it may now be seen by
anyone who cares to pass that way.

The work consists of about forty figures in all, not
counting Cupids, and is divided into four main divi-
sions. First, there is the large public sitting-room or
drawing-room of the College, where the elder young
ladies are engaged in various elegant employments.
Three, at a table to the left, are making a mitre
for the Bishop, as may be seen from the model on the
table. Some are merely spinning or about to spin.
One young lady, sitting rather apart from the others,
is doing an elaborate piece of needlework at a tambour-
frame near the window ; others are making lace or
slippers, probably for the new curate ; another is
struggling with a letter, or perhaps a theme, which

seems to be giving her a good deal of trouble, but which, when done, will, I am sure, be beautiful. One dear little girl is simply reading *Paul and Virginia* underneath the window, and is so concealed that I hardly think she can be seen from the outside at all, though from inside she is delightful; it was with great regret that I could not get her into any photograph. One most amiable young woman has got a child's head on her lap, the child having played itself to sleep. All are industriously and agreeably employed in some way or other; all are plump; all are nice-looking; there is not one Becky Sharp in the whole school; on the contrary, as in "Pious Orgies," all is pious—or sub-pious—and all, if not great, is at least eminently respectable. One feels that St. Joachim and St. Anne could not have chosen a school more judiciously, and that if one had a daughter oneself this is exactly where one would wish to place her. If there is a fault of any kind in the arrangements, it is that they do not keep cats enough. The place is overrun with mice, though what these can find to eat I know not. It occurs to me also that the young ladies might be kept a little more free of spiders' webs; but in all these chapels, bats, mice, and spiders are troublesome.

Off the main drawing-room on the side facing the window there is a daïs, which is approached by a large raised semicircular step, higher than the rest of the floor, but lower than the daïs itself. The daïs is, of course, reserved for the venerable Lady Principal and the under-mistresses, one of whom, by the way, is a little more *mondaine* than might have been expected, and is admiring herself in a looking-glass—unless, indeed, she is only looking to see if there is a spot of ink on her face. The Lady Principal is seated near a table, on which lie some books in expensive bindings, which I imagine to have been presented to her by the parents of pupils who were leaving school. One has given her a photographic album ; another a large scrapbook, for illustrations of all kinds ; a third volume has red edges, and is presumably of a devotional character. If I dared venture another criticism, I should say it would be better not to keep the ink-pot on the top of these books. The Lady Principal is being read to by the monitress for the week, whose duty it was to recite selected passages from the most approved Hebrew writers ; she appears to be a good deal outraged, possibly at the faulty intonation of the reader, which she has long tried vainly to correct ; or perhaps she has been hearing of the atrocious way in which her forefathers had treated the prophets, and is explaining to the young ladies how impossible it would be, in their own more enlightened age, for a prophet to fail of recognition.

On the half-daïs, as I suppose the large semicircular step between the main room and the daïs should be called, we find, first, the monitress for the week, who stands up while she recites ; and secondly, the Virgin herself, who is the only pupil allowed a seat so near to the august presence of the Lady Principal. She is ostensibly doing a piece of embroidery which is stretched on a cushion on her lap, but I should say that she was chiefly interested in the nearest of four pretty little Cupids, who are all trying to attract her attention, though they pay no court to any other young lady. I have sometimes wondered whether the obviously scandalized gesture of the Lady Principal might not be directed at these Cupids, rather than at anything the monitress may have been reading, for she would surely find them disquieting. Or she may be saying, " Why, bless me ! I do declare the Virgin has got another hamper, and St. Anne's cakes are always so terribly rich ! " Certainly the hamper is there, close to the Virgin, and the Lady Principal's action may be well directed at it, but it may have been sent to some other young lady, and be put on the sub-daïs for public exhibition. It looks as if it might have come from Fortnum and Mason's, and I half expected to find a label, addressing it to " The Virgin Mary, Temple College, Jerusalem," but if ever there was one the mice have long since eaten it. The Virgin herself does not seem to care much about it, but if she has a fault it· is that she is generally a little apathetic.

Whose the hamper was, however, is a point we shall never now certainly determine, for the best fossil is worse than the worst living form. Why, alas ! was not Mr. Edison alive when this chapel was made ? We might the.. have had a daily phonographic recital of the conversation, and an announcement might be put outside the chapels, telling us at what hours the figures would speak.

On either side of the main room there are two annexes opening out from it ; these are reserved chiefly for the younger children, some of whom, I think, are little boys. In the left annex, behind the ladies who are making a mitre, there is a child who has got a cake, and another has some fruit—possibly given them by the Virgin—and a third child is begging for some of it. The light failed so completely here that I was not able to photograph any of these figures. It was a dull September afternoon, and the clouds had settled thick round the chapel, which is never very light, and is nearly 4000 feet above the sea. I waited till such twilight as made it hopeless that more detail could be got—and a queer ghostly place enough it was to wait in—but after giving the plate an exposure of fifty minutes, I saw I could get no more, and desisted.

These long photographic exposures have the advantage that one is compelled to study a work in detail through mere lack of other employment, and that one can take one's notes in peace without being tempted to hurry over them ; but even so I continually find I have omitted to note, and have clean forgotten, much that I want later on.

In the other annex there are also one or two younger children, but it seems to have been set apart for conversation and relaxation more than any other part of the establishment.

I have already said that the work is signed by an inscription inside the chapel, to the effect that the sculptures are by Pietro Aureggio Termine di Biella. It will be seen that the young ladies are exceedingly like one another, and that the artist aimed at nothing more than a faithful rendering of the life of his own times. Let us be thankful that he aimed at nothing less. Perhaps his wife kept a girls' school ; or he may have had a large family of fat, good-natured daughters, whose little ways he had studied attentively ; at all events the work is full of spontaneous incident, and cannot fail to become more and more interesting as the age it renders falls farther back into the past. It is to be regretted that many artists, better-known men, have not been satisfied with the humbler ambitions of this most amiable and interesting sculptor. If he has left us no laboured life-studies, he has at least done something for us which we can find nowhere else, which we should be very sorry not to have, and the

M

fidelity of which to Italian life at the beginning of the eighteenth century will not be disputed.

The eighth chapel is that of the *Sposalizio*, is certainly not by Aureggio, and I should say was mainly by the same sculptor who did the Presentation in the Temple.   On going inside I found the figures had come from more than one source ; some of them are constructed so absolutely on Valsesian principles, as regards technique, that it may be assumed they came from Varallo.   Each of these last figures is in three pieces, that are baked separately and cemented together afterwards, hence they are more easily transported ; no more clay is used than is absolutely necessary ; and the off-side of the figure is neglected ; they will be found chiefly, if not entirely, at the top of the steps.   The other figures are more solidly built, and do not remind me in their business features of anything in the Valsesia.   There was a sculptor, Francesco Sala, of Locarno (doubtless the village a short distance below Varallo, and not the Locarno on the Lago Maggiore), who made designs for some of the Oropa chapels, and some of whose letters are still preserved, but whether the Valsesian figures in this present work are by him or not I cannot say.

The statues are twenty-five in number ; I could find no date or signature ; the work reminds me of Montrigone ; several of the figures are not at all bad, and several have horsehair for hair, as at Varallo.   The effect of the whole composition is better than we have a right to expect from any sculpture dating from the beginning of the eighteenth century.

The ninth chapel, the Annunciation, presents no feature of interest ; nor yet does the tenth, the Visit of Mary to Elizabeth. The eleventh, the Nativity, though rather better, is still not remarkable.

The twelfth, the Purification, is absurdly bad, but I do not know whether the expression of strong personal dislike to the Virgin which the High Priest wears is intended as prophetic, or whether it is the result of incompetence, or whether it is merely a smile gone wrong in the baking. It is amusing to find Marocco, who has not been strict about archæological accuracy hitherto, complain here that there is an anachronism, inasmuch as some young ecclesiastics are dressed as they would be at present, and one of them actually carries a wax candle. This is not as it should be ; in works like those at Oropa, where implicit reliance is justly placed on the earnest endeavours that have been so successfully made to thoroughly and carefully and patiently ensure the accuracy of the minutest details, it is a pity that even a single error should have escaped detection ; this, however, has most unfortunately happened here, and Marocco feels it his duty to put us on our guard. He explains that the mistake arose from the sculptor's having taken both his general arrangement and his details from some picture of the fourteenth or fifteenth century, when the value of the strictest historical accuracy was not yet so fully understood.

It seems to me that in the matter of accuracy, priests and men of science whether lay or regular on the one hand, and plain people whether lay or regular on the other, are trying to play a different game, and fail to understand one another because they do not see that their objects are not the same. The cleric and the man of science (who is only the cleric in his latest development) are trying to develop a throat with two distinct passages—one that shall refuse to pass even the smallest gnat, and another that shall gracefully gulp even the largest camel ; whereas we men of the street desire but one throat, and are content that this shall swallow nothing bigger than a pony. Everyone knows that there is no such effectual means of developing the power to swallow camels as incessant watchfulness for opportunities of straining at gnats, and this should explain many passages that puzzle us in the work both of our clerics and our scientists. I, not being a man of science, still continue to do what I said I did in *Alps and Sanctuaries*, and make it a rule to earnestly and patiently and carefully swallow a few of the smallest gnats I can find several times a day, as the best astringent for the throat I know of.

The thirteenth chapel is the Marriage Feast at Cana of Galilee. This is the best chapel as a work of art ; indeed, it is the only one which can claim to be taken quite seriously. Not that all the figures are very good ; those to the left of the composition are commonplace enough ; nor are the Christ and the giver of the feast at all remarkable ; but the ten or dozen figures of guests and attendants at the right-hand end of the work are as good as anything of their kind can be, and remind me so strongly of Tabachetti that I cannot doubt they were done by someone who was indirectly influenced by that great sculptor's work. It is not likely that Tabachetti was alive long after 1640, by which time he would have been about eighty years old ; and the foundations of this chapel were not laid till about 1690 ; the statues are probably a few years later ; they can hardly, therefore, be by one who had even studied under Tabachetti ; but until I found out the dates, and went inside the chapel to see the way in

which the figures had been constructed, I was inclined
to think they might be by Tabachetti himself, of whom,
indeed, they are not unworthy. On examining the
figures I found them more heavily constructed than
Tabachetti's are, with smaller holes for taking out
superfluous clay, and more finished on the off-sides.
Marocco says the sculptor is not known. I looked in
vain for any date or signature. Possibly the right-
hand figures (for the left-hand ones can hardly be by
the same hand) may be by some sculptor from Crea,
which is at no very great distance from Oropa, who
was penetrated by Tabachetti's influence ; but whether
as regards action and concert with one another, or as
regards excellence in detail, I do not see how anything
can be more realistic, and yet more harmoniously
composed. The placing of the musicians in a minstrels'
gallery helps the effect ; these musicians are six in
number, and the other figures are twenty-three. Under
the table, between Christ and the giver of the feast,
there is a cat.

The fourteenth chapel, the Assumption of the Virgin
Mary, is without interest.

The fifteenth, the Coronation of the Virgin, contains
forty-six angels, twenty-six cherubs, fifty-six saints,
the Holy Trinity, the Madonna herself, and twenty-four
innocents, making 156 statues in all. Of these I am
afraid there is not one of more than ordinary merit ;
the most interesting is a half-length nude life-study
of Disma—the good thief. After what had been
promised him it was impossible to exclude him, but it
was felt that a half-length nude figure would be as much
as he could reasonably expect.

Behind the sanctuary there is a semi-ruinous and
wholly valueless work, which shows the finding of the

black image, which is now in the church, but is only shown on great festivals.

This leads us to a consideration that I have delayed till now. The black image is the central feature of Oropa ; it is the *raison d'être* of the whole place, and all else is a mere incrustation, so to speak, around it. According to this image, then, which was carved by St. Luke himself, and than which nothing can be better authenticated, both the Madonna and the infant Christ were as black as anything can be conceived. It is not likely that they were as black as they have been painted ; no one yet ever was so black as that ; yet, even allowing for some exaggeration on St. Luke's part, they must have been exceedingly black if the portrait is to be accepted ; and uncompromisingly black they accordingly are on most of the wayside chapels for many a mile around Oropa. Yet in the chapels we have been hitherto considering—works in which, as we know, the most punctilious regard has been shown to accuracy—both the Virgin and Christ are uncompromisingly white. As in the shops under the Colonnade where devotional knick-knacks are sold, you can buy a black china image or a white one, whichever you like ; so with the pictures—the black and white are placed side by side—*pagando il danaro si può scegliere.* It rests not with history or with the Church to say whether the Madonna and Child were black or white, but you may settle it for yourself, whichever way you please, or rather you are required, with the acquiescence of the Church, to hold that they were both black and white at one and the same time.

It cannot be maintained that the Church leaves the matter undecided, and by tolerating both types proclaims the question an open one, for she acquiesces in the portrait by St. Luke as genuine. How, then, justify the whiteness of the Holy Family in the chapels ? If the portrait is not known as genuine, why set such a stumbling-block in our paths as to show us a black Madonna and a white one, both as historically accurate, within a few yards of one another ?

I ask this not in mockery, but as knowing that the Church must have an explanation to give, if she would only give it, and as myself unable to find any, even the most far-fetched, that can bring what we see at Oropa, Loreto and elsewhere into harmony with modern conscience, either intellectual or ethical.

I see, indeed, from an interesting article in the *Atlantic Monthly* for September, 1889, entitled " The Black Madonna of Loreto," that black Madonnas were so frequent in ancient Christian art that " some of the early writers of the Church felt obliged to account for it by explaining that the Virgin was of a very dark complexion, as might be proved by the verse of Canticles which says, ' I am black, but comely, O ye daughters of Jerusalem.' Others maintained that she became black during her sojourn in Egypt. . . . Priests, of to-day, say that extreme age and exposure to the smoke of countless altar-candles have caused that change in complexion which the more naïve fathers of the Church attributed to the power of an Egyptian sun " ; but the writer ruthlessly disposes of this supposition by pointing out that in nearly all the instances of black Madonnas it is the flesh alone that is entirely black, the crimson of the lips, the white of the eyes, and the draperies having preserved their original colour. The authoress of the article (Mrs. Hilliard) goes on to tell us that Pausanias mentions two statues of the black Venus, and says that the oldest statue of Ceres among the Phigalenses was black. She adds that Minerva Aglaurus, the daughter of Cecrops, at Athens, was black ; that Corinth had a black Venus, as also the Thespians ; that the oracles of Dodona and Delphi were founded by black doves, the emissaries of Venus, and that the Isis Multimammia in the Capitol at Rome is black.

Sometimes I have asked myself whether the Church does not intend to suggest that the whole story falls outside the domain of history, and is to be held as the one great epos, or myth, common to all mankind ; adaptable by each nation according to its own several needs ; translatable, so to speak, into the facts of each individual nation, as the written word is translatable into its language, but appertaining to the realm of the imagination rather than to that of the understanding, and precious for spiritual rather than literal truths. More briefly, I have wondered whether she may not intend that such details as whether the Virgin was white or black are of very little importance in comparison with the basing of ethics on a story that shall appeal to black races as well as to white ones.

If so, it is time we were made to understand this more clearly. If the Church, whether of Rome or England, would lean to some such view as this— tainted though it be with mysticism—if we could see either great branch of the Church make a frank, authoritative attempt to bring its teaching into greater harmony with the educated understanding and conscience of the time, instead of trying to fetter that understanding with bonds that gall it daily more and more profoundly ; then I, for one, in view of the difficulty and graciousness of the task, and in view of the great importance of historical continuity, would gladly sink much of my own private opinion as to the value of the Christian ideal, and would gratefully help either Church or both, according to the best of my very feeble ability. On these terms, indeed, I could swallow not a few camels myself cheerfully enough.

Can we, however, see any signs as though either Rome or England will stir hand or foot to meet us? Can any step be pointed to as though either Church wished to make things easier for men holding the opinions held by the late Mr. Darwin, or by Mr. Herbert Spencer and Professor Huxley? How can those who accept evolution with any thoroughness accept such doctrines as the Incarnation or the Redemption with any but a quasi-allegorical and poetical interpretation? Can we conceivably accept these doctrines in the literal sense in which the Church advances them? And can the leaders of the Church be bl:nd to the resistlessness of the current that has set against those literal interpretations which she seems to hug more and more closely the more religious life is awakened at all? The clergyman is wanted as supplementing the doctor and the lawyer in all civilized communities ; these three keep watch on one another, and prevent one another from becoming too powerful. I, who distrust the *doctrinaire* in science even more than the *doctrinaire* in religion, should view with dismay the abolition of the Church of England, as knowing that a blatant bastard science would instantly step into her shoes ; but if some such deplorable consummation is to be avoided in England, it can only be through more evident leaning on the part of our clergy to such an interpretation of the Sacred History as the presence of a black and white Madonna almost side by side at Oropa appears to suggest.

I fear that in these last paragraphs I may have trenched on dangerous ground, but it is not possible to go to such places as Oropa without asking oneself what they mean and involve. As for the average Italian pilgrims, they do not appear to give the matter so much as a thought. They love Oropa, and flock to it in thousands during the summer ; the President of the Administration assured me that they lodged, after a fashion, as many as ten thousand pilgrims on the 15th of last August. It is astonishing how living the statues are to these people, and how the wicked are upbraided and the good applauded. At Varallo, since I took the photographs I published in my book *Ex Voto,* an angry pilgrim has smashed the nose of the dwarf in Tabachetti's Journey to Calvary, for no other reason than inability to restrain his indignation against one who was helping to inflict pain on Christ. It is the real hair and the painting up to nature that does this. Here at Oropa I found a paper on the floor of the *Sposalizio* Chapel, which ran as follows :—

" By the grace of God and the will of the administrative chapter of this sanctuary, there have come here to work —— ——, mason, —— ——, carpenter, and —— ——, plumber, all of Chiavazza, on the twenty-first day of January, 1886, full of cold (*pieni di freddo*).

" They write these two lines to record their visit. They pray the Blessed Virgin that she will maintain them safe and sound from everything equivocal that may befall them (*sempre sani e salvi da ogni equivoco li possa accadere*). Oh, farewell ! We reverently salute all the present statues, and especially the Blessed Virgin, and the reader."

Through the *Universal Review*, I suppose, all its readers are to consider themselves saluted ; at any rate, these good fellows, in the effusiveness of their hearts, actually wrote the above in pencil. I was sorely tempted to steal it, but, after copying it, left it in the Chief Priest's hands instead.

Art in the Valley of Saas[1]

HAVING been told by Mr. Fortescue, of the British Museum, that there were some chapels at Saas-Fée which bore analogy to those at Varallo, described in my book *Ex Voto*, I went to Saas during this last summer, and venture now to lay my conclusions before the reader.

The chapels are fifteen in number, and lead up to a larger and singularly graceful one, rather more than half-way between Saas and Saas-Fée. This is commonly but wrongly called the chapel of St. Joseph, for it is dedicated to the Virgin, and its situation is of such extreme beauty—the great Fée glaciers showing through the open portico—that it is in itself worth a pilgrimage. It is surrounded by noble larches and overhung by rock ; in front of the portico there is a small open space covered with grass, and a huge larch, the stem of which is girt by a rude stone seat. The portico itself contains seats for worshippers, and a pulpit from which the preacher's voice can reach the many who must stand outside. The walls of the inner chapel are hung with votive pictures, some of them very quaint and pleasing, and not overweighted by those qualities that are usually dubbed by the name of artistic merit. Innumerable wooden and waxen representations of arms, legs, eyes, ears and babies

---

[1] Published in the *Universal Review*, November, 1890.

tell of the cures that have been effected during two centuries of devotion, and can hardly fail to awaken a kindly sympathy with the long dead and forgotten folks who placed them where they are.

The main interest, however, despite the extreme loveliness of the St. Mary's Chapel, centres rather in the small and outwardly unimportant oratories (if they should be so called) that lead up to it. These begin immediately with the ascent from the level ground on which the village of Saas-im-Grund is placed, and contain scenes in the history of the Redemption, represented by rude but spirited wooden figures, each about two feet high, painted, gilt, and rendered as life-like in all respects as circumstances would permit. The figures have suffered a good deal from neglect, and are still not a little misplaced. With the assistance, however, of the Rev. E. J. Selwyn, English Chaplain at Saas-im-Grund, I have been able to replace many of them in their original positions, as indicated by the parts of the figures that are left rough-hewn and unpainted. They vary a good deal in interest, and can be easily sneered at by those who make a trade of sneering. Those, on the other hand, who remain unsophisticated by overmuch art-culture will find them full of character in spite of not a little rudeness of execution, and will be surprised at coming across such works in a place so remote from any art-centre as Saas must have been at the time these chapels were made. It will be my business therefore to throw what light I can upon the questions how they came to be made at all, and who was the artist who designed them.

The only documentary evidence consists in a chronicle of the valley of Saas written in the early years of this century by the Rev. Peter Jos. Ruppen, and published at Sion in 1851. This work makes frequent reference to a manuscript by the Rev. Peter Joseph Clemens Lommatter, *curé* of Saas-Fée from 1738 to 1751, which has unfortunately been lost, so that we have no means of knowing how closely it was adhered to. The Rev. Jos. Ant. Ruppen, the present excellent *curé* of Saas-im-Grund, assures me that there is no reference to the Saas-Fée oratories in the " Actes de l'Eglise " at Saas, which I understand go a long way back ; but I have not seen these myself. Practically, then, we have no more documentary evidence than is to be found in the published chronicle above referred to.

We there find it stated that the large chapel, commonly, but as above explained, wrongly called St. Joseph's, was built in 1687, and enlarged by subscription in 1747. These dates appear on the building itself, and are no doubt accurate. The writer adds that there was no actual edifice on this site before the one now existing was built, but there was a miraculous picture of the Virgin placed in a mural niche, before which the pious herdsmen and devout inhabitants of the valley worshipped under the vault of heaven.[1] A miraculous (or miracle-working) picture was always more or less rare and important ; the present site, therefore, seems

[1] M. Ruppen's words run : " 1687 wurde die Kapelle zur hohen Stiege gebaut, 1747 durch Zusatz vergrössert und 1755 mit Orgeln ausgestattet. Anton Ruppen, ein geschickter Steinhauer und Maurermeister leitete den Kapellebau, und machte darin das kleinere Altärlein. Bei der hohen Stiege war früher kein Gebetshäuslein ; nur ein wunderthätiges Bildlein der Mutter Gottes stand da in einer Mauer vor dem fromme Hirten und viel andächtiges Volk unter freiem Himmel beteten.

" 1709 wurden die kleinen Kapellelein die 15 Geheimnisse des Psalters vorstellend auf dem Wege zur hohen Stiege gebaut. Jeder Haushalter des Viertels Fée übernahm den Bau eines dieser Geheimnisskapellen, und ein besonderer Gutthäter dieser frommen Unternehmung war Heinrich Andenmatten, nachher Bruder der Gesellschaft Jesu."

to have been long one of peculiar sanctity. Possibly
the name Fée may point to still earlier pagan mysteries
on the same site.

As regards the fifteen small chapels, the writer says
they illustrate the fifteen mysteries of the Psalter,
and were built in 1709, each householder of the Saas-
Fée contributing one chapel. He adds that Heinrich
Andenmatten, afterwards a brother of the Society of
Jesus, was an especial benefactor or promoter of the
undertaking. One of the chapels, the Ascension (No. 12
of the series), has the date 1709 painted on it ; but
there is no date on any other chapel, and there
seems no reason why this should be taken as governing
the whole series.

Over and above this, there exists in Saas a tradition,
as I was told immediately on my arrival, by an English
visitor, that the chapels were built in consequence of a
flood, but I have vainly endeavoured to trace this
story to an indigenous source.

The internal evidence of the wooden figures themselves—nothing analogous to which, it should be
remembered, can be found in the chapel of 1687—
points to a much earlier date. I have met with no
school of sculpture belonging to the early part of the
eighteenth century to which they can be plausibly
assigned ; and the supposition that they are the work
of some unknown local genius who was not led up to
and left no successors may be dismissed, for the work
is too scholarly to have come from anyone but a trained
sculptor. I refer of course to those figures which the
artist must be supposed to have executed with his
own hand, as, for example, the central figure of the
Crucifixion group and those of the Magdalene and St.
John. The greater number of the figures were probably,

as was suggested to me by Mr. Ranshaw, of Lowth, executed by a local wood-carver from models in clay and wax furnished by the artist himself. Those who examine the play of line in the hair, mantle, and sleeve of the Magdalene in the Crucifixion group, and contrast it with the greater part of the remaining draperies, will find little hesitation in concluding that this was the case, and will ere long readily distinguish the two hands from which the figures have mainly come. I say "mainly," because there is at least one other sculptor who may well have belonged to the year 1709, but who fortunately has left us little. Examples of his work may perhaps be seen in the nearest villain with a big hat in the Flagellation chapel, and in two cherubs in the Assumption of the Virgin.

We may say, then, with some certainty, that the designer was a cultivated and practised artist. We may also not less certainly conclude that he was of Flemish origin, for the horses in the Journey to Calvary and Crucifixion chapels, where alone there are any horses at all, are of Flemish breed, with no trace of the Arab blood adopted by Gaudenzio at Varallo. The character, moreover, of the villains is Northern—of the Quentin Matsys, Martin Schongauer type, rather than Italian ; the same sub-Rubensesque feeling which is apparent in more than one chapel at Varallo is not less evident here—especially in the Journey to Calvary and Crucifixion chapels. There can hardly, therefore, be a doubt that the artist was a Fleming who had worked for several years in Italy.

It is also evident that he had Tabachetti's work at Varallo well in his mind. For not only does he adopt certain details of costume (I refer particularly to the treatment of soldiers' tunics) which are peculiar to

Tabachetti at Varallo, but whenever he treats a subject which Tabachetti had treated at Varallo, as in the Flagellation, Crowning with Thorns, and Journey to Calvary chapels, the work at Saas is evidently nothing but a somewhat modified abridgment of that at Varallo. When, however, as in the Annunciation, the Nativity, the Crucifixion, and other chapels, the work at Varallo is by another than Tabachetti, no allusion is made to it. The Saas artist has Tabachetti's Varallo work at his finger-ends, but betrays no acquaintance whatever with Gaudenzio Ferrari, Gio. Ant. Paracca, or Giovanni d'Enrico.

Even, moreover, when Tabachetti's work at Varallo is being most obviously drawn from, as in the Journey to Calvary chapel, the Saas version differs materially from that at Varallo, and is in some respects an improvement on it. The idea of showing other horsemen and followers coming up from behind, whose heads can be seen over the crown of the interposing hill, is singularly effective as suggesting a number of others that are unseen, nor can I conceive that anyone but the original designer would follow Tabachetti's Varallo design with as much closeness as it has been followed here, and yet make such a brilliantly successful modification. The stumbling, again, of one horse (a detail almost hidden, according to Tabachetti's wont) is a touch which Tabachetti himself might add, but which no Saas wood-carver who was merely adapting from a reminiscence of Tabachetti's Varallo chapel would be likely to introduce. These considerations have convinced me that the designer of the chapels at Saas is none other than Tabachetti himself, who, as has been now conclusively shown, was a native of Dinant, in Belgium.

N

The Saas chronicler, indeed, avers that the chapels were not built till 1709—a statement apparently corroborated by a date now visible on one chapel ; but we must remember that the chronicler did not write until a century or so later than 1709, and though indeed, his statement may have been taken from the lost earlier manuscript of 1738, we know nothing about this either one way or the other. The writer may have gone by the still existing 1709 on the Ascension chapel, whereas this date may in fact have referred to a restoration, and not to an original construction. There is nothing, as I have said, in the choice of the chapel on which the date appears, to suggest that it was intended to govern the others. I have explained that the work is isolated and exotic. It is by one in whom Flemish and Italian influences are alike equally predominant ; by one who was saturated with Tabachetti's Varallo work, and who can improve upon it, but over whom the other Varallo sculptors have no power. The style of the work is of the sixteenth and not of the eighteenth century—with a few obvious exceptions that suit the year 1709 exceedingly well. Against such considerations as these, a statement made at the beginning of this century referring to a century earlier and a promiscuous date upon one chapel, can carry but little weight. I shall assume, therefore, henceforward, that we have here groups designed in a plastic material by Tabachetti, and reproduced in wood by the best local wood-sculptor available, with the exception of a few figures cut by the artist himself.

We ask, then, at what period in his life did Tabachetti design these chapels, and what led to his coming to such an out-of-the-way place as Saas at all ? We should remember that, according both to Fassola and Torrotti (writing in 1671 and 1686 respectively), Tabachetti[1] became insane about the year 1586 or early in 1587, after having just begun the Salutation chapel. I have explained in *Ex Voto* that I do not believe this story. I have no doubt that Tabachetti was declared to be mad, but I believe this to have been due to an intrigue, set on foot in order to get a foreign artist out of the way, and to secure the Massacre of the Innocents chapel, at that precise time undertaken, for Gio. Ant. Paracca, who was an Italian.

Or he may have been sacrificed in order to facilitate the return of the workers in stucco whom he had superseded on the Sacro Monte. He may have been goaded into some imprudence which was seized upon as a pretext for shutting him up ; at any rate, the fact that when in 1587 he inherited his father's property at Dinant, his trustee (he being expressly stated to be " *expatrié* ") was " *datif*," " *dativus*," appointed not by himself but by the court, lends colour to the statement that he was not his own master at the time ; for in later kindred deeds, now at Namur, he appoints his own trustee. I suppose, then, that Tabachetti was shut up in a madhouse at Varallo for a considerable time, during which I can find no trace of him, but that eventually he escaped or was released.

Whether he was a fugitive, or whether he was let out from prison, he would in either case, in all reasonable

---

[1] The story of Tabachetti's insanity and imprisonment is very doubtful, and it is difficult to make his supposed visit to Saas fit in with the authentic facts of his life. Cavaliere Negri, to whose pamphlet on Tabachetti I have already referred the reader, mentions neither. Tabachetti left his native Dinant in 1585, and from that date until his death he appears to have lived chiefly at Varallo and Crea. In 1588 he was working at Crea ; in 1590 he was at Varallo and again in 1594, 1599, and 1602. He died in 1615, possibly during a visit to Varallo, though his home at the time was at Costigliole, near Asti.—R. A. S.

probability, turn his face homeward. If he was escaping, he would make immediately for the Savoy frontier, within which Saas then lay. He would cross the Baranca above Fobello, coming down on to Ponte Grande in the Val Anzasca. He would go up the Val Anzasca to Macugnaga, and over the Monte Moro, which would bring him immediately to Saas. Saas, therefore, is the nearest and most natural place for him to make for, if he were flying from Varallo, and here I suppose him to have halted.

It so happened that on the 9th of September, 1589, there was one of the three great outbreaks of the Mattmark See that have from time to time devastated the valley of Saas.[1] It is probable that the chapels were decided upon in consequence of some grace shown by the miraculous picture of the Virgin, which had mitigated a disaster occurring so soon after the anniversary of her own Nativity. Tabachetti, arriving at this juncture, may have offered to undertake them if the Saas people would give him an asylum. Here, at any rate, I suppose him to have stayed till some time in 1590, probably the second half of it ; his design of eventually returning home, if he ever entertained it, being then interrupted by a summons to Crea near Casale, where I believe him to have worked with a few brief interruptions thenceforward for little if at all short of half a century, or until about the year 1640. I admit, however, that the evidence for assigning him so long a life rests solely on the supposed identity of

[1] This is thus chronicled by M. Ruppen : "1589 den 9 September war eine Wassergrösse, die viel Schaden verursachte.   Die Thalstrasse, die von den Steinmatten an bis zur Kirche am Ufer der Visp lag, wurde ganz zerstört.   Man ward gezwungen eine neue Strasse in einiger Entfernung vom Wasser durch einen alten Fussweg auszuhauen welche vier und einerhalben Viertel der Klafter, oder 6 Schuh und 9 Zoll breit sollte" (p. 43).

the figure known as " Il Vecchietto," in the Varallo
Descent from the Cross chapel, with the portrait of
Tabachetti himself in the Ecce Homo chapel, also at
Varallo.

I find additional reason for thinking the chapels owe
their origin to the inundation of 9th September, 1589,
in the fact that the 8th of September is made a day
of pilgrimage to the Saas-Fée chapels throughout the
whole valley of Saas.   It is true the 8th of September
is the festival of the Nativity of the Virgin Mary, so
that under any circumstances this would be a great
day, but the fact that not only the people of Saas, but
the whole valley down to Visp, flock to this chapel on
the 8th of September, points to the belief that some
special act of grace on the part of the Virgin was
vouchsafed on this day in connection with this chapel.
A belief that it was owing to the intervention of St.
Mary of Fée that the inundation was not attended with
loss of life would be very likely to lead to the foundation
of a series of chapels leading up to the place where her
miraculous picture was placed, and to the more special
celebration of her Nativity in connection with this spot
throughout the valley of Saas.   I have discussed the
subject with the Rev. Jos. Ant. Ruppen, and he told
me he thought the fact that the great *fête* of the year
in connection with the Saas-Fée chapels was on the
8th of September pointed rather strongly to the supposition that there was a connection between these
and the recorded flood of 9th September, 1589.

Turning to the individual chapels they are as
follows :—

1. The Annunciation.   The treatment here presents
no more analogy to that of the same subject at Varallo
than is inevitable in the nature of the subject.   The

Annunciation figures at Varallo have proved to be mere draped dummies with wooden heads ; Tabachetti, even though he did the heads, which he very likely did, would take no interest in the Varallo work with the same subject. The Annunciation, from its very simplicity as well as from the transcendental nature of the subject, is singularly hard to treat, and the work here, whatever it may once have been, is now no longer remarkable.

2. The Salutation of Mary by Elizabeth. This group, again, bears no analogy to the Salutation chapel at Varallo, in which Tabachetti's share was so small that it cannot be considered as in any way his. It is not to be expected, therefore, that the Saas chapel should follow the Varallo one. The figures, four in number, are pleasing and well arranged. St. Joseph, St. Elizabeth, and St. Zacharias are all talking at once. The Virgin is alone silent.

3. The Nativity is much damaged and hard to see. The treatment bears no analogy to that adopted by Gaudenzio Ferrari at Varallo. There is one pleasing young shepherd standing against the wall, but some figures have no doubt (as in others of the chapels) disappeared, and those that remain have been so shifted from their original positions that very little idea can be formed of what the group was like when Tabachetti left it.

4. The Purification. I can hardly say why this chapel should remind me, as it does, of the Circumcision chapel at Varallo, for there are more figures here than space at Varallo will allow. It cannot be pretended that any single figure is of extraordinary merit, but amongst them they tell their story with excellent effect. Two, those of St. Joseph and St. Anna (?), that doubt-

less were once more important factors in the drama, are now so much in corners near the window that they can hardly be seen.

5. The Dispute in the Temple. This subject is not treated at Varallo. Here at Saas there are only six doctors now ; whether or no there were originally more cannot be determined.

6. The Agony in the Garden. Tabachetti had no chapel with this subject at Varallo, and there is no resemblance between the Saas chapel and that by D'Enrico. The figures are no doubt approximately in their original positions, but I have no confidence that I have rearranged them correctly. They were in such confusion when I first saw them that the Rev. E. J. Selwyn and myself determined to rearrange them. They have doubtless been shifted more than once since Tabachetti left them. The sleeping figures are all good. St. James is perhaps a little prosaic. One Roman soldier who is coming into the garden with a lantern, and motioning silence with his hand, does duty for the others that are to follow him. I should think more than one of these figures is actually carved in wood by Tabachetti, allowance being made for the fact that he was working in a material with which he was not familiar, and which no sculptor of the highest rank has ever found congenial.

7. The Flagellation. Tabachetti has a chapel with this subject at Varallo, and the Saas group is obviously a descent with modification from his work there. The figure of Christ is so like the one at Varallo that I think it must have been carved by Tabachetti himself. The man with the hooked nose, who at Varallo is stooping to bind his rods, is here upright : it was probably the intention to emphasize him in the succeeding scenes as

well as this, in the same way as he has been emphasized at Varallo, but his nose got pared down in the cutting of later scenes, and could not easily be added to. The man binding Christ to the column at Varallo is repeated (*longo intervallo*) here, and the whole work is one inspired by that at Varallo, though no single figure except that of the Christ is adhered to with any very great closeness. I think the nearer malefactor, with a goitre, and wearing a large black hat, is either an addition of the year 1709, or was done by the journey-man of the local sculptor who carved the greater number of the figures. The man stooping down to bind his rods can hardly be by the same hand as either of the two black-hatted malefactors, but it is impossible to speak with certainty. The general effect of the chapel is excellent, if we consider the material in which it is executed, and the rudeness of the audience to whom it addresses itself.

8. The Crowning with Thorns. Here again the inspiration is derived from Tabachetti's Crowning with Thorns at Varallo. The Christs in the two chapels are strikingly alike, and the general effect is that of a residuary impression left in the mind of one who had known the Varallo Flagellation exceedingly well.

9. Sta. Veronica. This and the next succeeding chapels are the most important of the series. Tabachetti's Journey to Calvary at Varallo is again the source from which the present work was taken, but, as I have already said, it has been modified in reproduction. Mount Calvary is still shown, as at Varallo, towards the left-hand corner of the work, but at Saas it is more towards the middle than at Varallo, so that horsemen and soldiers may be seen coming up behind

it—a stroke that deserves the name of genius none the less for the manifest imperfection with which it has been carried into execution. There are only three horses fully shown, and one partly shown. They are all of the heavy Flemish type adopted by Tabachetti at Varallo. The man kicking the fallen Christ and the goitred man (with the same teeth missing), who are so conspicuous in the Varallo Journey to Calvary, reappear here, only the kicking man has much less nose than at Varallo, probably because (as explained) the nose got whittled away and could not be whittled back again. I observe that the kind of lapelled tunic which Tabachetti, and only Tabachetti, adopts at Varallo, is adopted for the centurion in this chapel, and indeed throughout the Saas chapels this particular form of tunic is the most usual for a Roman soldier. The work is still a very striking one, notwithstanding its translation into wood and the decay into which it has been allowed to fall ; nor can it fail to impress the visitor who is familiar with this class of art as coming from a man of extraordinary dramatic power and command over the almost impossible art of composing many figures together effectively in all-round sculpture. Whether all the figures are even now as Tabachetti left them I cannot determine, but Mr. Selwyn has restored Simon the Cyrenian to the position in which he obviously ought to stand, and between us we have got the chapel into something more like order.

10. The Crucifixion. This subject was treated at Varallo not by Tabachetti but by Gaudenzio Ferrari. It confirms therefore my opinion as to the designer of the Saas chapels to find in them no trace of the Varallo Crucifixion, while the kind of tunic which at Varallo is only found in chapels wherein Tabachetti

worked again appears here. The work is in a deplorable
state of decay. Mr. Selwyn has greatly improved the
arrangement of the figures, but even now they are not,
I imagine, quite as Tabachetti left them. The figure of
Christ is greatly better in technical execution than
that of either of the two thieves ; the folds of the
drapery alone will show this even to an unpractised eye.
I do not think there can be a doubt but that Tabachetti
cut this figure himself, as also those of the Magdalene
and St. John, who stand at the foot of the cross. The
thieves are coarsely executed, with no very obvious
distinction between the penitent and the impenitent
one, except that there is a fiend painted on the ceiling
over the impenitent thief. The one horse introduced
into the composition is again of the heavy Flemish
type adopted by Tabachetti at Varallo. There is
great difference in the care with which the folds on the
several draperies have been cut, some being stiff and
poor enough, while others are done very sufficiently.
In spite of smallness of scale, ignoble material, dis-
arrangement and decay, the work is still striking.

11. The Resurrection. There being no chapel at
Varallo with any of the remaining subjects treated at
Saas, the sculptor has struck out a line for himself.
The Christ in the Resurrection Chapel is a carefully
modelled figure, and if better painted might not be
ineffective. Three soldiers, one sleeping, alone remain.
There were probably other figures that have been lost.
The sleeping soldier is very pleasing.

12. The Ascension is not remarkably interesting ;
the Christ appears to be, but perhaps is not, a much
more modern figure than the rest.

13. The Descent of the Holy Ghost. Some of the
figures along the end wall are very good, and were, I

should imagine, cut by Tabachetti himself. Those against the two side walls are not so well cut.

14. The Assumption of the Virgin Mary. The two large cherubs here are obviously by a later hand, and the small ones are not good. The figure of the Virgin herself is unexceptionable. There were doubtless once other figures of the Apostles which have disappeared ; of these a single St. Peter (?), so hidden away in a corner near the window that it can only be seen with difficulty, is the sole survivor.

15. The Coronation of the Virgin is of later date, and has probably superseded an earlier work. It can hardly be by the designer of the other chapels of the series. Perhaps Tabachetti had to leave for Crea before all the chapels at Saas were finished.

Lastly, we have the larger chapel dedicated to St. Mary, which crowns the series. Here there is nothing of more than common artistic interest, unless we except the stone altar mentioned in Ruppen's chronicle. This is of course classical in style, and is, I should think, very good.

Once more I must caution the reader against expecting to find highly finished gems of art in the chapels I have been describing. A wooden figure not more than two feet high clogged with many coats of paint can hardly claim to be taken very seriously, and even those few that were cut by Tabachetti himself were not meant to have attention concentrated on themselves alone. As mere wood-carving the Saas-Fée chapels will not stand comparison, for example, with the triptych of unknown authorship in the Church of St. Anne at Gliss, close to Brieg. But, in the first place, the work at Gliss is worthy of Holbein himself ; I know no wood-carving that can so rivet the attention ; moreover it is coloured with water-colour and not oil, so that it is tinted, not painted ; and, in the second place, the Gliss triptych belongs to a date (1519) when artists held neither time nor impressionism as objects, and hence, though greatly better than the Saas-Fée chapels as regards a certain Japanese curiousness of finish and *naïveté* of literal transcription, it cannot even enter the lists with the Saas work as regards *élan* and dramatic effectiveness. The difference between the two classes of work is much that between, say, John Van Eyck or Memling and Rubens or Rembrandt, or, again, between Giovanni Bellini and Tintoretto ; the aims of the one class of work are incompatible with those of the other. Moreover, in the Gliss triptych the intention of the designer is carried out (whether by himself or no) with admirable skill ; whereas at Saas the wisdom of the workman is rather of Ober-Ammergau than of the Egyptians, and the voice of the poet is not a little drowned in that of his mouthpiece. If, however, the reader will bear in mind these somewhat obvious considerations, and will also remember the pathetic circumstances under which the chapels were designed—for Tabachetti when he reached Saas was no doubt shattered in body and mind by his four years' imprisonment—he will probably be not less attracted to them than I observed were many of the visitors both at Saas-Grund and Saas-Fée with whom I had the pleasure of examining them.

I will now run briefly through the other principal works in the neighbourhood to which I think the reader would be glad to have his attention directed.

At Saas-Fée itself the main altar-piece is without interest, as also one with a figure of St. Sebastian. The Virgin and Child above the remaining altar are, so far as I remember them, very good, and greatly superior to the smaller figures of the same altar-piece.

At Almagel, an hour's walk or so above Saas-Grund —a village, the name of which, like those of the Alphubel, the Monte Moro, and more than one other neighbouring site, is supposed to be of Saracenic origin —the main altar-piece represents a female saint with folded arms being beheaded by a vigorous man to the left. These two figures are very good. There are two somewhat inferior elders to the right, and the composition is crowned by the Assumption of the Virgin. I like the work, but have no idea who did it. Two bishops flanking the composition are not so good. There are two other altars in the church : the right-hand one has some pleasing figures, not so the left-hand.

In St. Joseph's Chapel, on the mule-road between Saas-Grund and Saas-Fée, the St. Joseph and the two children are rather nice. In the churches and chapels which I looked into between Saas and Stalden, I saw many florid extravagant altar-pieces, but nothing that impressed me favourably.

In the parish church at Saas-Grund there are two altar-pieces which deserve attention. In the one over the main altar the arrangement of the Last Supper in a deep recess half-way up the composition is very pleasing and effective ; in that above the right-hand altar of the two that stand in the body of the church there are a number of round lunettes, about eight inches in diameter, each containing a small but spirited group of wooden figures. I have lost my notes on these altar-pieces and can only remember that the main one has been restored, and now belongs to two different dates, the earlier date being, I should imagine,

about 1670. A similar treatment of the Last Supper
may be found near Brieg in the church of Naters,
and no doubt the two altar-pieces are by the same man.
There are, by the way, two very ambitious altars on
either side the main arch leading to the chancel in the
church at Naters, of which the one on the south side
contains obvious reminiscences of Gaudenzio Ferrari's
Sta. Maria frescoes at Varallo ; but none of the four
altar-pieces in the two transepts tempted me to give
them much attention. As regards the smaller altar-
piece at Saas-Grund, analogous work may be found at
Cravagliana, half-way between Varallo and Fobello,
but this last has suffered through the inveterate habit
which Italians have of showing their hatred towards
the enemies of Christ by mutilating the figures that
represent them. Whether the Saas work is by a
Valsesian artist who came over to Switzerland, or
whether the Cravagliana work is by a Swiss who had
come to Italy, I cannot say without further consideration and closer examination than I have been able to
give. The altar-pieces of Mairengo, Chiggiogna, and,
I am told, Lavertezzo, all in the Canton Ticino, are by a
Swiss or German artist who has migrated southward ;
but the reverse migration was equally common.

Being in the neighbourhood, and wishing to assure
myself whether the sculptor of the Saas-Fée chapels
had or had not come lower down the valley, I examined every church and village which I could hear of
as containing anything that might throw light on this
point. I was thus led to Vispertimenen, a village some
three hours above either Visp or Stalden. It stands
very high, and is an almost untouched example of a
medieval village. The altar-piece of the main church
is even more floridly ambitious in its abundance of

carving and gilding than the many other ambitious
altar-pieces with which the Canton Valais abounds.
The Apostles are receiving the Holy Ghost on the first
storey of the composition, and they certainly are
receiving it with an overjoyed alacrity and hilarious
ecstasy of *allegria spirituale* which it would not be easy
to surpass. Above the village, reaching almost to the
limits beyond which there is no cultivation, there stands
a series of chapels like those I have been describing at
Saas-Fée, only much larger and more ambitious. They
are twelve in number, including the church that crowns
the series. The figures they contain are of wood (so I
was assured, but I did not go inside the chapels) : they
are life-size, and in some chapels there are as many as a
dozen figures. I should think they belonged to the later
half of the eighteenth century, and here, one would say,
sculpture touches the ground ; at least, it is not easy to
see how cheap exaggeration can sink an art more deeply.
The only things that at all pleased me were a smiling
donkey and an ecstatic cow in the Nativity chapel.
Those who are not allured by the prospect of seeing
perhaps the very worst that can be done in its own line,
need not be at the pains of climbing up to Vispertimenen. Those, on the other hand, who may find this
sufficient inducement will not be disappointed, and
they will enjoy magnificent views of the Weisshorn
and the mountains near the Dom.

I have already referred to the triptych at Gliss.
This is figured in Wolf's work on Chamonix and the
Canton Valais, but a larger and clearer reproduction
of such an extraordinary work is greatly to be desired.
The small wooden statues above the triptych, as also
those above its modern companion in the south
transept, are not less admirable than the triptych

itself. I know of no other like work in wood, and have no clue whatever as to who the author can have been beyond the fact that the work is purely German and eminently Holbeinesque in character.

I was told of some chapels at Rarogne, five or six miles lower down the valley than Visp. I examined them, and found they had been stripped of their figures. The few that remained satisfied me that we have had no loss. Above Brieg there are two other like series of chapels. I examined the higher and more promising of the two, but found not one single figure left. I was told by my driver that the other series, close to the Pont Napoléon on the Simplon road, had been also stripped of its figures, and, there being a heavy storm at the time, have taken his word for it that this was so.

Thought and Language[1]

THREE well-known writers, Professor Max Müller, Professor Mivart, and Mr. Alfred Russel Wallace, have lately maintained that though the theory of descent with modification accounts for the development of all vegetable life, and of all animals lower than man, yet that man cannot—not at least in respect of the whole of his nature—be held to have descended from any animal lower than himself, inasmuch as none lower than man possesses even the germs of language. Reason, it is contended—more especially by Professor Max Müller in his *Science of Thought*, to which I propose confining our attention this evening—is so inseparably connected with language, that the two are in point of fact identical ; hence it is argued that, as the lower animals have no germs of language, they can have no germs of reason, and the inference is drawn that man cannot be conceived as having derived his own reasoning powers and command of language through descent from beings in which no germ of either can be found. The relations therefore between thought and language, interesting in themselves, acquire additional importance from the fact of their having become the battle-ground between those who say that

[1] A lecture delivered at the Working Men's College in Great Ormond Street, March 15th, 1890 ; rewritten and delivered again at the Somerville Club, February 13th, 1894.

the theory of descent breaks down with man, and those who maintain that we are descended from some ape-like ancestor long since extinct.

The contention of those who refuse to admit man unreservedly into the scheme of evolution is comparatively recent. The great propounders of evolution, Buffon, Erasmus Darwin and Lamarck—not to mention a score of others who wrote at the close of the last and early part of this present century—had no qualms about admitting man into their system. They have been followed in this respect by the late Mr. Charles Darwin, and by the greatly more influential part of our modern biologists, who hold that whatever loss of dignity we may incur through being proved to be of humble origin, is compensated by the credit we may claim for having advanced ourselves to such a high pitch of civilization ; this bids us expect still further progress, and glorifies our descendants more than it abases our ancestors. But to whichever view we may incline on sentimental grounds the fact remains that, while Charles Darwin declared language to form no impassable barrier between man and the lower animals, Professor Max Müller calls it the Rubicon which no brute dare cross, and deduces hence the conclusion that man cannot have descended from an unknown but certainly speechless ape.

It may perhaps be expected that I should begin a lecture on the relations between thought and language with some definition of both these things ; but thought, as Sir William Grove said of motion, is a phenomenon " so obvious to simple apprehension that to define it would make it more obscure."[1] Definitions are useful where things are new to us, but they are super-

[1] *Correlation of Forces*, Longmans, 1874, p. 15.

fluous about those that are already familiar, and mischievous, so far as they are possible at all, in respect of all those things that enter so profoundly and intimately into our being that in them we must either live or bear no life. To vivisect the more vital processes of thought is to suspend, if not to destroy them ; for thought can think about everything more healthily and easily than about itself. It is like its instrument the brain, which knows nothing of any injuries inflicted upon itself. As regards what is new to us, a definition will sometimes dilute a difficulty, and help us to swallow that which might choke us undiluted ; but to define when we have once well swallowed is to unsettle, rather than settle, our digestion. Definitions, again, are like steps cut in a steep slope of ice, or shells thrown on to a greasy pavement ; they give us foothold, and enable us to advance, but when we are at our journey's end we want them no longer. Again, they are useful as mental fluxes, and as helping us to fuse new ideas with our older ones. They present us with some tags and ends of ideas that we have already mastered, on to which we can hitch our new ones ; but to multiply them in respect of such a matter as thought, is like scratching the bite of a gnat ; the more we scratch the more we want to scratch ; the more we define the more we shall have to go on defining the words we have used in our definitions, and shall end by setting up a serious mental raw in the place of a small uneasiness that was after all quite endurable. We know too well what thought is, to be able to know that we know it, and I am persuaded there is no one in this room but understands what is meant by thought and thinking well enough for all the purposes of this discussion. Whoever does not know this without

words will not learn it for all the words and definitions that are laid before him. The more, indeed, he
hears, the more confused he will become. I shall,
therefore, merely premise that I use the word
" thought " in the same sense as that in which it is
generally used by people who say that they think this
or that. At any rate, it will be enough if I take
Professor Max Müller's own definition, and say that its
essence consists in a bringing together of mental images
and ideas with deductions therefrom, and with a
corresponding power of detaching them from one
another. Hobbes, the Professor tells us, maintained
this long ago, when he said that all our thinking consists of addition and subtraction—that is to say, in
bringing ideas together, and in detaching them from
one another.

Turning from thought to language, we observe that
the word is derived from the French *langue*, or *tongue*.
Strictly, therefore, it means *tonguage*. This, however,
takes account of but a very small part of the ideas that
underlie the word. It does, indeed, seize a familiar
and important detail of everyday speech, though it
may be doubted whether the tongue has more to do
with speaking than lips, teeth and throat have, but it
makes no attempt at grasping and expressing the
essential characteristic of speech. Anything done
with the tongue, even though it involve no speaking at
all, is *tonguage ;* eating oranges is as much tonguage as
speech is. The word, therefore, though it tells us in
part how speech is effected, reveals nothing of that
ulterior meaning which is nevertheless inseparable
from any right use of the words either " speech " or
" language." It presents us with what is indeed a very
frequent adjunct of conversation, but the use of written

characters, or the finger-speech of deaf mutes, is enough
to show that the word " language " omits all reference
to the most essential characteristics of the idea, which
in practice it nevertheless very sufficiently presents to
us. I hope presently to make it clear to you how and
why it should do so. The word is incomplete in the
first place, because it omits all reference to the ideas
which words, speech or language are intended to convey,
and there can be no true word without its actually or
potentially conveying an idea. Secondly, it makes no
allusion to the person or persons to whom the ideas
are to be conveyed. Language is not language unless
it not only expresses fairly definite and coherent ideas,
but unless it also conveys these ideas to some other
living intelligent being, either man or brute, that can
understand them. We may speak to a dog or horse, but
not to a stone. If we make pretence of doing so we
are in reality only talking to ourselves. The person or
animal spoken to is half the battle—a half, moreover,
which is essential to there being any battle at all. It
takes two people to say a thing—a sayee as well as a
sayer. The one is as essential to any true saying as the
other. A. may have spoken, but if B. has not heard
there has been nothing said, and he must speak again.
True, the belief on A.'s part that he had a *bona fide*
sayee in B., saves his speech *qua* him, but it has been
barren and left no fertile issue. It has failed to fulfil
the conditions of true speech, which involve not only
that A. should speak, but also that B. should hear.
True, again, we often speak of loose, incoherent,
indefinite language ; but by doing so we imply, and
rightly, that we are calling that language which is not
true language at all. People, again, sometimes talk to
themselves without intending that any other person

should hear them, but this is not well done, and does harm to those who practise it. It is abnormal, whereas our concern is with normal and essential characteristics ; we may, therefore, neglect both delirious babblings, and the cases in which a person is regarding him or herself, as it were, from outside, and treating himself as though he were someone else.

Inquiring, then, what are the essentials, the presence of which constitutes language, while their absence negatives it altogether, we find that Professor Max Müller restricts them to the use of grammatical articulate words that we can write or speak, and denies that anything can be called language unless it can be written or spoken in articulate words and sentences. He also denies that we can think at all unless we do so in words ; that is to say, in sentences with verbs and nouns. Indeed, he goes so far as to say upon his title-page that there can be no reason—which I imagine comes to much the same thing as thought—without language, and no language without reason.

Against the assertion that there can be no true language without reason I have nothing to say. But when the Professor says that there can be no reason, or thought, without language, his opponents contend, as it seems to me, with greater force, that thought, though infinitely aided, extended and rendered definite through the invention of words, nevertheless existed so fully as to deserve no other name thousands, if not millions of years before words had entered into it at all. Words, they say, are a comparatively recent invention, for the fuller expression of something that was already in existence.

Children, they urge, are often evidently thinking and reasoning, though they can neither think nor speak in words. If you ask me to define reason, I answer as before that this can no more be done than thought, truth or motion can be defined. Who has answered the question, " What is truth ? " Man cannot see God and live. We cannot go so far back upon ourselves as to undermine our own foundations ; if we try to do so we topple over, and lose that very reason about which we vainly try to reason. If we let the foundations be, we know well enough that they are there, and we can build upon them in all security. We cannot, then, define reason nor crib, cabin and confine it within a thus-far-shalt-thou-go-and-no-further. Who can define heat or cold, or night or day ? Yet, so long as we hold fast by current consent, our chances of error for want of better definition are so small that no sensible person will consider them. In like manner, if we hold by current consent or common sense, which is the same thing, about reason, we shall not find the want of an academic definition hinder us from a reasonable conclusion. What nurse or mother will doubt that her infant child can reason within the limits of its own experience, long before it can formulate its reason in articulately worded thought ? If the development of any given animal is, as our opponents themselves admit, an epitome of the history of its whole anterior development, surely the fact that speech is an accomplishment acquired after birth so artificially that children who have gone wild in the woods lose it if they have ever learned it, points to the conclusion that man's ancestors only learned to express themselves in articulate language at a comparatively recent period. Granted that they learn to think and reason continually the more and more fully for having done so, will common sense permit us to suppose that they could neither think nor reason at all till they could convey their ideas in words ?

I will return later to the reason of the lower animals, but will now deal with the question what it is that constitutes language in the most comprehensive sense that can be properly attached to it. I have said already that language to be language at all must not only convey fairly definite coherent ideas, but must also convey them to another living being. Whenever two living beings have conveyed and received ideas, there has been language, whether looks or gestures or words spoken or written have been the vehicle by means of which the ideas have travelled. Some ideas crawl, some run, some fly ; and in this case words are the wings they fly with, but they are only the wings of thought or of ideas, they are not the thought or ideas themselves, nor yet, as Professor Max Müller would have it, inseparably connected with them. Last summer I was at an inn in Sicily, where there was a deaf and dumb waiter ; he had been born so, and could neither write nor read. What had he to do with words or words with him ? Are we to say, then, that this most active, amiable and intelligent fellow could neither think nor reason ? One day I had had my dinner and had left the hotel. A friend came in, and the waiter saw him look for me in the place I generally occupied. He instantly came up to my friend and moved his two forefingers in a way that suggested two people going about together, this meant " your friend "; he then moved his forefingers horizontally across his eyes, this meant, " who wears divided spectacles " ; he made two fierce marks over the sockets of his eyes, this meant, " with the heavy eyebrows " ; he pulled his chin, and then touched his white shirt, to say that

my beard was white. Having thus identified me as a
friend of the person he was speaking to, and as having
a white beard, heavy eyebrows, and wearing divided
spectacles, he made a munching movement with his
jaws to say that I had had my dinner ; and finally, by
making two fingers imitate walking on the table, he
explained that I had gone away. My friend, however,
wanted to know how long I had been gone, so he
pulled out his watch and looked inquiringly. The
man at once slapped himself on the back, and held up
the five fingers of one hand, to say it was five minutes
ago. All this was done as rapidly as though it had been
said in words ; and my friend, who knew the man well,
understood without a moment's hesitation. Are we
to say that this man had no thought, nor reason, nor
language, merely because he had not a single word of
any kind in his head, which I am assured he had not ;
for, as I have said, he could not speak with his fingers ?
Is it possible to deny that a dialogue—an intelligent
conversation—had passed between the two men ?
And if conversation, then surely it is technical and
pedantic to deny that all the essential elements of
language were present. The signs and tokens used by
this poor fellow were as rude an instrument of expression, in comparison with ordinary language, as going
on one's hands and knees is in comparison with walking,
or as walking compared with going by train ; but it is
as great an abuse of words to limit the word " language " to mere words written or spoken, as it would be
to limit the idea of a locomotive to a railway engine.
This may indeed pass in ordinary conversation, where
so much must be suppressed if talk is to be got through
at all, but it is intolerable when we are inquiring about
the relations between thought and words. To do so is

to let words become as it were the masters of thought, on the ground that the fact of their being only its servants and appendages is so obvious that it is generally allowed to go without saying.

If all that Professor Max Müller means to say is, that no animal but man commands an articulate language, with verbs and nouns, or is ever likely to command one (and I question whether in reality he means much more than this), no one will differ from him. No dog or elephant has one word for bread, another for meat, and another for water. Yet, when we watch a cat or dog dreaming, as they often evidently do, can we doubt that the dream is accompanied by a mental image of the thing that is dreamed of, much like what we experience in dreams ourselves, and much doubtless like the mental images which must have passed through the mind of my deaf and dumb waiter ? If they have mental images in sleep, can we doubt that waking, also, they picture things before their mind's eyes, and see them much as we do—too vaguely indeed to admit of our thinking that we actually see the objects themselves, but definitely enough for us to be able to recognize the idea or object of which we are thinking, and to connect it with any other idea, object, or sign that we may think appropriate ?

Here we have touched on the second essential element of language. We laid it down, that its essence lay in the communication of an idea from one intelligent being to another ; but no ideas can be communicated at all except by the aid of conventions to which both parties have agreed to attach an identical meaning. The agreement may be very informal, and may pass so unconsciously from one generation to another that its existence can only be recognized by the aid of much

introspection, but it will be always there. A sayer, a
sayee, and a convention, no matter what, agreed upon
between them as inseparably attached to the idea
which it is intended to convey—these comprise all the
essentials of language. Where these are present there
is language ; where any of them are wanting there is
no language. It is not necessary for the sayee to be
able to speak and become a sayer. If he comprehends
the sayer—that is to say, if he attaches the same
meaning to a certain symbol as the sayer does—if he
is a party to the bargain whereby it is agreed upon by
both that any given symbol shall be attached invariably
to a certain idea, so that in virtue of the principle of
associated ideas the symbol shall never be present
without immediately carrying the idea along with it,
then all the essentials of language are complied with,
and there has been true speech though never a word
was spoken.

The lower animals, therefore, many of them, possess
a part of our own language, though they cannot
speak it, and hence do not possess it so fully as we do.
They cannot say " bread," " meat," or " water," but
there are many that readily learn what ideas they ought
to attach to these symbols when they are presented to
them. It is idle to say that a cat does not know what
the cat's-meat man means when he says " meat."
The cat knows just as well, neither better nor worse
than the cat's-meat man does, and a great deal better
than I myself understand much that is said by some
very clever people at Oxford or Cambridge. There is
more true employment of language, more *bona fide*
currency of speech, between a sayer and a sayee who
understand each other, though neither of them can
speak a word, than between a sayer who can speak

with the tongues of men and of angels without being
clear about his own meaning, and a sayee who can
himself utter the same words, but who is only in
imperfect agreement with the sayer as to the ideas
which the words or symbols that he utters are intended
to convey. The nature of the symbols counts for
nothing ; the gist of the matter is in the perfect
harmony between sayer and sayee as to the significance
that is to be associated with them.

Professor Max Müller admits that we share with the
lower animals what he calls an emotional language,
and continues that we may call their interjections and
imitations language if we like, as we speak of the
language of the eyes or the eloquence of mute nature,
but he warns us against mistaking metaphor for fact.
It is indeed mere metaphor to talk of the eloquence of
mute nature, or the language of winds and waves.
There is no intercommunion of mind with mind by
means of a covenanted symbol ; but it is only an
apparent, not a real, metaphor to say that two pairs of
eyes have spoken when they have signalled to one
another something which they both understand. A
schoolboy at home for the holidays wants another plate
of pudding, and does not like to apply officially for
more. He catches the servant's eye and looks at the
pudding ; the servant understands, takes his plate
without a word, and gets him some. Is it metaphor to
say that the boy asked the servant to do this, or is it
not rather pedantry to insist on the letter of a bond
and deny its spirit, by denying that language passed,
on the ground that the symbols covenanted upon and
assented to by both were uttered and received by eyes
and not by mouth and ears ? When the lady drank
to the gentleman only with her eyes, and he pledged

with his, was there no conversation because there was neither noun nor verb ? Eyes are verbs, and glasses of wine are good nouns enough as between those who understand one another. Whether the ideas underlying them are expressed and conveyed by eyeage or by tonguage is a detail that matters nothing.

But everything we say is metaphorical if we choose to be captious. Scratch the simplest expressions, and you will find the metaphor. Written words are handage, inkage and paperage ; it is only by metaphor, or substitution and transposition of ideas, that we can call them language. They are indeed potential language, and the symbols employed presuppose nouns, verbs, and the other parts of speech ; but for the most part it is in what we read between the lines that the profounder meaning of any letter is conveyed. There are words unwritten and untranslatable into any nouns that are nevertheless felt as above, about and underneath the gross material symbols that lie scrawled upon the paper ; and the deeper the feeling with which anything is written the more pregnant will it be of meaning which can be conveyed securely enough, but which loses rather than gains if it is squeezed into a sentence, and limited by the parts of speech. The language is not in the words but in the heart-to-heartness of the thing, which is helped by words, but is nearer and farther than they. A correspondent wrote to me once, many years ago, " If I could think to you without words you would understand me better." But surely in this he was thinking to me, and without words, and I did understand him better. . . . So it is not by the words that I am too presumptuously venturing to speak to-night that your opinions will be formed or modified. They will be formed or modified,

if either, by something that you will feel, but which
I have not spoken, to the full as much as by anything
that I have actually uttered. You may say that this
borders on mysticism. Perhaps it does, but there
really is some mysticism in nature.

To return, however, to *terra firma*. I believe I am
right in saying that the essence of language lies in the
intentional conveyance of ideas from one living being to
another through the instrumentality of arbitrary tokens
or symbols agreed upon and understood by both as
being associated with the particular ideas in question.
The nature of the symbol chosen is a matter of indiffer-
ence ; it may be anything that appeals to human
senses, and is not too hot or too heavy ; the essence of
the matter lies in a mutual covenant that whatever it is
shall stand invariably for the same thing, or nearly so.

We shall see this more easily if we observe the
differences between written and spoken language.
The written word " stone," and the spoken word, are
each of them symbols arrived at in the first instance
arbitrarily. They are neither of them more like the
other than they are to the idea of a stone which rises
before our minds, when we either see or hear the word,
or than this idea again is like the actual stone itself, but
nevertheless the spoken symbol and the written one
each alike convey with certainty the combination of
ideas to which we have agreed to attach them.

The written symbol is formed with the hand, appeals
to the eye, leaves a material trace as long as paper and
ink last, can travel as far as paper and ink can travel,
and can be imprinted on eye after eye practically *ad
infinitum* both as regards time and space.

The spoken symbol is formed by means of various
organs in or about the mouth, appeals to the ear, not

the eye, perishes instantly without material trace, and
if it lives at all does so only in the minds of those who
heard it. The range of its action is no wider than that
within which a voice can be heard ; and every time a
fresh impression is wanted the type must be set up
anew.

The written symbol extends infinitely, as regards
time and space, the range within which one mind can
communicate with another ; it gives the writer's mind
a life limited by the duration of ink, paper and readers,
as against that of his flesh and blood body. On the
other hand, it takes longer to learn the rules so as to be
able to apply them with ease and security, and even
then they cannot be applied so quickly and easily as
those attaching to spoken symbols. Moreover, the
spoken symbols admit of a hundred quick and subtle
adjuncts by way of action, tone and expression, so that
no one will use written symbols unless either for the
special advantages of permanence and travelling
power, or because he is incapacitated from using
spoken ones. This, however, is hardly to the point ;
the point is that these two conventional combinations
of symbols, that are as unlike one another as the
Hallelujah Chorus is to St. Paul's Cathedral, are the
one as much language as the other ; and we therefore
inquire what this very patent fact reveals to us about
the more essential characteristics of language itself.
What is the common bond that unites these two classes
of symbols that seem at first sight to have nothing in
common, and makes the one raise the idea of language
in our minds as readily as the other ? The bond lies
in the fact that both are a set of conventional tokens
or symbols, agreed upon between the parties to whom
they appeal as being attached invariably to the same

ideas, and because they are being made as a means of communion between one mind and another—for a memorandum made for a person's own later use is nothing but a communication from an earlier mind to a later and modified one ; it is therefore in reality a communication from one mind to another as much as though it had been addressed to another person.

We see, therefore, that the nature of the outward and visible sign to which the inward and spiritual idea of language is attached does not matter. It may be the firing of a gun ; it may be an old semaphore telegraph ; it may be the movements of a needle ; a look, a gesture, the breaking of a twig by an Indian to tell someone that he has passed that way : a twig broken designedly with this end in view is a letter addressed to whomsoever it may concern, as much as though it had been written out in full on bark or paper. It does not matter one straw what it is, provided it is agreed upon in concert, and stuck to. Just as the lowest forms of life nevertheless present us with all the essential characteristics of livingness, and are as much alive in their own humble way as the most highly developed organisms, so the rudest intentional and effectual communication between two minds through the instrumentality of a concerted symbol is as much language as the most finished oratory of Mr. Gladstone. I demur therefore to the assertion that the lower animals have no language, inasmuch as they cannot themselves articulate a grammatical sentence. I do not indeed pretend that when the cat calls upon the tiles it uses what it consciously and introspectively recognizes as language ; it says what it has to say without introspection, and in the ordinary course of business, as one of the common forms of courtship.

It no more knows that it has been using language than M. Jourdain knew he had been speaking prose, but M. Jourdain's knowing or not knowing was neither here nor there.

Anything which can be made to hitch on invariably to a definite idea that can carry some distance—say an inch at the least, and which can be repeated at pleasure, can be pressed into the service of language. Mrs. Bentley, wife of the famous Dr. Bentley of Trinity College, Cambridge, used to send her snuff-box to the college buttery when she wanted beer, instead of a written order. If the snuff-box came the beer was sent, but if there was no snuff-box there was no beer. Wherein did the snuff-box differ more from a written order, than a written order differs from a spoken one ? The snuff-box was for the time being language. It sounds strange to say that one might take a pinch of snuff out of a sentence, but if the servant had helped him or herself to a pinch while carrying it to the buttery this is what would have been done ; for if a snuff-box can say " Send me a quart of beer," so efficiently that the beer is sent, it is impossible to say that it is not a *bona fide* sentence. As for the recipient of the message, the butler did not probably translate the snuff-box into articulate nouns and verbs ; as soon as he saw it he just went down into the cellar and drew the beer, and if he thought at all, it was probably about something else. Yet he must have been thinking without words, or he would have drawn too much beer or too little, or have spilt it in the bringing it up, and we may be sure that he did none of these things.

You will, of course, observe that if Mrs. Bentley had sent the snuff-box to the buttery of St. John's College instead of Trinity, it would not have been

P

language, for there would have been no covenant
between sayer and sayee as to what the symbol should
represent, there would have been no previously established association of ideas in the mind of the butler of
St. John's between beer and snuff-box ; the connection
was artificial, arbitrary, and by no means one of those
in respect of which an impromptu bargain might be
proposed by the very symbol itself, and assented to
without previous formality by the person to whom it
was presented. More briefly, the butler of St. John's
would not have been able to understand and read it
aright. It would have been a dead letter to him—a
snuff-box and not a letter ; whereas to the butler of
Trinity it was a letter and not a snuff-box. You will
also note that it was only at the moment when he was
looking at it and accepting it as a message that it
flashed forth from snuff-box-hood into the light and
life of living utterance. As soon as it had kindled the
butler into sending a single quart of beer, its force
was spent until Mrs. Bentley threw her soul into it
again and charged it anew by wanting more beer, and
sending it down accordingly.

Again, take the ring which the Earl of Essex sent to
Queen Elizabeth, but which the queen did not receive.
This was intended as a sentence, but failed to become
effectual language because the sensible material
symbol never reached those sentient organs which it
was intended to affect. A book, again, however full of
excellent words it may be, is not language when it is
merely standing on a bookshelf. It speaks to no one,
unless when being actually read, or quoted from by
an act of memory. It is potential language as a
lucifer-match is potential fire, but it is no more
language till it is in contact with a recipient mind,

than a match is fire till it is struck, and is being consumed.

A piece of music, again, without any words at all, or a song with words that have nothing in the world to do with the ideas which it is nevertheless made to convey, is very often effectual language. Much lying, and all irony depends on tampering with covenanted symbols, and making those that are usually associated with one set of ideas convey by a sleight of mind others of a different nature. That is why irony is intolerably fatiguing unless very sparingly used. Take the song which Blondel sang under the window of King Richard's prison. There was not one syllable in it to say that Blondel was there, and was going to help the king to get out of prison. It was about some silly love affair, but it was a letter all the same, and the king made language of what would otherwise have been no language, by guessing the meaning, that is to say, by perceiving that he was expected to enter then and there into a new covenant as to the meaning of the symbols that were presented to him, understanding what this covenant was to be, and acquiescing in it.

On the other hand, no ingenuity can torture "language" into being a fit word to use in connection with either sounds or any other symbols that have not been intended to convey a meaning, or again in connection with either sounds or symbols in respect of which there has been no covenant between sayer and sayee. When we hear people speaking a foreign language— we will say Welsh—we feel that though they are no doubt using what is very good language as between themselves, there is no language whatever as far as we are concerned. We call it lingo, not language. The

Chinese letters on a tea-chest might as well not be there, for all that they say to us, though the Chinese find them very much to the purpose. They are a covenant to which we have been no parties—to which our intelligence has affixed no signature.

We have already seen that it is in virtue of such an understood covenant that symbols so unlike one another as the written word " stone " and the spoken word alike at once raise the idea of a stone in our minds. See how the same holds good as regards the different languages that pass current in different nations. The letters p, i, e, r, r, e convey the idea of a stone to a Frenchman as readily as s, t, o, n, e do to ourselves. And why ? because that is the covenant that has been struck between those who speak and those who are spoken to. Our " stone " conveys no idea to a Frenchman, nor his " pierre " to us, unless we have done what is commonly called acquiring one another's language. To acquire a foreign language is only to learn and adhere to the covenants in respect of symbols which the nation in question has adopted and adheres to. Till we have done this we neither of us know the rules, so to speak, of the game that the other is playing, and cannot, therefore, play together ; but the convention being once known and consented to, it does not matter whether we raise the idea of a stone by the words " lapis," or by " lithos," " pietra," " pierre," " stein," " stane " or " stone " ; we may choose what symbols written or spoken we choose, and one set, unless they are of unwieldy length, will do as well as another, if we can get other people to choose the same and stick to them ; it is the accepting and sticking to them that matters, not the symbols. The whole power of spoken language is vested in the invariableness with which certain symbols are associated with certain ideas. If we are strict in always connecting the same symbols with the same ideas, we speak well, keep our meaning clear to ourselves, and convey it readily and accurately to anyone who is also fairly strict. If, on the other hand, we use the same combination of symbols for one thing one day and for another the next, we abuse our symbols instead of using them, and those who indulge in slovenly habits in this respect ere long lose the power alike of thinking and of expressing themselves correctly. The symbols, however, in the first instance, may be anything in the wide world that we have a fancy for. They have no more to do with the ideas they serve to convey than money has with the things that it serves to buy.

The principle of association, as everyone knows, involves that whenever two things have been associated sufficiently together, the suggestion of one of them to the mind shall immediately raise a suggestion of the other. It is in virtue of this principle that language, as we so call it, exists at all, for the essence of language consists, as I have said perhaps already too often, in the fixity with which certain ideas are invariably connected with certain symbols. But this being so, it is hard to see how we can deny that the lower animals possess the germs of a highly rude and unspecialized, but still true language, unless we also deny that they have any ideas at all ; and this I gather is what Professor Max Müller in a quiet way rather wishes to do. Thus he says, " It is easy enough to show that animals communicate, but this is a fact which has never been doubted. Dogs who growl and bark leave no doubt in the minds of other dogs or cats, or even of man, of what they mean, but growling and barking are not language, nor do they even contain the elements of language."[1]

I observe the Professor says that animals communicate without saying what it is that they communicate. I believe this to have been because if he said that the lower animals communicate their ideas, this would be to admit that they have ideas ; if so, and if, as they present every appearance of doing, they can remember, reflect upon, modify these ideas according to modified surroundings, and interchange them with one another, how is it possible to deny them the germs of thought, language, and reason—not to say a good deal more than the germs ? It seems to me that not knowing what else to say that animals communicated if it was not ideas, and not knowing what mess he might not get into if he admitted that they had ideas at all, he thought it safer to omit his accusative case altogether.

That growling and barking cannot be called a very highly specialized language goes without saying ; they are, however, so much diversified in character, according to circumstances, that they place a considerable number of symbols at an animal's command, and he invariably attaches the same symbol to the same idea. A cat never purrs when she is angry, nor spits when she is pleased. When she rubs her head against anyone affectionately it is her symbol for saying that she is very fond of him, and she expects, and usually finds that it will be understood. If she sees her mistress raise her hand as though to pretend to strike her, she knows that it is the symbol her mistress invariably attaches to the idea of sending her away, and as such she accepts it. Granted that the symbols in use among the lower animals are fewer and less highly differenti-

[1] *Three Lectures on the Science of Language*, Longmans, 1889, p. 4.

ated than in the case of any known human language, and therefore that animal language is incomparably less subtle and less capable of expressing delicate shades of meaning than our own, these differences are nevertheless only those that exist between highly developed and inchoate language ; they do not involve those that distinguish language from no language. They are the differences between the undifferentiated protoplasm of the amœba and our own complex organization ; they are not the differences between life and no life. In animal language as much as in human there is a mind intentionally making use of a symbol accepted by another mind as invariably attached to a certain idea, in order to produce that idea in the mind which it is desired to affect—more briefly, there is a sayer, a sayee, and a covenanted symbol designedly applied. Our own speech is vertebrated and articulated by means of nouns, verbs, and the rules of grammar. A dog's speech is invertebrate, but I do not see how it is possible to deny that it possesses all the essential elements of language.

I have said nothing about Professor R. L. Garner's researches into the language of apes, because they have not yet been so far verified and accepted as to make it safe to rely upon them ; but when he lays it down that all voluntary sounds are the products of thought, and that, if they convey a meaning to another, they perform the functions of human speech, he says what I believe will commend itself to any unsophisticated mind. I could have wished, however, that he had not limited himself to sounds, and should have preferred his saying what I doubt not he would readily accept — I mean, that all symbols or tokens of whatever kind, if voluntarily adopted as such, are the products of thought, and perform the functions of human speech ; but I cannot too often remind you that nothing can be considered as fulfilling the conditions of language, except a voluntary application of a recognized token in order to convey a more or less definite meaning, with the intention doubtless of thus purchasing as it were some other desired meaning and consequent sensation. It is astonishing how closely in this respect money and words resemble one another. Money indeed may be considered as the most universal and expressive of all languages. For gold and silver coins are no more money when not in the actual process of being voluntarily used in purchase, than words not so in use are language. Pounds, shillings and pence are recognized covenanted tokens, the outward and visible signs of an inward and spiritual purchasing power, but till in actual use they are only potential money, as the symbols of language, whatever they may be, are only potential language till they are passing between two minds. It is the power and will to apply the symbols that alone gives life to money, and as long as these are in abeyance the money is in abeyance also ; the coins may be safe in one's pocket, but they are as dead as a log till they begin to burn in it, and so are our words till they begin to burn within us.

The real question, however, as to the substantial underlying identity between the language of the lower animals and our own, turns upon that other question whether or no, in spite of an immeasurable difference of degree, the thought and reason of man and of the lower animals is essentially the same. No one will expect a dog to master and express the varied ideas that are incessantly arising in connection with human affairs. He is a pauper as against a millionaire. To ask him to do so would be like giving a street-boy sixpence and telling him to go and buy himself a founder's share in the New River Company. He would not even know what was meant, and even if he did it would take several millions of sixpences to buy one. It is astonishing what a clever workman will do with very modest tools, or again how far a thrifty housewife will make a very small sum of money go, or again in like manner how many ideas an intelligent brute can receive and convey with its very limited vocabulary ; but no one will pretend that a dog's intelligence can ever reach the level of a man's. What we do maintain is that, within its own limited range, it is of the same essential character as our own, and that though a dog's ideas in respect of human affairs are both vague and narrow, yet in respect of canine affairs they are precise enough and extensive enough to deserve no other name than thought or reason. We hold moreover that they communicate their ideas in essentially the same manner as we do—that is to say, by the instrumentality of a code of symbols attached to certain states of mind and material objects, in the first instance arbitrarily, but so persistently, that the presentation of the symbol immediately carries with it the idea which it is intended to convey. Animals can thus receive and impart ideas on all that most concerns them. As my great name-sake said some two hundred years ago, they know " what's what, and that's as high as metaphysic wit can fly." And they not only know what's what them-selves, but can impart to one another any new what's-whatness that they may have acquired, for they are notoriously able to instruct and correct one another.

Against this Professor Max Müller contends that we can know nothing of what goes on in the mind of any lower animal, inasmuch as we are not lower animals ourselves. " We can imagine anything we like about what passes in the mind of an animal," he writes, " we can know absolutely nothing." [1] It is something to have it in evidence that he conceives animals as having a mind at all, but it is not easy to see how they can be supposed to have a mind, without being able to acquire ideas, and having acquired, to read, mark, learn and inwardly digest them. Surely the mistake of requiring too much evidence is hardly less great than that of being contented with too little. We, too, are animals, and can no more refuse to infer reason from certain visible actions in their case than we can in our own. If Professor Max Müller's plea were allowed, we should have to deny our right to infer confidently what passes in the mind of anyone not ourselves, inasmuch as we are not that person. We never, indeed, can obtain irrefragable certainty about this or any other matter, but we can be sure enough in many cases to warrant our staking all that is most precious to us on the soundness of our opinion. Moreover, if the Professor denies our right to infer that animals reason, on the ground that we are not animals enough ourselves to be able to form an opinion, with what right does he infer so confidently himself that they do not reason ? And how, if they present every one of those appearances which we are accustomed to connect with the communication of an idea from one mind to another, can we deny that they have a language of their own, though it is one which in most cases we can neither speak nor understand ? How can we say that a sentinel rook, when it sees a man with a gun and warns the other rooks by a concerted note which they all

[1] *Science of Thought*, Longmans, 1887, p. 9.

show that they understand by immediately taking flight, should not be credited both with reason and the germs of language ?

After all, a professor, whether of philology, psychology, biology, or any other ology, is hardly the kind of person to whom we should appeal on such an elementary question as that of animal intelligence and language. We might as well ask a botanist to tell us whether grass grows, or a meteorologist to tell us if it has left off raining. If it is necessary to appeal to anyone, I should prefer the opinion of an intelligent gamekeeper to that of any professor, however learned. The keepers, again, at the Zoological Gardens, have exceptional opportunities for studying the minds of animals—modified, indeed, by captivity, but still minds of animals. Grooms, again, and dog-fanciers, are to the full as able to form an intelligent opinion on the reason and language of animals as any University Professor, and so are cat's-meat men. I have repeatedly asked gamekeepers and keepers at the Zoological Gardens whether animals could reason and converse with one another, and have always found myself regarded somewhat contemptuously for having even asked the question. I once said to a friend, in the hearing of a keeper at the Zoological Gardens, that the penguin was very stupid. The man was furious, and jumped upon me at once. "He's not stupid at all," said he ; " he's very intelligent."

Who has not seen a cat, when it wishes to go out, raise its fore paws on to the handle of the door, or as near as it can get, and look round, evidently asking someone to turn it for her ? Is it reasonable to deny that a reasoning process is going on in the cat's mind, whereby she connects her wish with the steps necessary for its fulfilment, and also with certain invariable symbols which she knows her master or mistress will interpret ? Once, in company with a friend, I watched a cat playing with a house-fly in the window of a ground-floor room. We were in the street, while the cat was inside. When we came up to the window she gave us one searching look, and, having satisfied herself that we had nothing for her, went on with her game. She knew all about the glass in the window, and was sure we could do nothing to molest her, so she treated us with absolute contempt, never even looking at us again.

The game was this. She was to catch the fly and roll it round and round under her paw along the window-sill, but so gently as not to injure it nor prevent it from being able to fly again when she had done rolling it. It was very early spring, and flies were scarce, in fact there was not another in the whole window. She knew that if she crippled this one, it would not be able to amuse her further, and that she would not readily get another instead, and she liked the feel of it under her paw. It was soft and living, and the quivering of its wings tickled the ball of her foot in a manner that she found particularly grateful ; so she rolled it gently along the whole length of the window-sill. It then became the fly's turn. He was to get up and fly about in the window, so as to recover himself a little ; then she was to catch him again, and roll him softly all along the window-sill, as she had done before.

It was plain that the cat knew the rules of her game perfectly well, and enjoyed it keenly. It was equally plain that the fly could not make head or tail of what it was all about. If it had been able to do so it would have gone to play in the upper part of the window, where the cat could not reach it.　Perhaps it was always hoping to get through the glass, and escape that way ; anyhow, it kept pretty much to the same pane, no matter how often it was rolled.　At last, however, the fly, for some reason or another, did not reappear on the pane, and the cat began looking everywhere to find it.　Her annoyance when she failed to do so was extreme.　It was not only that she had lost her fly, but that she could not conceive how she should have ever come to do so.　Presently she noted a small knot in the woodwork of the sill, and it flashed upon her that she had accidentally killed the fly, and that this was its dead body.　She tried to move it gently with her paw, but it was no use, and for the time she satisfied herself that the knot and the fly had nothing to do with one another.　Every now and then, however, she returned to it as though it were the only thing she could think of, and she would try it again.　She seemed to say she was certain there had been no knot there before—she must have seen it if there had been ; and yet, the fly could hardly have got jammed so firmly into the wood.　She was puzzled and irritated beyond measure, and kept looking in the same place again and again, just as we do when we have mislaid something. She was rapidly losing temper and dignity when suddenly we saw the fly reappear from under the cat's stomach and make for the window-pane, at the very moment when the cat herself was exclaiming for the fiftieth time that she wondered where that stupid fly ever could have got to.　No man who has been hunting twenty minutes for his spectacles could be more delighted when he suddenly finds them on his own forehead.　" So that's where you were," we seemed to hear her say, as she proceeded to catch it, and again began rolling it very softly without hurting it, under her paw.

My friend and I both noticed that the cat, in spite of her perplexity, never so much as hinted that we were the culprits. The question whether anything outside the window could do her good or harm had long since been settled by her in the negative, and she was not going to reopen it ; she simply cut us dead, and though her annoyance was so great that she was manifestly ready to lay the blame on anybody or anything with or without reason, and though she must have perfectly well known that we were watching the whole affair with amusement, she never either asked us if we had happened to see such a thing as a fly go down our way lately, or accused us of having taken it from her—both of which ideas she would, I am confident, have been very well able to convey to us if she had been so minded.

Now what are thought and reason if the processes that were going through this cat's mind were not both, one and the other ? It would be childish to suppose that the cat thought in words of its own, or in anything like words. Its thinking was probably conducted through the instrumentality of a series of mental images. We so habitually think in words ourselves that we find it difficult to realize thought without words at all ; our difficulty, however, in imagining the particular manner in which the cat thinks has nothing to do with the matter. We must answer the question whether she thinks or no, not according to our own ease or difficulty in understanding the particular manner of her thinking, but according as her action does or does not appear to be of the same character as other action that we commonly call thoughtful. To say that the cat is not intelligent, merely on the ground that we cannot ourselves fathom her intelligence—this, as I have elsewhere said, is to make intelligence mean the power of being understood, rather than the power of understanding. This nevertheless is what, for all our boasted intelligence, we generally do. The more we can understand an animal's ways, the more intelligent we call it, and the less we can understand these, the more stupid do we declare it to be. As for plants—whose punctuality and attention to all the details and routine of their somewhat restricted lines of business is as obvious as it is beyond all praise—we understand the working of their minds so little that by common consent we declare them to have no intelligence at all.

Before concluding I should wish to deal a little more fully with Professor Max Müller's contention that there can be no reason without language, and no language without reason. Surely when two practised pugilists are fighting, parrying each other's blows, and watching keenly for an unguarded point, they are thinking and reasoning very subtly the whole time, without doing so in words. The machination of their thoughts, as well as its expression, is actual—I mean, effectuated and expressed by action and deed, not words. They are unaware of any logical sequence of thought that they could follow in words as passing through their minds at all. They may perhaps think consciously in words now and again, but such thought will be intermittent, and the main part of the fighting will be done without any internal concomitance of articulated phrases. Yet we cannot doubt that their action, however much we may disapprove of it, is guided by intelligence and reason ; nor should we doubt that a reasoning process of the same character goes on in the minds of two dogs or fighting-cocks when they are striving to master their opponents.

Do we think in words, again, when we wind up our watches, put on our clothes, or eat our breakfasts? If we do, it is generally about something else. We do these things almost as much without the help of words as we wink or yawn, or perform any of those other actions that we call reflex, as it would almost seem because they are done without reflection. They are not, however, the less reasonable because wordless.

Even when we think we are thinking in words, we do so only in half measure. A running accompaniment of words no doubt frequently attends our thoughts; but, unless we are writing or speaking, this accompaniment is of the vaguest and most fitful kind, as we often find out when we try to write down or say what we are thinking about, though we have a fairly definite notion of it, or fancy that we have one, all the time. The thought is not steadily and coherently governed by and moulded in words, nor does it steadily govern them. Words and thought interact upon and help one another, as any other mechanical appliances interact on and help the invention that first hit upon them; but reason or thought, for the most part, flies along over the heads of words, working its own mysterious way in paths that are beyond our ken, though whether some of our departmental personalities are as unconscious of what is passing, as that central government is which we alone dub with the name of " we " or " us," is a point on which I will not now touch.

I cannot think, then, that Professor Max Müller's contention that thought and language are identical—and he has repeatedly affirmed this—will ever be generally accepted. Thought is no more identical with language than feeling is identical with the nervous system. True, we can no more feel without a nervous system than we can discern certain minute organisms without a microscope. Destroy the nervous system, and we destroy feeling. Destroy the microscope, and we can no longer see the animalcules; but our sight of the animalcules is not the microscope, though it is effectuated by means of the microscope, and our feeling is not the nervous system, though the nervous system is the instrument that enables us to feel.

The nervous system is a device which living beings have gradually perfected—I believe I may say quite truly—through the will and power which they have derived from a fountain-head, the existence of which we can infer, but which we can never apprehend. By the help of this device, and in proportion as they have perfected it, living beings feel ever with great definiteness, and hence formulate their feelings in thought with more and more precision. The higher evolution of thought has reacted on the nervous system, and the consequent higher evolution of the nervous system has again reacted upon thought. These things are as power and desire, or supply and demand, each one of which is continually outstripping, and being in turn outstripped by the other ; but, in spite of their close connection and interaction, power is not desire, nor demand supply. Language is a device evolved sometimes by leaps and bounds, and sometimes exceedingly slowly, whereby we help ourselves alike to greater ease, precision, and complexity of thought, and also to more convenient interchange of thought among ourselves. Thought found rude expression, which gradually among other forms assumed that of words. These reacted upon

Q

thought, and thought again on them, but thought is no more identical with words than words are with the separate letters of which they are composed.

To sum up, then, and to conclude. I would ask you to see the connection between words and ideas as in the first instance arbitrary. No doubt in some cases an imitation of the cry of some bird or wild beast would suggest the name should be attached to it ; occasionally the sound of an operation such as grinding may have influenced the choice of the letters g, r, as the root of many words that denote a grinding, grating, grasping, crushing action ; but I understand that the number of words due to direct imitation is comparatively few in number, and that they have been mainly coined as the result of connections so far-fetched and fanciful as to amount practically to no connection at all. Once chosen, however, they were adhered to for a considerable time among the dwellers in any given place, so as to become acknowledged as the vulgar tongue, and raise readily in the mind of the inhabitants of that place the ideas with which they had been artificially associated.

As regards our being able to think and reason without words, the Duke of Argyll has put the matter as soundly as I have yet seen it stated. " It seems to me," he wrote, " quite certain that we can and do constantly think of things without thinking of any sound or word as designating them. Language seems to me to be necessary for the progress of thought, but not at all for the mere act of thinking. It is a product of thought, an expression of it, a vehicle for the communication of it, and an embodiment which is essential to its growth and continuity; but it seems to me altogether erroneous to regard it as an inseparable part of cogitation."

The following passages, again, are quoted from Sir William Hamilton in Professor Max Müller's own book, with so much approval as to lead one to suppose that the differences between himself and his opponents are in reality less than he believes them to be.

" Language," says Sir W. Hamilton, " is the attribution of signs to our cognitions of things. But as a cognition must have already been there before it could receive a sign, consequently that knowledge which is denoted by the formation and application of a word must have preceded the symbol that denotes it. A sign, however, is necessary to give stability to our intellectual progress—to establish each step in our advance as a new starting-point for our advance to another beyond. A country may be overrun by an armed host, but it is only conquered by the establishment of fortresses. Words are the fortresses of thought. They enable us to realize our dominion over what we have already overrun in thought ; to make every intellectual conquest the base of operations for others still beyond."

" This," says Professor Max Müller, " is a most happy illustration." and he proceeds to quote the following, also from Sir William Hamilton, which he declares to be even happier still.

" You have all heard," says Sir William Hamilton, " of the process of tunnelling through a sandbank. In this operation it is impossible to succeed unless every foot, nay, almost every inch of our progress be secured by an arch of masonry before we attempted the excavation of another. Now language is to the mind precisely what the arch is to the tunnel. The power of thinking and the power of excavation are not dependent on the words in the one case or on the mason-work in the other ; but without these subsidiaries neither could be carried on beyond its rudimentary commencement. Though, therefore, we allow that every movement forward in language must be determined by an antecedent movement forward in thought, still, unless thought be accompanied at each point of its evolutions by a corresponding evolution of language, its further development is arrested."

Man has evolved an articulate language, whereas the lower animals seem to be without one. Man, therefore, has far outstripped them in reasoning faculty as well as in power of expression. This, however, does not bar the communications which the lower animals make to one another from possessing all the essential characteristics of language, and, as a matter of fact, wherever we can follow them we find such communications effectuated by the aid of arbitrary symbols covenanted upon by the living beings that wish to communicate, and persistently associated with certain corresponding feelings, states of mind, or material objects. Human language is nothing more than this in principle, however much further the principle has been carried in our own case than in that of the lower animals.

This being admitted, we should infer that the thought or reason on which the language of men and animals is alike founded differs as between men and brutes in degree but not in kind. More than this cannot be claimed on behalf of the lower animals, even by their most enthusiastic admirer.

The
Deadlock in Darwinism[1]

Part I

IT will be readily admitted that of all living writers
Mr. Alfred Russel Wallace is the one the peculiar
turn of whose mind best fits him to write on the subject
of natural selection, or the accumulation of fortunate
but accidental variations through descent and the
struggle for existence. His mind in all its more
essential characteristics closely resembles that of the
late Mr. Charles Darwin himself, and it is no doubt due
to this fact that he and Mr. Darwin elaborated their
famous theory at the same time, and independently
of one another. I shall have occasion in the course of
the following article to show how misled and misleading
both these distinguished men have been, in spite of
their unquestionable familiarity with the whole range
of animal and vegetable phenomena. I believe it will
be more respectful to both of them to do this in the
most outspoken way. I believe their work to have
been as mischievous as it has been valuable, and as
valuable as it has been mischievous ; and higher,
whether praise or blame, I know not how to give.
Nevertheless I would in the outset, and with the utmost
sincerity, admit concerning Messrs. Wallace and

[1] Published in the *Universal Review*, April, May, and June, 1890.

Darwin that neither can be held as the more profound and conscientious thinker ; neither can be put forward as the more ready to acknowledge obligation to the great writers on evolution who had preceded him, or to place his own developments in closer and more conspicuous historical connection with earlier thought upon the subject ; neither is the more ready to welcome criticism and to state his opponent's case in the most pointed and telling way in which it can be put ; neither is the more quick to encourage new truth ; neither is the more genial, generous adversary, or has the profounder horror of anything even approaching literary or scientific want of candour ; both display the same inimitable power of putting their opinions forward in the way that shall best ensure their acceptance ; both are equally unrivalled in the tact that tells them when silence will be golden, and when on the other hand a whole volume of facts may be advantageously brought forward.   Less than the foregoing tribute both to Messrs. Darwin and Wallace I will not, and more I cannot pay.

Let us now turn to the most authoritative exponent of latter-day evolution—I mean to Mr. Wallace, whose work, entitled *Darwinism*, though it should have been entitled *Wallaceism*, is still so far Darwinistic that it develops the teaching of Mr. Darwin in the direction given to it by Mr. Darwin himself—so far, indeed, as this can be ascertained at all—and not in that of Lamarck.   Mr. Wallace tells us, on the first page of his preface, that he has no intention of dealing even in outline with the vast subject of evolution in general, and has only tried to give such an account of the theory of natural selection as may facilitate a clear conception of Darwin's work.   How far he has succeeded is a point on which opinion will probably be divided. Those who find Mr. Darwin's works clear will also find no difficulty in understanding Mr. Wallace; those, on the other hand, who find Mr. Darwin puzzling are little likely to be less puzzled by Mr. Wallace. He continues :—

"The objections now made to Darwin's theory apply solely to the particular means by which the change of species has been brought about, not to the fact of that change."

But "Darwin's theory"—as Mr. Wallace has elsewhere proved that he understands—has no reference "to the fact of that change"—that is to say, to the fact that species have been modified in course of descent from other species. This is no more Mr. Darwin's theory than it is the reader's or my own. Darwin's theory is concerned only with "the particular means by which the change of species has been brought about"; his contention being that this is mainly due to the natural survival of those individuals that have happened by some accident to be born most favourably adapted to their surroundings, or, in other words, through accumulation in the common course of nature of the more lucky variations that chance occasionally purveys. Mr. Wallace's words, then, in reality amount to this, that the objections now made to Darwin's theory apply solely to Darwin's theory, which is all very well as far as it goes, but might have been more easily apprehended if he had simply said, "There are several objections now made to Mr. Darwin's theory."

It must be remembered that the passage quoted above occurs on the first page of a preface dated March, 1889, when the writer had completed his task, and was most fully conversant with his subject.

Nevertheless, it seems indisputable either that he is still confusing evolution with Mr. Darwin's theory, or that he does not know when his sentences have point and when they have none.

I should perhaps explain to some readers that Mr. Darwin did not modify the main theory put forward, first by Buffon, to whom it indisputably belongs, and adopted from him by Erasmus Darwin, Lamarck, and many other writers in the latter half of the eighteenth century and the earlier years of the nineteenth. The early evolutionists maintained that all existing forms of animal and vegetable life, including man, were derived in course of descent with modification from forms resembling the lowest now known.

Mr. Darwin went as far as this, and farther no one can go. The point at issue between him and his predecessors involves neither the main fact of evolution, nor yet the geometrical ratio of increase, and the struggle for existence consequent thereon. Messrs. Darwin and Wallace have each thrown invaluable light upon these last two points, but Buffon, as early as 1756, had made them the keystone of his system. "The movement of nature," he then wrote, "turns on two immovable pivots : one, the illimitable fecundity which she has given to all species : the other, the innumerable difficulties which reduce the results of that fecundity." Erasmus Darwin and Lamarck followed in the same sense. They thus admit the survival of the fittest as fully as Mr. Darwin himself, though they do not make use of this particular expression. The dispute turns not upon natural selection, which is common to all writers on evolution, but upon the nature and causes of the variations that are supposed to be selected from and thus accumulated.

Are these mainly attributable to the inherited effects of use and disuse, supplemented by occasional sports and happy accidents ? Or are they mainly due to sports and happy accidents, supplemented by occasional inherited effects of use and disuse ?

The Lamarckian system has all along been maintained by Mr. Herbert Spencer, who, in his *Principles of Biology*, published in 1865, showed how impossible it was that accidental variations should accumulate at all. I am not sure how far Mr. Spencer would consent to being called a Lamarckian pure and simple, nor yet how far it is strictly accurate to call him one ; nevertheless, I can see no important difference in the main positions taken by him and by Lamarck.

The question at issue between the Lamarckians, supported by Mr. Spencer and a growing band of those who have risen in rebellion against the Charles-Darwinian system on the one hand, and Messrs. Darwin and Wallace with the greater number of our more prominent biologists on the other, involves the very existence of evolution as a workable theory. For it is plain that what Nature can be supposed able to do by way of choice must depend on the supply of the variations from which she is supposed to choose. She cannot take what is not offered to her ; and so again she cannot be supposed able to accumulate unless what is gained in one direction in one generation, or series of generations, is little likely to be lost in those that presently succeed. Now variations ascribed·mainly to use and disuse can be supposed capable of being accumulated, for use and disuse are fairly constant for long periods among the individuals of the same species, and often over large areas ; moreover, conditions of existence involving changes of habit, and thus of organization, come for the most part gradually ; so that time is given during which the organism can endeavour to adapt itself in the requisite respects, instead of being shocked out of existence by too sudden change. Variations, on the other hand, that are ascribed to mere chance cannot be supposed as likely to be accumulated, for chance is notoriously inconstant, and would not purvey the variations in sufficiently unbroken succession, or in a sufficient number of individuals, modified similarly in all the necessary correlations at the same time and place to admit of their being accumulated. It is vital therefore to the theory of evolution, as was early pointed out by the late Professor Fleeming Jenkin and by Mr. Herbert Spencer, that variations should be supposed to have a definite and persistent principle underlying them, which shall tend to engender similar and simultaneous modification, however small, in the vast majority of individuals composing any species. The existence of such a principle and its permanence is the only thing that can be supposed capable of acting as rudder and compass to the accumulation of variations, and of making it hold steadily on one course for each species, till eventually many havens, far remote from one another, are safely reached.

It is obvious that the having fatally impaired the theory of his predecessors could not warrant Mr. Darwin in claiming, as he most fatuously did, the theory of evolution. That he is still generally believed to have been the originator of this theory is due to the fact that he claimed it, and that a powerful literary backing at once came forward to support him. It seems at first sight improbable that those who too zealously urged his claims were unaware that so much had been written on the subject, but when we find even Mr. Wallace himself as profoundly ignorant on this subject as he still either is, or affects to be, there is no limit assignable to the ignorance or affected ignorance of the kind of biologists who would write reviews in leading journals thirty years ago. Mr. Wallace writes :—

" A few great naturalists, struck by the very slight difference between many of these species, and the numerous links that exist between the most different forms of animals and plants, and also observing that a great many species do vary considerably in their forms, colours and habits, conceived the idea that they might be all produced one from the other. The most eminent of these writers was a great French naturalist, Lamarck, who published an elaborate work, the *Philosophie Zoologique*, in which he endeavoured to prove that all animals whatever are descended from other species of animals. He attributed the change of species chiefly to the effect of changes in the conditions of life—such as climate, food, etc. ; and especially to the desires and efforts of the animals themselves to improve their condition, leading to a modification of form or size in certain parts, owing to the well-known physiological law that all organs are strengthened by constant use, while they are weakened or even completely lost by disuse. . . .

" The only other important work dealing with the question was the celebrated *Vestiges of Creation*, published anonymously, but now acknowledged to have been written by the late Robert Chambers."

None are so blind as those who will not see, and it would be waste of time to argue with the invincible ignorance of one who thinks Lamarck and Buffon

252 The Deadlock in Darwinism

conceived that all species were produced from one
another, more especially as I have already dealt at
some length with the early evolutionists in my work
Evolution, Old and New, first published ten years ago,
and not, so far as I am aware, detected in serious
error or omission. If, however, Mr. Wallace still
thinks it safe to presume so far on the ignorance of his
readers as to say that the only two important works
on evolution before Mr. Darwin's were Lamarck's
Philosophie Zoologique and the *Vestiges of Creation*,
how fathomable is the ignorance of the average
reviewer likely to have been thirty years ago, when the
Origin of Species was first published ? Mr. Darwin
claimed evolution as his own theory. Of course, he
would not claim it if he had no right to it. Then by all
means give him the credit of it. This was the most
natural view to take, and it was generally taken. It
was not, moreover, surprising that people failed to
appreciate all the niceties of Mr. Darwin's " distinctive
feature " which, whether distinctive or no, was
assuredly not distinct, and was never frankly contrasted with the older view, as it would have been by
one who wished it to be understood and judged upon
its merits. It was in consequence of this omission that
people failed to note how fast and loose Mr. Darwin
played with his distinctive feature, and how readily
he dropped it on occasion.

It may be said that the question of what was
thought by the predecessors of Mr. Darwin is, after all,
personal, and of no interest to the general public,
comparable to that of the main issue—whether we are
to accept evolution or not. Granted that Buffon,
Erasmus Darwin, and Lamarck bore the burden and
heat of the day before Mr. Charles Darwin was born,

they did not bring people round to their opinion, whereas Mr. Darwin and Mr. Wallace did, and the public cannot be expected to look beyond this broad and indisputable fact.

The answer to this is, that the theory which Messrs. Darwin and Wallace have persuaded the public to accept is demonstrably false, and that the opponents of evolution are certain in the end to triumph over it. Paley, in his *Natural Theology*, long since brought forward far too much evidence of design in animal organization to allow of our setting down its marvels to the accumulation of fortunate accident, undirected by will, effort and intelligence. Those who examine the main facts of animal and vegetable organization without bias will, no doubt, ere long conclude that all animals and vegetables are derived ultimately from unicellular organisms, but they will not less readily perceive that the evolution of species without the concomitance and direction of mind and effort is as inconceivable as is the independent creation of every individual species. The two facts, evolution and design, are equally patent to plain people. There is no escaping from either. According to Messrs. Darwin and Wallace, we may have evolution, but are on no account to have it as mainly due to intelligent effort, guided by ever higher and higher range of sensations, perceptions, and ideas. We are to set it down to the shuffling of cards, or the throwing of dice without the play, and this will never stand.

According to the older men, cards did indeed count for much, but play counted for more. They denied the teleology of the time—that is to say, the teleology that saw all adaptation to surroundings as part of a plan devised long ages since by a quasi-anthropomorphic being who schemed everything out much as a man would do, but on an infinitely vaster scale. This conception they found repugnant alike to intelligence and conscience, but, though they do not seem to have perceived it, they left the door open for a design more true and more demonstrable than that which they excluded. By making their variations mainly due to effort and intelligence, they made organic development run on all-fours with human progress, and with inventions which we have watched growing up from small beginnings. They made the development of man from the amœba part and parcel of the story that may be read, though on an infinitely smaller scale, in the development of our most powerful marine engines from the common kettle, or of our finest microscopes from the dew-drop.

The development of the steam-engine and the microscope is due to intelligence and design, which did indeed utilize chance suggestions, but which improved on these, and directed each step of their accumulation, though never foreseeing more than a step or two ahead, and often not so much as this. The fact, as I have elsewhere urged, that the man who made the first kettle did not foresee the engines of the *Great Eastern*, or that he who first noted the magnifying power of the dew-drop had no conception of our present microscopes—the very limited amount, in fact, of design and intelligence that was called into play at any one point —this does not make us deny that the steam-engine and microscope owe their development to design. If each step of the road was designed, the whole journey was designed, though the particular end was not designed when the journey was begun. And so is it, according to the older view of evolution, with the development of those living organs, or machines, that are born with us, as part of the perambulating carpenter's chest we call our bodies. The older view gives us our design, and gives us our evolution too. If it refuses to see a quasi-anthropomorphic God modelling each species from without as a potter models clay, it gives us God as vivifying and indwelling in all His creatures—He in them, and they in Him. If it refuses to see God outside the universe, it equally refuses to see any part of the universe as outside God. If it makes the universe the body of God, it also makes God the soul of the universe. The question at issue, then, between the Darwinism of Erasmus Darwin and the neo-Darwinism of his grandson, is not a personal one, nor anything like a personal one. It not only involves the existence of evolution, but it affects the view we take of life and things in an endless variety of most interesting and important ways. It is imperative, therefore, on those who take any interest in these matters, to place side by side in the clearest contrast the views of those who refer the evolution of species mainly to accumulation of variations that have no other inception than chance, and of that older school which makes design perceive and develop still further the goods that chance provides.

But over and above this, which would be in itself sufficient, the historical mode of studying any question is the only one which will enable us to comprehend it effectually. The personal element cannot be eliminated from the consideration of works written by living persons for living persons. We want to know who is who—whom we can depend upon to have no other end than the making things clear to himself and his readers, and whom we should mistrust as having an ulterior aim

on which he is more intent than on the furthering of
our better understanding. We want to know who is
doing his best to help us, and who is only trying to make
us help him, or to bolster up the system in which his
interests are vested. There is nothing that will throw
more light upon these points than the way in which a
man behaves towards those who have worked in the
same field with himself, and, again, than his style. A
man's style, as Buffon long since said, is the man
himself. By style, I do not, of course, mean grammar
or rhetoric, but that style of which Buffon again said
that it is like happiness, and *vient de la douceur de
l'âme*. When we find a man concealing worse than
nullity of meaning under sentences that sound plausibly
enough, we should distrust him much as we should
a fellow-traveller whom we caught trying to steal our
watch. We often cannot judge of the truth or false-
hood of facts for ourselves, but we most of us know
enough of human nature to be able to tell a good
witness from a bad one.

However this may be, and whatever we may think
of judging systems by the directness or indirectness
of those who advance them, biologists, having com-
mitted themselves too rashly, would have been more
than human if they had not shown some pique towards
those who dared to say, first, that the theory of Messrs.
Darwin and Wallace was unworkable ; and secondly,
that even though it were workable it would not justify
either of them in claiming evolution. When biologists
show pique at all they generally show a good deal of
pique, but pique or no pique, they shunned Mr.
Spencer's objection above referred to with a persistency
more unanimous and obstinate than I ever remember
to have seen displayed even by professional truth-

seekers. I find no rejoinder to it from Mr. Darwin
himself, between 1865 when it was first put forward,
and 1882 when Mr. Darwin died. It has been similarly
" ostrichized " by all the leading apologists of Darwinism, so far at least as I have been able to observe, and
I have followed the matter closely for many years.
Mr. Spencer has repeated and amplified it in his recent
work *The Factors of Organic Evolution*, but it still
remains without so much as an attempt at serious
answer, for the perfunctory and illusory remarks of
Mr. Wallace at the end of his *Darwinism* cannot be
counted as such. The best proof of its irresistible
weight is that Mr. Darwin, though maintaining silence
in respect to it, retreated from his original position in
the direction that would most obviate Mr. Spencer's
objection.

Yet this objection has been repeatedly urged by the
more prominent anti-Charles-Darwinian authorities,
and there is no sign that the British public is becoming
less rigorous in requiring people either to reply to
objections repeatedly urged by men of even moderate
weight, or to let judgment go by default. As regards
Mr. Darwin's claim to the theory of evolution generally,
Darwinians are beginning now to perceive that this
cannot be admitted, and either say with some hardi-
hood that Mr. Darwin never claimed it, or after a few
saving clauses to the effect that this theory refers only
to the particular means by which evolution has been
brought about, imply forthwith thereafter none the
less that evolution is Mr. Darwin's theory. Mr.
Wallace has done this repeatedly in his recent *Darwinism*. Indeed, I should be by no means sure that on the
first page of his preface, in the passage about " Darwin's
theory," which I have already somewhat severely

R

criticized, he was not intending evolution by " Darwin's
theory," if in his preceding paragraph he had not so
clearly shown that he knew evolution to be a theory
of greatly older date than Mr. Darwin's.

The history of science—well exemplified by that of
the development theory—is the history of eminent
men who have fought against light and have been
worsted. The tenacity with which Darwinians stick
to their accumulation of fortuitous variations is on
a par with the like tenacity shown by the illustrious
Cuvier, who did his best to crush evolution altogether.
It always has been thus, and always will be ; nor is it
desirable in the interests of Truth herself that it should
be otherwise. Truth is like money—lightly come,
lightly go ; and if she cannot hold her own against
even gross misrepresentation, she is herself not worth
holding. Misrepresentation in the long run makes
Truth as much as it mars her ; hence our law courts
do not think it desirable that pleaders should speak
their *bona fide* opinions, much less that they should
profess to do so. Rather let each side hoodwink judge
and jury as best it can, and let truth flash out from
collision of defence and accusation. When either side
will not collide, it is an axiom of controversy that it
desires to prevent the truth from being elicited.

Let us now note the courses forced upon biologists
by the difficulties of Mr. Darwin's distinctive feature.
Mr. Darwin and Mr. Wallace, as is well known, brought
the feature forward simultaneously and independently
of one another, but Mr. Wallace always believed in it
more firmly than Mr. Darwin did. Mr. Darwin as a
young man did not believe in it. He wrote before 1839,
" Nature, by making habit omnipotent and its effects
hereditary, has fitted the Fuegian for the climate and

productions of his country,"[1] a sentence than which
nothing can coincide more fully with the older view
that use and disuse were the main purveyors of
variations, or conflict more fatally with his own
subsequent distinctive feature. Moreover, as I showed
in my last work on evolution,[2] in the peroration to his
Origin of Species, he discarded his accidental variations
altogether, and fell back on the older theory, so that
the body of the *Origin of Species* supports one theory,
and the peroration another that differs from it *toto
cælo*. Finally, in his later editions, he retreated
indefinitely from his original position, edging always
more and more continually towards the theory of his
grandfather and Lamarck. These facts convince me
that he was at no time a thoroughgoing Darwinian,
but was throughout an unconscious Lamarckian,
though ever anxious to conceal the fact alike from
himself and from his readers.

Not so with Mr. Wallace, who was both more outspoken in the first instance, and who has persevered
along the path of Wallaceism just as Mr. Darwin with
greater sagacity was ever on the retreat from Darwinism. Mr. Wallace's profounder faith led him in the
outset to place his theory in fuller daylight than Mr.
Darwin was inclined to do. Mr. Darwin just waved
Lamarck aside, and said as little about him as he could,
while in his earlier editions Erasmus Darwin and
Buffon were not so much as named. Mr. Wallace,
on the contrary, at once raised the Lamarckian spectre,
and declared it exorcized. He said the Lamarckian
hypothesis was " quite unnecessary." The giraffe did
not " acquire its long neck by desiring to reach the

---

[1] *Voyages of the " Adventure " and " Beagle*," iii. p. 237.
[2] *Luck or Cunning*, pp. 170, 180.

foliage of the more lofty shrubs, and constantly stretching its neck for this purpose, but because any varieties which occurred among its antitypes with a longer neck than usual at once secured a fresh range of pasture over the same ground as their shorter-necked companions, and on the first scarcity of food were thus enabled to outlive them." [1]

" Which occurred " is evidently " which happened to occur " by some chance of accident unconnected with use and disuse. The word " accident " is never used, but Mr. Wallace must be credited with this instance of a desire to give his readers a chance of perceiving that according to his distinctive feature evolution is an affair of luck, rather than of cunning. Whether his readers actually did understand this as clearly as Mr. Wallace doubtless desired that they should, and whether greater development at this point would not have helped them to fuller apprehension, we need not now inquire. What was gained in distinctness might have been lost in distinctiveness, and after all he did technically put us upon our guard.

Nevertheless, he too at a pinch takes refuge in Lamarckism. In relation to the manner in which the eyes of soles, turbots, and other flat-fish travel round the head so as to become in the end unsymmetrically placed, he says :—

" The eyes of these fish are curiously distorted in order that both eyes may be upon the upper side, where alone they would be of any use. . . . Now if we suppose this process, which in the young is completed in a few days or weeks, to have been spread over thousands of generations during the development of these fish,

---

[1] *Journals of the Proceedings of the Linnean Society* (*Zoology*, vol. iii.), 1859, p. 62.

those usually surviving *whose eyes retained more and more of the position into which the young fish tried to twist them* [italics mine], the change becomes intelligible." [1] When it was said by Professor Ray Lankester—who knows as well as most people what Lamarck taught—that this was " flat Lamarckism," Mr. Wallace rejoined that it was the survival of the modified individuals that did it all, not the efforts of the young fish to twist their eyes, and the transmission to descendants of the effects of those efforts. But this, as I said in my book *Evolution, Old and New*, is like saying that horses are swift runners, not by reason of the causes, whatever they were, that occasioned the direct line of their progenitors to vary towards ever greater and greater swiftness, but because their more slow-going uncles and aunts go away. Plain people will prefer to say that the main cause of any accumulation of favourable modifications consists rather in that which brings about the initial variations, and in the fact that these can be inherited at all, than in the fact that the unmodified individuals were not successful. People do not become rich because the poor in large numbers go away, but because they have been lucky, or provident, or more commonly both. If they would keep their wealth when they have made it they must exclude luck thenceforth to the utmost of their power and their children must follow their example, or they will soon lose their money. The fact that the weaker go to the wall does not bring about the greater strength of the stronger ; it is the consequence of this last and not the cause—unless, indeed, it be contended that a knowledge that the weak go to the wall stimulates the strong to exertions which they would not otherwise so

[1] *Darwinism* (Macmillan, 1889), p. 129.

make, and that these exertions produce inheritable modifications. Even in this case, however, it would be the exertions, or use and disuse, that would be the main agents in the modification. But it is not often that Mr. Wallace thus backslides. His present position is that acquired (as distinguished from congenital) modifications are not inherited at all. He does not indeed put his faith prominently forward and pin himself to it as plainly as could be wished, but under the heading " The Non-Heredity of Acquired Characters," he writes as follows on p. 440 of his recent work in reference to Professor Weismann's Theory of Heredity :—

" Certain observations on the embryology of the lower animals are held to afford direct proof of this theory of heredity, but they are too technical to be made clear to ordinary readers. A logical result of the theory is the impossibility of the transmission of acquired characters, since the molecular structure of the germ-plasm is already determined within the embryo ; and Weismann holds that there are no facts which really prove that acquired characters can be inherited, although their inheritance has, by most writers, been considered so probable as hardly to stand in need of direct proof.

" We have already seen in the earlier part of this chapter that many instances of change, imputed to the inheritance of acquired variations, are really cases of selection."

And the rest of the remarks tend to convey the impression that Mr. Wallace adopts Professor Weismann's view, but, curiously enough, though I have gone through Mr. Wallace's book with a special view to this particular point, I have not been able to find him definitely committing himself either to the assertion that acquired modifications never are inherited, or that they sometimes are so. It is abundantly laid down that Mr. Darwin laid too much stress on use and disuse, and a residuary impression is left that Mr. Wallace is endorsing Professor Weismann's view, but I have found it impossible to collect anything that enables me to define his position confidently in this respect.

This is natural enough, for Mr. Wallace has entitled his book *Darwinism*, and a work denying that use and disuse produced any effect could not conceivably be called Darwinism. Mr. Herbert Spencer has recently collected many passages from *The Origin of Species* and from *Animals and Plants under Domestication*,"[1] which show how largely, after all, use and disuse entered into Mr. Darwin's system, and we know that in his later years he attached still more importance to them. It was out of the question, therefore, that Mr. Wallace should categorically deny that their effects were inheritable. On the other hand, the temptation to adopt Professor Weismann's view must have been overwhelming to one who had been already inclined to minimize the effects of use and disuse. On the whole, one does not see what Mr. Wallace could do, other than what he has done—unless, of course, he changed his title, or had been no longer Mr. Wallace.

Besides, thanks to the works of Mr. Spencer, Professor Mivart, Professor Semper, and very many others, there has for some time been a growing perception that the Darwinism of Charles Darwin was doomed. Use and disuse must either do even more than is officially recognized in Mr. Darwin's later concessions,

---

[1] See *Nature*, March 6, 1890.

or they must do a great deal less. If they can do as
much as Mr. Darwin himself said they did, why should
they not do more ? Why stop where Mr. Darwin did ?
And again, where in the name of all that is reasonable
did he really stop ? He drew no line, and on what
principle can we say that so much is possible as effect
of use and disuse, but so much more impossible ? If,
as Mr. Darwin contended, disuse can so far reduce an
organ as to render it rudimentary, and in many cases get
rid of it altogether, why cannot use create as much as
disuse can destroy, provided it has anything, no matter
how low in structure, to begin with ? Let us know
where we stand. If it is admitted that use and disuse
can do a good deal, what does a good deal mean ?
And what is the proportion between the shares attributable to use and disuse and to natural selection respectively ? If we cannot be told with absolute precision,
let us at any rate have something more definite than
the statement that natural selection is "the most
important means of modification."

Mr. Darwin gave us no help in this respect ; and
worse than this, he contradicted himself so flatly as to
show that he had very little definite idea upon the
subject at all. Thus in respect to the winglessness of
the Madeira beetles he wrote :—

"In some cases we might easily put down to disuse
modifications of structure, which are wholly or mainly
due to natural selection. Mr. Wollaston has discovered
the remarkable fact that 200 beetles, out of the 550
species (but more are now known) inhabiting Madeira,
are so far deficient in wings that they cannot fly ; and
that of the 29 endemic genera no less than 23 have all
their species in this condition ! Several facts—namely,
that beetles in many parts of the world are frequently

blown out to sea and perish ; that the beetles in Madeira, as observed by Mr. Wollaston, lie much concealed until the wind lulls and the sun shines ; that the proportion of wingless beetles is larger on the exposed Desertas than in Madeira itself ; and especially the extraordinary fact, so strongly insisted on by Mr. Wollaston, that certain large groups of beetles, elsewhere excessively numerous, which absolutely require the use of their wings are here almost entirely absent ; —these several considerations make me believe that the wingless condition of so many Madeira beetles is mainly due to the action of natural selection, *combined probably with disuse* [italics mine]. For during many successive generations each individual beetle which flew least, either from its wings having been ever so little less perfectly developed or from indolent habit, will have had the best chance of surviving, from not being blown out to sea ; and, on the other hand, those beetles which most readily took to flight would oftenest have been blown to sea, and thus destroyed."[1]

We should like to know, first, somewhere about how much disuse was able to do after all, and moreover why, if it can do anything at all, it should not be able to do all. Mr. Darwin says : "Any change in structure and function which can be effected by small stages is within the power of natural selection." "And why not," we ask, "within the power of use and disuse ? " Moreover, on a later page we find Mr. Darwin saying :—

"*It appears probable that disuse has been the main agent in rendering organs rudimentary* [italics mine]. It would at first lead by slow steps to the more and more complete reduction of a part, until at last it has

[1] *Origin of Species*, sixth edition, 1888, vol. i. p. 168.

become rudimentary—as in the case of the eyes of animals inhabiting dark caverns, and of the wings of birds inhabiting oceanic islands, which have seldom been forced by beasts of prey to take flight, and have ultimately lost the power of flying. Again, an organ, useful under certain conditions, might become injurious under others, *as with the wings of beetles living on small and exposed islands ;* and in this case natural selection will have aided in reducing the organ, until it was rendered harmless and rudimentary [italics mine]."[1]

So that just as an undefined amount of use and disuse was introduced on the earlier page to supplement the effects of natural selection in respect of the wings of beetles on small and exposed islands, we have here an undefined amount of natural selection introduced to supplement the effects of use and disuse in respect of the identical phenomena. In the one passage we find that natural selection has been the main agent in reducing the wings, though use and disuse have had an appreciable share in the result ; in the other, it is use and disuse that have been the main agents, though an appreciable share in the result must be ascribed to natural selection.

Besides, who has seen the uncles and aunts going away with the uniformity that is necessary for Mr. Darwin's contention ? We know that birds and insects do often get blown out to sea and perish, but in order to establish Mr. Darwin's position we want the evidence of those who watched the reduction of the wings during the many generations in the course of which it was being effected, and who can testify that all, or the overwhelming majority, of the beetles born with fairly well-developed wings got blown out

---

[1] *Origin of Species*, sixth edition, 1888, vol. ii. p. 261.

to sea, while those alone survived whose wings were congenitally degenerate. Who saw them go, or can point to analogous cases so conclusive as to compel assent from any equitable thinker ?

Darwinians of the stamp of Mr. Thiselton Dyer, Professor Ray Lankester, or Mr. Romanes, insist on their pound of flesh in the matter of irrefragable demonstration. They complain of us for not bringing forward someone who has been able to detect the movement of the hour-hand of a watch during a second of time, and when we fail to do so, declare triumphantly that we have no evidence that there is any connection between the beating of a second and the movement of the hour-hand. When we say that rain comes from the condensation of moisture in the atmosphere, they demand of us a rain-drop from moisture not yet condensed. If they stickle for proof and cavil on the ninth part of a hair, as they do when we bring forward what we deem excellent instances of the transmission of an acquired characteristic, why may not we, too, demand at any rate some evidence that the unmodified beetles actually did always, or nearly always, get blown out to sea, during the reduction above referred to, and that it is to this fact, and not to the masterly inactivity of their fathers and mothers, that the Madeira beetles owe their winglessness ? If we begin stickling for proof in this way, our opponents would not be long in letting us know that absolute proof is unattainable on any subject, that reasonable presumption is our highest certainty, and that crying out for too much evidence is as bad as accepting too little. Truth is like a photographic sensitized plate, which is equally ruined by over and by under exposure, and the just exposure for which can never be absolutely determined.

Surely if disuse can be credited with the vast powers involved in Mr. Darwin's statement that it has probably " been the main agent in rendering organs rudimentary," no limits are assignable to the accumulated effects of habit, provided the effects of habit, or use and disuse, are supposed, as Mr. Darwin supposed them, to be inheritable at all. Darwinians have at length woke up to the dilemma in which they are placed by the manner in which Mr. Darwin tried to sit on the two stools of use and disuse, and natural selection of accidental variations, at the same time. The knell of Charles-Darwinism is rung in Mr. Wallace's present book, and in the general perception on the part of biologists that we must either assign to use and disuse such a predominant share in modification as to make it the feature most proper to be insisted on, or deny that the modifications, whether of mind or body, acquired during a single lifetime, are ever transmitted at all. If they can be inherited at all, they can be accumulated. If they can be accumulated at all, they can be so, for anything that appears to the contrary, to the extent of the specific and generic differences with which we are surrounded. The only thing to do is to pluck them out root and branch : they are as a cancer which, if the smallest fibre be left unexcised, will grow again, and kill any system on to which it is allowed to fasten. Mr. Wallace, therefore, may well be excused if he casts longing eyes towards Weismannism.

And what was Mr. Darwin's system ? Who can make head or tail of the inextricable muddle in which he left it ? The *Origin of Species* in its latest shape is the reduction of hedging to an absurdity. How did Mr. Darwin himself leave it in the last chapter of the last edition of the *Origin of Species* ? He wrote :—

" I have now recapitulated the facts and considerations which have thoroughly convinced me that species have been modified during a long course of descent. This has been effected chiefly through the natural selection of numerous, successive, slight, favourable variations ; aided in an important manner by the inherited effects of the use and disuse of parts, and in an unimportant manner—that is, in relation to adaptive structures whether past or present—by the direct action of external conditions, and by variations which seem to us in our ignorance to arise spontaneously. It appears that I formerly underrated the frequency and value of these latter forms of variation, as leading to permanent modifications of structure independently of natural selection."

The " numerous, successive, slight, favourable variations " above referred to are intended to be fortuitous, accidental, spontaneous. It is the essence of Mr. Darwin's theory that this should be so. Mr. Darwin's solemn statement, therefore, of his theory, after he had done his best or his worst with it, is, when stripped of surplusage, as follows :—

" The modification of species has been mainly effected by accumulation of spontaneous variations ; it has been aided in an important manner by accumulation of variations due to use and disuse, and in an unimportant manner by spontaneous variations ; I do not even now think that spontaneous variations have been very important, but I used once to think them less important than I do now."

It is a discouraging symptom of the age that such a system should have been so long belauded, and it is a sign of returning intelligence that even he who has been more especially the *alter ego* of Mr. Darwin should have felt constrained to close the chapter of Charles-Darwinism as a living theory, and relegate it to the important but not very creditable place in history which it must henceforth occupy. It is astonishing, however, that Mr. Wallace should have quoted the extract from the *Origin of Species* just given, as he has done on p. 412 of his *Darwinism*, without betraying any sign that he has caught its driftlessness—for drift, other than a desire to hedge, it assuredly has not got. The battle now turns on the question whether modifications of either structure or instinct due to use or disuse are ever inherited, or whether they are not. Can the effects of habit be transmitted to progeny at all ? We know that more usually they are not transmitted to any perceptible extent, but we believe also that occasionally, and indeed not infrequently, they are inherited and even intensified. What are our grounds for this opinion ? It will be my object to put these forward in the following number of the *Universal Review*.

The
Deadlock in Darwinism[1]

Part II

AT the close of my article in last month's number
of the *Universal Review*, I said I would in this
month's issue show why the opponents of Charles-
Darwinism believe the effects of habits acquired
during the lifetime of a parent to produce an effect
on their subsequent offspring, in spite of the fact that
we can rarely find the effect in any one generation, or
even in several, sufficiently marked to arrest our
attention.

I will now show that offspring can be, and not very
infrequently is, affected by occurrences that have

[1] Mr. J. T. Cunningham, of the Marine Biological Laboratory,
Plymouth, has called my attention to the fact that I have ascribed to
Professor Ray Lankester a criticism on Mr. Wallace's remarks upon the
eyes of certain flat-fish, which Professor Ray Lankester was, in reality,
only adopting—with full acknowledgment—from Mr. Cunningham. Mr.
Cunningham has left it to me whether to correct my omission publicly
or not, but he would so plainly prefer my doing so that I consider myself
bound to insert this note. Curiously enough, I find that in my book
Evolution, Old and New I gave what Lamarck actually said upon the eyes
of flat-fish, and, having been led to return to the subject, I may as well
quote his words. He wrote :—

" Need—always occasioned by the circumstances in which an animal is
placed, and followed by sustained efforts at gratification—can not only
modify an organ—that is to say, augment or reduce it—but can change its
position when the case requires its removal.

" Ocean fishes have occasion to see what is on either side of them, and
have their eyes accordingly placed on either side of their head. Some

produced a deep impression on the parent organism—
the effect produced on the offspring being such as
leaves no doubt that it is to be connected with the
impression produced on the parent.   Having thus
established the general proposition, I will proceed to
the more particular one—that habits, involving use
and disuse of special organs, with the modifications of
structure thereby engendered, produce also an effect
upon offspring, which, though seldom perceptible
as regards structure in a single, or even in
several generations, is nevertheless capable of being
accumulated in successive generations till it amounts
to specific and generic difference.   I have found the
first point as much as I can treat within the limits of
this present article, and will avail myself of the hospitality of the *Universal Review* next month to deal with
the second.

The proposition which I have to defend is one which
no one till recently would have questioned, and even
now those who look most askance at it do not venture
to dispute it unreservedly ; they every now and then
admit it as conceivable, and even in some cases
probable ;   nevertheless they seek to minimize it,
and to make out that there is little or no connection
between the great mass of the cells of which the body

fishes, however, have their abode near coasts on submarine banks and
inclinations, and are thus forced to flatten themselves as much as possible
in order to get as near as they can to the shore.   In this situation they
receive more light from above than from below, and find it necessary to pay
attention to whatever happens to be above them ; this need has involved
the displacement of their eyes, which now take the remarkable position
which we observe in the case of soles, turbots, plaice, etc.   The transfer
of position is not even yet complete in the case of these fishes, and the eyes
are not, therefore, symmetrically placed ; but they are so with the skate,
whose head and whole body are equally disposed on either side a longi-
tudinal section.   Hence the eyes of this fish are placed symmetrically upon
the uppermost side."—*Philosophie Zoologique*, tom. i. pp. 250, 251.
Edition C. Martins.   Paris, 1873.

is composed, and those cells that are alone capable of reproducing the entire organism. The tendency is to assign to these last a life of their own, apart from, and unconnected with that of the other cells of the body, and to cheapen all evidence that tends to prove any response on their part to the past history of the individual, and hence ultimately of the race.

Professor Weismann is the foremost exponent of those who take this line. He has naturally been welcomed by English Charles-Darwinians ; for if his view can be sustained, then it can be contended that use and disuse produce no transmissible effect, and the ground is cut from under Lamarck's feet ; if, on the other hand, his view is unfounded, the Lamarckian reaction, already strong, will gain still further strength. The issue, therefore, is important, and is being fiercely contested by those who have invested their all of reputation for discernment in Charles-Darwinian securities.

Professor Weismann's theory is, that at every new birth a part of the substance which proceeds from parents and which goes to form the new embryo is not used up in forming the new animal, but remains apart to generate the germ-cells—or perhaps I should say " germ-plasm "—which the new animal itself will in due course issue.

Contrasting the generally received view with his own, Professor Weismann says that according to the first of these " the organism produces germ-cells afresh again and again, and that it produces them entirely from its own substance." While by the second " the germ-cells are no longer looked upon as the product of the parent's body, at least as far as their essential part —the specific germ-plasm—is concerned ; they are rather considered as something which is to be placed in

s

contrast with the *tout ensemble* of the cells which make up the parent's body, and the germ-cells of succeeding generations stand in a similar relation to one another as a series of generations of unicellular organisms arising by a continued process of cell-division."[1]

On another page he writes :—

"I believe that heredity depends upon the fact that a small portion of the effective substance of the germ, the germ-plasm, remains unchanged during the development of the ovum into an organism, and that this part of the germ-plasm serves as a foundation from which the germ-cells of the new organism are produced. There is, therefore, continuity of the germ-plasm from one generation to another. One might represent the germ-plasm by the metaphor of a long creeping root-stock from which plants arise at intervals, these latter representing the individuals of successive generations."[2]

Mr. Wallace, who does not appear to have read Professor Weismann's essays themselves, but whose remarks are, no doubt, ultimately derived from the sequel to the passage just quoted from page 266 of Professor Weismann's book, contends that the impossibility of the transmission of acquired characters follows as a logical result from Professor Weismann's theory, inasmuch as the molecular structure of the germ-plasm that will go to form any succeeding generation is already predetermined within the still unformed embryo of its predecessor ; "and Weismann," continues Mr. Wallace, "holds that there are no facts which really prove that acquired characters can be inherited, although their inheritance has, by most

[1] *Essays on Heredity*, etc., Oxford, 1889, p. 171.
[2] *Ibid.*, p. 266.

writers, been considered so probable as hardly to stand in need of direct proof."[1]

Professor Weismann, in passages too numerous to quote, shows that he recognizes this necessity, and acknowledges that the non-transmission of acquired characters "forms the foundation of the views" set forth in his book, p. 291.

Professor Ray Lankester does not commit himself absolutely to this view, but lends it support by saying (*Nature*, December 12, 1889) : "It is hardly necessary to say that it has never yet been shown experimentally that *anything* acquired by one generation is transmitted to the next (putting aside diseases)."

Mr. Romanes, writing in *Nature*, March 13, 1890, and opposing certain details of Professor Weismann's theory, so far supports it as to say that "there is the gravest possible doubt lying against the supposition that any really inherited decrease is due to the inherited effects of disuse." The "gravest possible doubt" should mean that Mr. Romanes regards it as a moral certainty that disuse has no transmitted effect in reducing an organ, and it should follow that he holds use to have no transmitted effect in its development. The sequel, however, makes me uncertain how far Mr. Romanes intends this, and I would refer the reader to the article which Mr. Romanes has just published on Weismann in the *Contemporary Review* for this current month.

The burden of Mr. Thiselton Dyer's controversy with the Duke of Argyll (see *Nature*, January 16, 1890, *et seq.*) was that there was no evidence in support of the transmission of any acquired modification. The orthodoxy of science, therefore, must be held as giving

[1] *Darwinism*, 1889, p. 440.

at any rate a provisional support to Professor Weismann, but all of them, including even Professor Weismann himself, shrink from committing themselves to the opinion that the germ-cells of any organisms remain in all cases unaffected by the events that occur to the other cells of the same organism, and until they do this they have knocked the bottom out of their case.

From among the passages in which Professor Weismann himself shows a desire to hedge I may take the following from page 170 of his book :—

" I am also far from asserting that the germ-plasm which, as I hold, is transmitted as the basis of heredity from one generation to another, is absolutely unchangeable or totally uninfluenced by forces residing in the organism within which it is transformed into germ-cells. I am also compelled to admit it as conceivable that organisms may exert a modifying influence upon their germ-cells, and even that such a process is to a certain extent inevitable. The nutrition and growth of the individual must exercise some influence upon its germ-cells . . ."

Professor Weismann does indeed go on to say that this influence must be extremely slight, but we do not care how slight the changes produced may be, provided they exist and can be transmitted. On an earlier page (p. 101) he said in regard to variations generally that we should not expect to find them conspicuous ; their frequency would be enough, if they could be accumulated. The same applies here, if stirring events that occur to the somatic cells can produce any effect at all on offspring. A very small effect, provided it can be repeated and accumulated in successive generations, is all that even the most exacting Lamarckian will ask for.

Having now made the reader acquainted with the position taken by the leading Charles-Darwinian authorities, I will return to Professor Weismann himself, who declares that the transmission of acquired characters " at first sight certainly seems necessary," and that " it appears rash to attempt to dispense with its aid." He continues :—

" Many phenomena only appear to be intelligible if we assume the hereditary transmission of such acquired characters as the changes which we ascribe to the use or disuse of particular organs, or to the direct influence of climate. Furthermore, how can we explain instinct as hereditary habit, unless it has gradually arisen by the accumulation, through heredity, of habits which were practised in succeeding generations ? "[1]

I may say in passing that Professor Weismann appears to suppose that the view of instinct just given is part of the Charles-Darwinian system, for on page 389 of his book he says " that many observers had followed Darwin in explaining them [instincts] as inherited habits." This was not Mr. Darwin's own view of the matter. He wrote :—

" If we suppose any habitual action to become in-herited—and I think it can be shown that this does sometimes happen—then the resemblance between what originally was a habit and an instinct becomes so close as not to be distinguished. . . . But it would be the most serious error to suppose that the greater number of instincts have been acquired by habit in one generation, and then transmitted by inheritance to succeeding generations. It can be clearly shown that the most wonderful instincts with which we are

[1] Page 83.

acquainted, namely, those of the hive-bee and of many ants, could not possibly have been thus acquired."—[*Origin of Species*, ed. 1859, p. 209.]

Again we read : " Domestic instincts are sometimes spoken of as actions which have become inherited solely from long-continued and compulsory habit, but this, I think, is not true."—*Ibid.*, p. 214.

Again : " I am surprised that no one has advanced this demonstrative case of neuter insects, against the well-known doctrine of inherited habit, as advanced by Lamarck."—[*Origin of Species*, ed. 1872, p. 233.]

I am not aware that Lamarck advanced the doctrine that instinct is inherited habit, but he may have done so in some work that I have not seen.

It is true, as I have more than once pointed out, that in the later editions of the *Origin of Species* it is no longer " the *most* serious " error to refer instincts generally to inherited habit, but it still remains " a serious error," and this slight relaxation of severity does not warrant Professor Weismann in ascribing to Mr. Darwin an opinion which he emphatically condemned. His tone, however, is so off-hand, that those who have little acquaintance with the literature of evolution would hardly guess that he is not much better informed on this subject than themselves.

Returning to the inheritance of acquired characters, Professor Weismann says that this has never been proved either by means of direct observation or by experiment. " It must be admitted," he writes, " that there are in existence numerous descriptions of cases which tend to prove that such mutilations as the loss of fingers, the scars of wounds, etc., are inherited by the offspring, but in these descriptions the previous history is invariably obscure, and hence the evidence loses all scientific value."

The experiments of M. Brown-Séquard throw so much light upon the question at issue that I will quote at some length from the summary given by Mr. Darwin in his *Variation of Animals and Plants under Domestication*."[1] Mr. Darwin writes :—

" With respect to the inheritance of structures mutilated by injuries or altered by disease, it was until lately difficult to come to any definite conclusion." [Then follow several cases in which mutilations practised for many generations are not found to be transmitted.] " Notwithstanding," continues Mr. Darwin, " the above several negative cases, we now possess conclusive evidence that the effects of operations are sometimes inherited.   Dr. Brown-Séquard gives the following summary of his observations on guinea-pigs, and this summary is so important that I will quote the whole :—

" ' 1st. Appearance of epilepsy in animals born of parents having been rendered epileptic by an injury to the spinal cord.

" ' 2nd. Appearance of epilepsy also in animals born of parents having been rendered epileptic by the section of the sciatic nerve.

" ' 3rd. A change in the shape of the ear in animals born of parents in which such a change was the effect of a division of the cervical sympathetic nerve.

" ' 4th. Partial closure of the eyelids in animals born of parents in which that state of the eyelids had been caused either by the section of the cervical sympathetic nerve or the removal of the superior cervical ganglion.

[1] Vol. i. p. 466, etc.   Ed. 1885.

" ' 5th. Exophthalmia in animals born of parents in which an injury to the restiform body had produced that protrusion of the eyeball. This interesting fact I have witnessed a good many times, and I have seen the transmission of the morbid state of the eye continue through four generations. In these animals modified by heredity, the two eyes generally protruded, although in the parents usually only one showed exophthalmia, the lesion having been made in most cases only on one of the corpora restiformia.

" ' 6th. Hæmatoma and dry gangrene of the ears in animals born of parents in which these ear-alterations had been caused by an injury to the restiform body near the nib of the calamus.

" ' 7th. Absence of two toes out of the three of the hind leg, and sometimes of the three, in animals whose parents had eaten up their hind-leg toes which had become anæsthetic from a section of the sciatic nerve alone, or of that nerve and also of the crural. Sometimes, instead of complete absence of the toes, only a part of one or two or three was missing in the young, although in the parent not only the toes but the whole foot was absent (partly eaten off, partly destroyed by inflammation, ulceration, or gangrene).

" ' 8th. Appearance of various morbid states of the skin and hair of the neck and face in animals born of parents having had similar alterations in the same parts, as effects of an injury to the sciatic nerve.'

" It should be especially observed that Brown-Séquard had bred during thirty years many thousand guinea-pigs from animals which had not been operated upon, and not one of these manifested the epileptic tendency. Nor has he ever seen a guinea-pig born without toes, which was not the offspring of parents which had gnawed off their own toes owing to the sciatic nerve having been divided. Of this latter fact thirteen instances were carefully recorded, and a greater number were seen ; yet Brown-Séquard speaks of such cases as one of the rarer forms of inheritance. It is a still more interesting fact, ' that the sciatic nerve in the congenitally toeless animal has inherited the power of passing through all the different morbid states which have occurred in one of its parents from the time of the division till after its reunion with the peripheric end. It is not, therefore, simply the power of performing an action which is inherited, but the power of performing a whole series of actions, in a certain order.'

" In most of the cases of inheritance recorded by Brown-Séquard only one of the two parents had been operated upon and was affected. He concludes by expressing his belief that ' what is transmitted is the morbid state of the nervous system,' due to the operation performed on the parents."

Mr. Darwin proceeds to give other instances of inherited effects of mutilations :—

" With the horse there seems hardly a doubt that exostoses on the legs, caused by too much travelling on hard roads, are inherited. Blumenbach records the case of a man who had his little finger on the right hand almost cut off, and which in consequence grew crooked, and his sons had the same finger on the same hand similarly crooked. A soldier, fifteen years before his marriage, lost his left eye from purulent ophthalmia, and his two sons were microphthalmic on the same side."

The late Professor Rolleston, whose competence as an observer no one is likely to dispute, gave Mr. Darwin two cases as having fallen under his own notice, one of a man whose knee had been severely wounded, and whose child was born with the same spot marked or scarred, and the other of one who was severely cut upon the cheek, and whose child was born scarred in the same place.   Mr. Darwin's conclusion was that "the effects of injuries, especially when followed by disease, or perhaps exclusively when thus followed, are occasionally inherited."

Let us now see what Professor Weismann has to say against this.   He writes :—

" The only cases worthy of discussion are the well-known experiments upon guinea-pigs conducted by the French physiologist, Brown-Séquard.   But the explanation of his results is, in my opinion, open to discussion.   In these cases we have to do with the apparent transmission of artificially produced malformations. . . .   All these effects were said to be transmitted to descendants as far as the fifth or sixth generation.

" But we must inquire whether these cases are really due to heredity, and not to simple infection.   In the case of epilepsy, at any rate, it is easy to imagine that the passage of some specific organism through the reproductive cells may take place, as in the case of syphilis.   We are, however, entirely ignorant of the nature of the former disease.   This suggested explanation may not perhaps apply to the other cases ; but we must remember that animals which have been subjected to such severe operations upon the nervous system have sustained a great shock, and if they are capable of breeding, it is only probable that they will produce weak descendants, and such as are easily affected by disease.   Such a result does not, however, explain why the offspring should suffer from the same disease as that which was artificially induced in the parents. But this does not appear to have been by any means invariably the case. Brown-Séquard himself says : 'The changes in the eye of the offspring were of a very variable nature, and were only occasionally exactly similar to those observed in the parents.'

" There is no doubt, however, that these experiments demand careful consideration, but before they can claim scientific recognition, they must be subjected to rigid criticism as to the precautions taken, the nature and number of the control experiments, etc.

" Up to the present time such necessary conditions have not been sufficiently observed. The recent experiments themselves are only described in short preliminary notices, which, as regards their accuracy, the possibility of mistake, the precautions taken, and the exact succession of individuals affected, afford no data on which a scientific opinion can be founded " (pp. 81, 82).

The line Professor Weismann takes, therefore, is to discredit the facts ; yet on a later page we find that the experiments have since been repeated by Obersteiner, " who has described them in a very exact and unprejudiced manner," and that " the fact "—(I imagine that Professor Weismann intends " the facts ")— " cannot be doubted."

On a still later page, however, we read :—

" If, for instance, it could be shown that artificial mutilation spontaneously reappears in the offspring with sufficient frequency to exclude all possibilities of chance, then such proof [i.e. that acquired characters can be transmitted] would be forthcoming. The transmission of mutilations has been frequently asserted, and has been even recently again brought forward, but all the supposed instances have broken down when carefully examined " (p. 390).

Here, then, we are told that proof of the occasional transmission of mutilations would be sufficient to establish the fact, but on p. 267 we find that no single fact is known which really proves that acquired characters can be transmitted, "*for the ascertained facts which seem to point to the transmission of artificially produced diseases cannot be considered as proof.*" [Italics mine.] Perhaps ; but it was mutilation in many cases that Professor Weismann practically admitted to have been transmitted when he declared that Obersteiner had verified Brown-Séquard's experiments.

That Professor Weismann recognizes the vital importance to his own theory of the question whether or no mutilations can be transmitted under any circumstances, is evident from a passage on p. 425 of his work, on which he says : " It can hardly be doubted that mutilations are acquired characters ; they do not arise from any tendency contained in the germ, but are merely the reaction of the body under certain external influences. They are, as I have recently expressed it, purely somatogenic characters—viz. characters which emanate from the body (*soma*) only, as opposed to the germ-cells ; they are, therefore, characters that do not arise from the germ itself.

" If mutilations must necessarily be transmitted " [which no one that I know of has maintained], " or even if they might occasionally be transmitted " [which cannot, I imagine, be reasonably questioned], " a powerful support would be given to the Lamarckian principle, and the transmission of functional hyper-

trophy or atrophy would thus become highly probable."

I have not found any further attempt in Professor
Weismann's book to deal with the evidence adduced by
Mr. Darwin to show that mutilations, if followed by
diseases, are sometimes inherited ; and I must leave
it to the reader to determine how far Professor Weismann has shown reason for rejecting Mr. Darwin's
conclusion. I do not, however, dwell upon these facts
now as evidence of a transmitted change of bodily
form, or of instinct due to use and disuse or habit ;
what they prove is that the germ-cells within the
parent's body do not stand apart from the other cells
of the body so completely as Professor Weismann
would have us believe, but that, as Professor Hering,
of Prague, has aptly said, they echo with more or less
frequency and force to the profounder impressions
made upon other cells.

I may say that Professor Weismann does not more
cavalierly wave aside the mass of evidence collected by
Mr. Darwin and a host of other writers, to the effect
that mutilations are sometimes inherited, than does
Mr. Wallace, who says that, " as regards mutilations,
it is generally admitted that they are not inherited, and
there is ample evidence on this point." It is indeed
generally admitted that mutilations, when not followed by disease, are very rarely, if ever, inherited ;
and Mr. Wallace's appeal to the " ample evidence "
which he alleges to exist on this head, is much as though
he should say that there is ample evidence to show
that the days are longer in summer than in winter.
" Nevertheless," he continues, " a few cases of apparent
inheritance of mutilations have been recorded, and
these, if trustworthy, are difficulties in the way of

the theory." . . . " The often-quoted case of a disease induced by mutilation being inherited (Brown-Séquard's epileptic guinea-pigs) has been discussed by Professor Weismann and shown to be not conclusive. The mutilation itself—a section of certain nerves—was never inherited, but the resulting epilepsy, or a general state of weakness, deformity, or sores, was sometimes inherited. It is, however, possible that the mere injury introduced and encouraged the growth of certain microbes, which, spreading through the organism, sometimes reached the germ-cells, and thus transmitted a diseased condition to the offspring."[1]

I suppose a microbe which made guinea-pigs eat their toes off was communicated to the germ-cells of an unfortunate guinea-pig which had been already microbed by it, and made the offspring bite its toes off too.   The microbe has a good deal to answer for.

On the case of the deterioration of horses in the Falkland Islands after a few generations, Professor Weismann says :—

" In such a case we have only to assume that the climate which is unfavourable, and nutriment which is insufficient for horses, affect not only the animal as a whole but also its germ-cells. This would result in the diminution in size of the germ-cells, the effects upon the offspring being still further intensified by the insufficient nourishment supplied during growth. But such results would not depend upon the transmission by the germ-cells of certain peculiarities due to the unfavourable climate, which only appear in the full-grown horse."

But Professor Weismann does not like such cases,

[1] *Darwinism*, p. 440.

and admits that he cannot explain the facts in connection with the climatic varieties of certain butterflies, except "by supposing the passive acquisition of characters produced by the direct influence of climate."

Nevertheless, in his next paragraph but one he calls such cases "doubtful," and proposes that for the moment they should be left aside. He accordingly leaves them, but I have not yet found what other moment he considered auspicious for returning to them. He tells us that "new experiments will be necessary, and that he has himself already begun to undertake them." Perhaps he will give us the results of these experiments in some future book—for that they will prove satisfactory to him can hardly, I think, be doubted. He writes :—

"Leaving on one side, for the moment, these doubtful and insufficiently investigated cases, we may still maintain that the assumption that changes induced by external conditions in the organism as a whole are communicated to the germ-cells after the manner indicated in Darwin's hypothesis of pangenesis, is wholly unnecessary for the explanation of these phenomena. Still we cannot exclude the possibility of such a transmission occasionally occurring, for even if the greater part of the effects must be attributable to natural selection, there might be a smaller part in certain cases which depends on this exceptional factor."

I repeatedly tried to understand Mr. Darwin's theory of pangenesis, and so often failed that I long since gave the matter up in despair. I did so with the less unwillingness because I saw that no one else appeared to understand the theory, and that even Mr. Darwin's warmest adherents regarded it with disfavour. If Mr.

Darwin means that every cell of the body throws off
minute particles that find their way to the germ-cells,
and hence into the new embryo, this is indeed difficult of
comprehension and belief. If he means that the
rhythms or vibrations that go on ceaselessly in every
cell of the body communicate themselves with greater
or less accuracy or perturbation, as the case may be,
to the cells that go to form offspring, and that since
the characteristics of matter are determined by
vibrations, in communicating vibrations they in effect
communicate matter, according to the view put forward
in the last chapter of my book *Luck or Cunning*, then
we can better understand it. I have nothing, however,
to do with Mr. Darwin's theory of pangenesis beyond
avoiding the pretence that I understand either the
theory itself or what Professor Weismann says about
it ; all I am concerned with is Professor Weismann's
admission, made immediately afterwards, that the
somatic cells may, and perhaps sometimes do, impart
characteristics to the germ-cells.

"A complete and satisfactory refutation of such
an opinion," he continues, "cannot be brought
forward at present "; so I suppose we must wait a
little longer, but in the meantime we may again
remark that, if we admit even occasional communication of changes in the somatic cells to the germ-cells,
we have let in the thin end of the wedge, as Mr. Darwin
did when he said that use and disuse did a good deal
towards modification. Buffon, in his first volume on
the lower animals,[1] dwells on the impossibility of
stopping the breach once made by admission of variation at all. "If the point," he writes, "were once
gained, that among animals and vegetables there had

[1] Tom. iv. p. 383.   Ed. 1753.

been, I do not say several species, but even a single one, which had been produced in the course of direct descent from another species ; if, for example, it could be once shown that the ass was but a degeneration from the horse—then there is no farther limit to be set to the power of Nature, and we should not be wrong in supposing that with sufficient time she could have evolved all other organized forms from one primordial type." So with use and disuse and transmission of acquired characteristics generally—once show that a single structure or instinct is due to habit in preceding generations, and we can impose no limit on the results achievable by accumulation in this respect, nor shall we be wrong in conceiving it as possible that all specialization, whether of structure or instinct, may be due ultimately to habit.

How far this can be shown to be probable is, of course, another matter, but I am not immediately concerned with this ; all I am concerned with now is to show that the germ-cells not unfrequently become permanently affected by events that have made a profound impression upon the somatic cells, in so far that they transmit an obvious reminiscence of the impression to the embryos which they go subsequently towards forming. This is all that is necessary for my case, and I do not find that Professor Weismann, after all, disputes it.

But here, again, comes the difficulty of saying what Professor Weismann does, and what he does not, dispute. One moment he gives all that is wanted for the Lamarckian contention, the next he denies common sense the bare necessaries of life. For a more exhaustive and detailed criticism of Professor Weismann's position, I would refer the reader to an admirably clear

T

article by Mr. Sidney H. Vines, which appeared in *Nature*, October 24, 1889. I can only say that while reading Professor Weismann's book, I feel as I do when I read those of Mr. Darwin, and of a good many other writers on biology whom I need not name. I become like a fly in a window-pane. I see the sunshine and freedom beyond, and buzz up and down their pages, ever hopeful to get through them to the fresh air without, but ever kept back by a mysterious something, which I feel but cannot either grasp or see. It was not thus when I read Buffon, Erasmus Darwin, and Lamarck ; it is not thus when I read such articles as Mr. Vines's just referred to. Love of self-display, and the want of singleness of mind that it inevitably engenders—these, I suppose, are the sins that glaze the casements of most men's minds ; and from these, no matter how hard he tries to free himself, nor how much he despises them, who is altogether exempt ?

Finally, then, when we consider the immense mass of evidence referred to briefly, but sufficiently, by Mr. Charles Darwin, and referred to without other, for the most part, than off-hand dismissal by Professor Weismann in the last of the essays that have been recently translated, I do not see how anyone who brings an unbiassed mind to the question can hesitate as to the side on which the weight of testimony inclines. Professor Weismann declares that " the transmission of mutilations may be dismissed into the domain of fable."[1] If so, then, whom can we trust ? What is the use of science at all if the conclusions of a man as competent as I readily admit Mr. Darwin to have been, on the evidence laid before him from countless sources, is to be set aside lightly and without giving the clearest

[1] Essays, etc., p. 447.

and most cogent explanation of the why and where-
fore ?   When we see a person " ostrichizing " the
evidence which he has to meet, as clearly as I believe
Professor Weismann to be doing, we shall in nine cases
out of ten be right in supposing that he knows the
evidence to be too strong for him.

The
Deadlock in Darwinism

Part III

NOW let me return to the recent division of biological opinion into two main streams—Lamarckism and Weismannism. Both Lamarckians and Weismannists, not to mention mankind in general, admit that the better adapted to its surroundings a living form may be, the more likely it is to outbreed its compeers. The world at large, again, needs not to be told that the normal course is not unfrequently deflected through the fortunes of war ; nevertheless, according to Lamarckians and Erasmus-Darwinians, habitual effort, guided by ever-growing intelligence—that is to say, by continued increase of power in the matter of knowing our likes and dislikes—has been so much the main factor throughout the course of organic development, that the rest, though not lost sight of, may be allowed to go without saying. According, on the other hand, to extreme Charles-Darwinians and Weismannists, habit, effort and intelligence acquired during the experience of any one life goes for nothing. Not even a little fraction of it endures to the benefit of offspring. It dies with him in whom it is acquired, and the heirs of a man's body take no interest therein. To state this doctrine is to arouse instinctive loathing ; it is my fortunate task to maintain that such a nightmare of waste and death is as baseless as it is repulsive.

The split in biological opinion occasioned by the deadlock to which Charles-Darwinism has been reduced, though comparatively recent, widens rapidly.   Ten years ago Lamarck's name was mentioned only as a byword for extravagance ; now, we cannot take up a number of *Nature* without seeing how hot the contention is between his followers and those of Weismann. This must be referred, as I implied earlier, to growing perception that Mr. Darwin should either have gone farther towards Lamarckism or not so far.   In admitting use and disuse as freely as he did, he gave Lamarckians leverage for the overthrow of a system based ostensibly on the accumulation of fortunate accidents. In assigning the lion's share of development to the accumulation of fortunate accidents, he tempted fortuitists to try to cut the ground from under Lamarck's feet by denying that the effects of use and disuse can be inherited at all.   When the public had once got to understand what Lamarck had intended, and wherein Mr. Charles Darwin had differed from him, it became impossible for Charles-Darwinians to remain where they were, nor is it easy to see what course was open to them except to cast about for a theory by which they could get rid of use and disuse altogether.   Weismannism, therefore, is the inevitable outcome of the straits to which Charles-Darwinians were reduced through the way in which their leader had halted between two opinions.

This is why Charles-Darwinians, from Professor Huxley downwards, have kept the difference between Lamarck's opinions and those of Mr. Darwin so much in the background. Unwillingness to make this understood is nowhere manifested more clearly than in Dr. Francis Darwin's life of his father. In this work Lamarck is sneered at once or twice and told to go away, but there is no attempt to state the two cases side by side ; from which, as from not a little else, I conclude that Dr. Francis Darwin has descended from his father with singularly little modification.

Proceeding to the evidence for the transmissions of acquired habits, I will quote two recently adduced examples from among the many that have been credibly attested. The first was contributed to *Nature* (March 14, 1889) by Professor Marcus M. Hartog, who wrote :—

" A. B. is moderately myopic and very astigmatic in the left eye ; extremely myopic in the right. As the left eye gave such bad images for near objects, he was compelled in childhood to mask it, and acquired the habit of leaning his head on his left arm for writing, so as to blind that eye, or of resting the left temple and eye on the hand, with the elbow on the table. At the age of fifteen the eyes were equalized by the use of suitable spectacles, and he soon lost the habit completely and permanently. He is now the father of two children, a boy and a girl, whose vision (tested repeatedly and fully) is emmetropic in both eyes, so that they have not inherited the congenital optical defect of their father. All the same, they have both of them inherited his early acquired habit, and need constant watchfulness to prevent their hiding the left eye when writing, by resting the head on the left forearm or hand. Imitation is here quite out of the question.

" Considering that every habit involves changes in the proportional development of the muscular and osseous systems, and hence probably of the nervous system also, the importance of inherited habits, natural or acquired, cannot be overlooked in the general theory of inheritance. I am fully aware that I shall be accused of flat Lamarckism, but a nickname is not an argument."

To this Professor Ray Lankester rejoined (*Nature*, March 21, 1889) :—

" It is not unusual for children to rest the head on the left forearm or hand when writing, and I doubt whether much value can be attached to the case described by Professor Hartog. The kind of observation which his letter suggests is, however, likely to lead to results either for or against the transmission of acquired characters. An old friend of mine lost his right arm when a schoolboy, and has ever since written with his left. He has a large family and grandchildren, but I have not heard of any of them showing a disposition to left-handedness."

From *Nature* (March 21, 1889) I take the second instance communicated by Mr. J. Jenner-Weir, who wrote as follows :—

" Mr. Marcus M. Hartog's letter of March 6th, inserted in last week's number (p. 462), is a very valuable contribution to the growing evidence that acquired characters may be inherited. I have long held the view that such is often the case, and I have myself observed several instances of the, at least I may say, apparent fact.

" Many years ago there was a very fine male of the *Capra megaceros* in the gardens of the Zoological Society. To restrain this animal from jumping over the fence of the enclosure in which he was confined, a long and heavy chain was attached to the collar round his neck. He was constantly in the habit of taking this chain up by his horns and moving it from one side to another over his back ; in doing this he threw his head very much back, his horns being placed in a line with the back. The habit had become quite chronic with him, and was very tiresome to look at. I was very much astonished to observe that his off-spring inherited the habit, and although it was not necessary to attach a chain to their necks, I have often seen a young male throwing his horns over his back and shifting from side to side an imaginary chain. The action was exactly the same as that of his ancestor. The case of the kid of this goat appears to me to be parallel to that of child and parent given by Mr. Hartog. I think at the time I made this observation I informed Mr. Darwin of the fact by letter, and he did not accuse me of ' flat Lamarckism.' "

To this letter there was no rejoinder. It may be said, of course, that the action of the offspring in each of these cases was due to accidental coincidence only. Anything can be said, but the question turns not on what an advocate can say, but on what a reasonably intelligent and disinterested jury will believe ; granted they might be mistaken in accepting the foregoing stories, but the world of science, like that of commerce, is based on the faith or confidence which both creates and sustains them. Indeed the universe itself is but the creature of faith, for assuredly we know of no other foundation. There is nothing so generally and reason-ably accepted—not even our own continued identity —but questions may be raised about it that will shortly prove unanswerable. We cannot so test every sixpence given us in change as to be sure that we never take a bad one, and had better sometimes be cheated

than reduce caution to an absurdity. Moreover, we
have seen from the evidence given in my preceding
article that the germ-cells issuing from a parent's body
can, and do, respond to profound impressions made on
the somatic cells. This being so, what impressions are
more profound, what needs engage more assiduous
attention than those connected with self-protection,
the procuring of food, and the continuation of the
species ? If the mere anxiety connected with an ill-
healing wound inflicted on but one generation is sometimes found to have so impressed the germ-cells that
they hand down its scars to offspring, how much more
shall not anxieties that have directed action of all
kinds from birth till death, not in one generation only
but in a longer series of generations than the mind can
realize to itself, modify, and indeed control, the
organization of every species ?

I see Professor S. H. Vines, in the article on Weismann's theory referred to in my preceding article,
says Mr. Darwin " held that it was not the sudden
variations due to altered external conditions which
become permanent, but those slowly produced by
what he termed ' the accumulative action of changed
conditions of life.' " Nothing can be more soundly
Lamarckian, and nothing should more conclusively
show that, whatever else Mr. Darwin was, he was not
a Charles-Darwinian ; but what evidence other than
inferential can from the nature of the case be adduced
in support of this, as I believe, perfectly correct
judgment ? None know better than they who clamour
for direct evidence that their master was right in
taking the position assigned to him by Professor Vines,
that they cannot reasonably look for it. With us, as
with themselves, modification proceeds very gradually,

and it violates our principles as much as their own to expect visible permanent progress, in any single generation, or indeed in any number of generations of wild species which we have yet had time to observe. Occasionally we can find such cases, as in that of *Branchipus stagnalis*, quoted by Mr. Wallace, or in that of the New Zealand Kea whose skin, I was assured by the late Sir Julius von Haast, has already been modified as a consequence of its change of food. Here we can show that in even a few generations structure is modified under changed conditions of existence, but as we believe these cases to occur comparatively rarely, so it is still more rarely that they occur when and where we can watch them. Nature is eminently conservative, and fixity of type, even under considerable change of conditions, is surely more important for the well-being of any species than an over-ready power of adaptation to, it may be, passing changes. There could be no steady progress if each generation were not mainly bound by the traditions of those that have gone before it. It is evolution and not incessant revolution that both parties are upholding ; and this being so, rapid visible modification must be the exception, not the rule. I have quoted direct evidence adduced by competent observers, which is, I believe, sufficient to establish the fact that offspring can be and is sometimes modified by the acquired habits of a progenitor. I will now proceed to the still more, as it appears to me, cogent proof afforded by general considerations.

What, let me ask, are the principal phenomena of heredity ? There must be physical continuity between parent, or parents, and offspring, so that the offspring is, as Erasmus Darwin well said, a kind of elongation of the life of the parent.

Erasmus Darwin put the matter so well that I may as well give his words in full ; he wrote :—

" Owing to the imperfection of language the offspring is termed a new animal, but is in truth a branch or elongation of the parent, since a part of the embryon animal is, or was, a part of the parent, and therefore, in strict language, cannot be said to be entirely new at the time of its production ; and therefore it may retain some of the habits of the parent system.

" At the earliest period of its existence the embryon would seem to consist of a living filament with certain capabilities of irritation, sensation, volition, and association, and also with some acquired habits or propensities peculiar to the parent ; the former of these are in common with other animals ; the latter seem to distinguish or produce the kind of animal, whether man or quadruped, with the similarity of feature or form to the parent." [1]

Those who accept evolution insist on unbroken physical continuity between the earliest known life and ourselves, so that we both are and are not personally identical with the unicellular organism from which we have descended in the course of many millions of years, exactly in the same ways as an octogenarian both is and is not personally identical with the microscopic impregnate ovum from which he grew up. Everything both is and is not. There is no such thing as strict identity between any two things in any two consecutive seconds. In strictness they are identical and yet not identical, so that in strictness they violate a fundamental rule of strictness—namely, that a thing shall never be itself and not itself at one and the same time ; we must choose between logic and dealing in

[1] *Zoonomia*, 1794, vol. i. p. 480.

a practical spirit with time and space ; it is not surprising, therefore, that logic, in spite of the show of respect outwardly paid to her, is told to stand aside when people come to practice. In practice identity is generally held to exist where continuity is only broken slowly and piecemeal; nevertheless, that occasional periods of even rapid change are not held to bar identity, appears from the fact that no one denies this to hold between the microscopically small impregnate ovum and the born child that springs from it, nor yet, therefore, between the impregnate ovum and the octogenarian into which the child grows; for both ovum and octogenarian are held personally identical with the new-born baby, and things that are identical with the same are identical with one another.

The first, then, and most important element of heredity is that there should be unbroken continuity, and hence sameness of personality, between parents and offspring, in neither more nor less than the same sense as that in which any other two personalities are said to be the same. The repetition, therefore, of its developmental stages by any offspring must be regarded as something which the embryo repeating them has already done once, in the person of one or other parent ; and if once, then, as many times as there have been generations between any given embryo now repeating it, and the point in life from which we started—say, for example, the amœba. In the case of asexually and sexually produced organisms alike, the offspring must be held to continue the personality of the parent or parents, and hence on the occasion of every fresh development, to be repeating something which in the person of its parent or parents it has done once, and if once, then any number of times, already.

It is obvious, therefore, that the germ-plasm (or whatever the fancy word for it may be) of any one generation is as physically identical with the germ-plasm of its predecessor as any two things can be. The difference between Professor Weismann and, we will say, Heringians consists in the fact that the first maintains the new germ-plasm when on the point of repeating its developmental processes to take practically no cognisance of anything that has happened to it since the last occasion on which it developed itself ; while the latter maintain that offspring takes much the same kind of account of what has happened to it in the persons of its parents since the last occasion on which it developed itself, as people in ordinary life take things that happen to them. In daily life people let fairly normal circumstances come and go without much heed as matters of course. If they have been lucky they make a note of it and try to repeat their success. If they have been unfortunate but have recovered rapidly they soon forget it ; if they have suffered long and deeply they grizzle over it and are scared and scarred by it for a long time. The question is one of cognisance or non-cognisance on the part of the new germs, of the more profound impressions made on them while they were one with their parents, between the occasion of their last preceding development and the new course on which they are about to enter. Those who accept the theory put forward independently by Professor Hering of Prague (whose work on this subject is translated in my book *Unconscious Memory*) and by myself in *Life and Habit*, believe in cognisance as do Lamarckians generally. Weismannites, and with them the orthodoxy of English science, find non-cognisance more acceptable.

If the Heringian view is accepted, that heredity is only a mode of memory, and an extension of memory from one generation to another, then the repetition of its development by any embryo thus becomes only the repetition of a lesson learned by rote ; and, as I have elsewhere said, our view of life is simplified by finding that it is no longer an equation of, say, a hundred unknown quantities, but of ninety-nine only, inasmuch as two of the unknown quantities prove to be sub-stantially identical. In this case the inheritance of acquired characteristics cannot be disputed, for it is postulated in the theory that each embryo takes note of, remembers and is guided by the profounder im-pressions made upon it while in the persons of its parents, between its present and last preceding de-velopment. To maintain this is to maintain use and disuse to be the main factors throughout organic development ; to deny it is to deny that use and disuse can have any conceivable effect. For the detailed reasons which led me to my own conclusions I must refer the reader to my books *Life and Habit* and *Unconscious Memory*, the conclusions of which have been often adopted, but never, that I have seen, disputed. A brief résumé of the leading points in the argument is all that space will here allow me to give.

We have seen that it is a first requirement of heredity that there shall be physical continuity between parents and offspring. This holds good with memory. There must be continued identity between the person re-membering and the person to whom the thing that is remembered happened. We cannot remember things that happened to someone else, and in our absence. We can only remember having heard of them. We have seen, however, that there is as much *bona-fide* sameness of personality between parents and offspring up to the time at which the offspring quits the parent's body, as there is between the different states of the parent himself at any two consecutive moments ; the offspring therefore, being one and the same person with its progenitors until it quits them, can be held to remember what happened to them within, of course, the limitations to which all memory is subject, as much as the progenitors can remember what happened earlier to themselves. Whether it does so remember can only be settled by observing whether it acts as living beings commonly do when they are acting under guidance of memory. I will endeavour to show that, though heredity and habit based on memory go about in different dresses, yet if we catch them separately— for they are never seen together—and strip them there is not a mole nor strawberry-mark nor trick nor leer of the one, but we find it in the other also.

What are the moles and strawberry-marks of habitual action, or actions remembered and thus repeated ? First, the more often we repeat them the more easily and unconsciously we do them. Look at reading, writing, walking, talking, playing the piano, etc. ; the longer we have practised any one of these acquired habits, the more easily, automatically and unconsciously, we perform it. Look, on the other hand, broadly, at the three points to which I called attention in *Life and Habit* :—

I. That we are most conscious of and have most control over such habits as speech, the upright position, the arts and sciences—which are acquisitions peculiar to the human race, always acquired after birth, and not common to ourselves and any ancestor who had not become entirely human.

II. That we are less conscious of and have less control over eating and drinking [provided the food be normal], swallowing, breathing, seeing, and hearing —which were acquisitions of our prehuman ancestry, and for which we had provided ourselves with all the necessary apparatus before we saw light, but which are still, geologically speaking, recent.

III. That we are most unconscious of and have least control over our digestion and circulation— powers possessed even by our invertebrate ancestry, and, geologically speaking, of extreme antiquity.

I have put the foregoing very broadly, but enough is given to show the reader the gist of the argument. Let it be noted that disturbance and departure, to any serious extent, from normal practice tends to induce resumption of consciousness even in the case of such old habits as breathing, seeing, and hearing, digestion and the circulation of the blood. So it is with habitual actions in general. Let a player be never so proficient on any instrument, he will be put out if the normal conditions under which he plays are too widely departed from, and will then do consciously, if indeed he can do it at all, what he had hitherto been doing unconsciously. It is an axiom as regards actions acquired after birth, that we never do them automatically save as the result of long practice ; the stages in the case of any acquired facility, the inception of which we have been able to watch, have invariably been from a nothingness of ignorant impotence to a little something of highly self-conscious, arduous performance, and thence to the unself-consciousness of easy mastery. I saw one year a poor blind lad of about eighteen sitting on a wall by the wayside at Varese, playing the concertina with his whole body, and snorting like a

child. The next year the boy no longer snorted, and
he played with his fingers only ; the year after that he
seemed hardly to know whether he was playing or not,
it came so easily to him. I know no exception to this
rule. Where is the intricate and at one time difficult art
in which perfect automatic ease has been reached except as the result of long practice ? If, then, wherever
we can trace the development of automatism we find
it to have taken this course, is it not most reasonable to infer that it has taken the same even when it
has risen in regions that are beyond our ken ? Ought we
not, whenever we see a difficult action performed automatically, to suspect antecedent practice ? Granted
that without the considerations in regard to identity
presented above it would not have been easy to see
where a baby of a day old could have had the practice
which enables it to do as much as it does unconsciously,
but even without these considerations it would have been
more easy to suppose that the necessary opportunities
had not been wanting, than that the easy performance
could have been gained without practice and memory.

When I wrote *Life and Habit* (originally published
in 1877) I said in slightly different words :—

" Shall we say that a baby of a day old sucks (which
involves the whole principle of the pump and hence a
profound practical knowledge of the laws of pneu-
matics and hydrostatics), digests, oxygenizes its blood
—millions of years before anyone had discovered
oxygen—sees and hears, operations that involve an
unconscious knowledge of the facts concerning optics
and acoustics compared with which the conscious
discoveries of Newton are insignificant—shall we say
that a baby can do all these things at once, doing them
so well and so regularly without being even able to

u

give them attention, and yet without mistake, and shall we also say at the same time that it has not learnt to do them, and never did them before ?

" Such an assertion would contradict the whole experience of mankind."

I have met with nothing during the thirteen years since the foregoing was published that has given me any qualms about its soundness. From the point of view of the law courts and everyday life it is, of course, nonsense ; but in the kingdom of thought, as in that of heaven, there are many mansions, and what would be extravagance in the cottage or farm-house, as it were, of daily practice, is but common decency in the palace of high philosophy, wherein dwells evolution. If we leave evolution alone, we may stick to common practice and the law courts ; touch evolution and we are in another world ; not higher, nor lower, but different as harmony from counterpoint. As, however, in the most absolute counterpoint there is still harmony, and in the most absolute harmony still counterpoint, so high philosophy should be still in touch with common sense, and common sense with high philosophy.

The common-sense view of the matter to people who are not over-curious and to whom time is money, will be that a baby is not a baby until it is born, and that when born it should be born in wedlock. Nevertheless, as a sop to high philosophy, every baby is allowed to be the offspring of its father and mother.

The high-philosophy view of the matter is that every human being is still but a fresh edition of the primordial cell with the latest additions and corrections; there has been no leap nor break in continuity anywhere ; the man of to-day is the primordial cell of millions of years ago as truly as he is the himself of yesterday; he can only be denied to be the one on grounds that will prove him not to be the other. Everyone is both himself and all his direct ancestors and descendants as well; therefore, if we would be logical, he is one also with all his cousins, no matter how distant, for he and they are alike identical with the primordial cell, and we have already noted it as an axiom that things which are identical with the same are identical with one another. This is practically making him one with all living things, whether animal or vegetable, that ever have existed or ever will—something of all which may have been in the mind of Sophocles when he wrote :—

> "Nor seest thou yet the gathering hosts of ill
> That shall en-one thee both with thine own self
> And with thine offspring."

And all this has come of admitting that a man may be the same person for two days running! As for sopping common sense it will be enough to say that these remarks are to be taken in a strictly scientific sense, and have no appreciable importance as regards life and conduct. True they deal with the foundations on which all life and conduct are based, but like other foundations they are hidden out of sight, and the sounder they are, the less we trouble ourselves about them.

What other main common features between heredity and memory may we note besides the fact that neither can exist without that kind of physical continuity which we call personal identity? First, the development of the embryo proceeds in an established order; so must all habitual actions based on memory. Disturb the normal order and the performance is arrested. The better we know " God save the Queen," the less easily can we play or sing it backwards. The return of memory again depends on the return of ideas associated with the particular thing that is remembered—we remember nothing but for the presence of these, and when enough of these are presented to us we remember everything. So, if the development of an embryo is due to memory, we should suppose the memory of the impregnate ovum to revert not to yesterday, when it was in the persons of its parents, but to the last occasion on which it was an impregnate ovum. The return of the old environment and the presence of old associations would at once involve recollection of the course that should be next taken, and the same should happen throughout the whole course of development. The actual course of development presents precisely the phenomena agreeable with this. For fuller treatment of this point I must refer the reader to the chapter on the abeyance of memory in my book *Life and Habit*, already referred to.

Secondly, we remember best our last few performances of any given kind, so our present performance will probably resemble some one or other of these ; we remember our earlier performances by way of residuum only, but every now and then we revert to an earlier habit. This feature of memory is manifested in heredity by the way in which offspring commonly resembles most its nearer ancestors, but sometimes reverts to earlier ones. Brothers and sisters, each as it were giving their own version of the same story, but in different words, should generally resemble each other more closely than more distant relations. And this is what actually we find.

Thirdly, the introduction of slightly new elements into a method already established varies it beneficially ;

the new is soon fused with the old, and the monotony ceases to be oppressive. But if the new be too foreign, we cannot fuse the old and the new— nature seeming to hate equally too wide a deviation from ordinary practice and none at all. This fact reappears in heredity as the beneficial effects of occasional crossing on the one hand, and on the other, in the generally observed sterility of hybrids. If heredity be an affair of memory, how can an embryo, say of a mule, be expected to build up a mule on the strength of but two mule-memories ? Hybridism causes a fault in the chain of memory, and it is to this cause that the usual sterility of hybrids must be referred.

Fourthly, it requires many repeated impressions to fix a method firmly, but when it has been engrained into us we cease to have much recollection of the manner in which it came to be so, or indeed of any individual repetition, but sometimes a single impression if prolonged as well as profound, produces a lasting impression and is liable to return with sudden force, and then to go on returning to us at intervals. As a general rule, however, abnormal impressions cannot long hold their own against the overwhelming pre- ponderance of normal authority. This appears in heredity as the normal non-inheritance of mutilations on the one hand, and on the other as their occasional inheritance in the case of injuries followed by disease.

Fifthly, if heredity and memory are essentially the same, we should expect that no animal would develop new structures of importance after the age at which its species begins ordinarily to continue its race ; for we cannot suppose offspring to remember anything that happens to the parent subsequently to the parent's ceasing to contain the offspring within itself. From the average age, therefore, of reproduction, offspring should cease to have any further steady, continuous memory to fall back upon ; what memory there is should be full of faults, and as such unreliable. An organism ought to develop as long as it is backed by memory—that is to say, until the average age at which reproduction begins ; it should then continue to go for a time on the impetus already received, and should eventually decay through failure of any memory to support it, and tell it what to do. This corresponds absolutely with what we observe in organisms generally, and explains, on the one hand, why the age of puberty marks the beginning of completed development—a riddle hitherto not only unexplained but, so far as I have seen, unasked ; it explains, on the other hand, the phenomena of old age—hitherto without even attempt at explanation.

Sixthly, those organisms that are the longest in reaching maturity should on the average be the longest-lived, for they will have received the most momentous impulse from the weight of memory behind them. This harmonizes with the latest opinion as to the facts. In his article of Weismann in the *Contemporary Review* for May, 1890, Mr. Romanes writes : " Professor Weismann has shown that there is throughout the metazoa a general correlation between the natural lifetime of individuals composing any given species, and the age at which they reach maturity or first become capable of procreation." This, I believe, has been the conclusion generally arrived at by biologists for some years past.

Lateness, then, in the average age of reproduction appears to be the principle underlying longevity. There does not appear at first sight to be much connection between such distinct and apparently disconnected phenomena as 1, the orderly normal progress of development ; 2, atavism and the resumption of feral characteristics ; 3, the more ordinary resemblance *inter se* of nearer relatives ; 4, the benefit of an occasional cross, and the usual sterility of hybrids ; 5, the unconsciousness with which alike bodily development and ordinary physiological functions proceed, so long as they are normal ; 6, the ordinary non-inheritance, but occasional inheritance of mutilations ; 7, the fact that puberty indicates the approach of maturity ; 8, the phenomena of middle life and old age ; 9, the principle underlying longevity.   These phenomena have no conceivable bearing on one another until heredity and memory are regarded as part of the same story.   Identify these two things, and I know no phenomenon of heredity that does not immediately become infinitely more intelligible.   Is it conceivable that a theory which harmonizes so many facts hitherto regarded as without either connection or explanation should not deserve at any rate consideration from those who profess to take an interest in biology ?

It is not as though the theory were unknown, or had been condemned by our leading men of science. Professor Ray Lankester introduced it to English readers in an appreciative notice of Professor Hering's address, which appeared in *Nature*, July 13, 1876.   He wrote to the *Athenæum*, March 24, 1884, and claimed credit for having done so, but I do not believe he has ever said more in pubiic about it than what I have here referred to.   Mr. Romanes did indeed try to crush it in *Nature*, January 27, 1881, but in 1883, in his *Mental Evolution in Animals*, he adopted its main conclusion without acknowledgment. The *Athenæum*, to my unbounded surprise, called him to task for this (March 1, 1884), and since that time he has given the Heringian theory a sufficiently wide berth. Mr. Wallace showed himself favourably enough disposed towards the view that heredity and memory are part of the same story when he reviewed my book *Life and Habit* in *Nature*, March 27, 1879, but he has never since betrayed any sign of being aware that such a theory existed. Mr. Herbert Spencer wrote to the *Athenæum* (April 5, 1884), and claimed the theory for himself, but, in spite of his doing this, he has never, that I have seen, referred to the matter again. I have dealt sufficiently with his claim in my book *Luck or Cunning*. Lastly, Professor Hering himself has never that I know of touched his own theory since the single short address read in 1870, and translated by me in 1881. Everyone, even its originator, except myself, seems afraid to open his mouth about it. Of course the inference suggests itself that other people have more sense than I have. I readily admit it ; but why have so many of our leaders shown such a strong hankering after the theory, if there is nothing in it ?

The deadlock that I have pointed out as existing in Darwinism will, I doubt not, lead ere long to a consideration of Professor Hering's theory. English biologists are little likely to find Weismann satisfactory for long, and if he breaks down there is nothing left for them but Lamarck, supplemented by the important and elucidatory corollary on his theory proposed by Professor Hering. When the time arrives for this to obtain a hearing it will be confirmed, doubtless, by arguments clearer and more forcible than any I have been able to adduce ; I shall then be delighted to

resign the championship which till then I shall continue, as for some years past, to have much pleasure
in sustaining. Heretofore my satisfaction has mainly
lain in the fact that more of our prominent men of
science have seemed anxious to claim the theory than
to refute it ; in the confidence thus engendered I leave
it to any fuller consideration which the outline I have
above given may incline the reader to bestow upon it.

THE END.